Second Edition

Guidance of Young Children

Marian Marion

University of Wisconsin—Stout

Merrill Publishing Company
A Bell & Howell Information Company
Columbus Toronto London Melbourne

Cover Photos: Merrill Publishing Company/Bruce Johnson

Published by Merrill Publishing Company
A Bell & Howell Information Company
Columbus, Ohio 43216

This book was set in Zapf Book.

Administrative Editor: Jennifer Knerr
Production Coordinator and Text Designer: Jeffrey Putnam
Cover Designer: Cathy Watterson

Photo credits (All photos copyrighted by the individuals or institutions
listed.): p. 5, Merrill Publishing; p. 27, Merrill Publishing/Bruce Johnson;
p. 45, Merrill Publishing/Bruce Johnson; p. 59, Merrill Publishing; p. 85,
Merrill Publishing /Bruce Johnson; p. 105, Strix Pix; p. 131, Merrill
Publishing; p. 153, Merrill Publishing; p. 171, Gale Zucker; p. 187,
Merrill Publishing; p. 205, Merrill Publishing. All other photos from the
Child and Family Study Center, University of Wisconsin–Stout.

Library of Congress Catalog Card Number: 86-62577
International Standard Book Number: 0-675-20709-6
Printed in the United States of America
  2 3 4 5 6 7 8 9 — 92 91 90 89 88 87

Contents

97379

Preface

The intention of the second edition of *Guidance of Young Children* is to help you reflect on the process of guiding young children. The textbook is based on the conviction that effective interaction with children does *not* "happen by magic," but develops when *a self-responsible adult*

☐ accepts the responsibility that goes along with having or working with children.

☐ believes that she or he has a choice about how to behave with children.

☐ understands how children develop.

☐ develops skills for effective guidance.

☐ has realistic expectations for himself or herself as well as for children.

☐ understands that a child exists in several different "systems," each of which affects the child's behavior.

☐ understands the long- and short-term goals of child guidance.

The process of child guidance has an immediate, short-term goal and a long-term goal. When you work with children you will undoubtedly be concerned about the short-term goal of figuring out how to control children's behavior on a daily basis. Because children are not born with self-control, you will have to stop them from hurting themselves, from damaging property, and from disturbing others. Guiding children involves confrontation with real problems and situations that demand your attention.

Guiding young children also involves long-term goals. As a self-responsible adult you will probably want to help children ultimately learn to control *themselves*, to become people who like and value themselves, who are humane, caring individuals, who are competent, independent and self-responsible, who stand up for their rights and negotiate conflicts without hurting others, and who are cooperative and helpful.

Guidance of Young Children was written for adults who currently live or work with young children or who are preparing to work with children. These groups of adults include parents, teachers, nurses, physicians and other health care professionals, home economists, parent educators, extension agents, church personnel and recreation/camp counselors. *CDA, or Child Development Associate candidates will find several of the chapters directly applicable to their program and modules: self-esteem, professionalism, guidance, discipline, and child development.*

This edition, like the first, includes three separate units with several chapters in each unit. The units focus on the guidance "system," special topics in child guidance and theoretical frameworks for child guidance. A few changes have been made in how chapters are constructed, changes aimed at helping you study and learn the material even more effectively. Each chapter

☐ starts with a list of objectives;

☐ has a "chapter overview" that, with the objectives, should serve as an "advance organizer" for your reading;

☐ has an observation at the end; (Use the observation to apply your knowledge and to have fun watching young children!)

☐ has a summary; read it both before studying the chapter and after you have finished the material;

☐ contains "boxed information," special features that target application of knowledge.

The content within each chapter has changed to reflect current research and theory. For example, the information on the child in the guidance system has been expanded to two chapters to accommodate the current research and emphasis on "cognizing" social development. Sections on social cognition and morality and justice have been added. Piaget's account of cognitive development has been retained and emphasized. The chapter on discipline has been restructured with an emphasis on positive discipline and skill development. The chapter on aggression has been retained and given an even greater "systems" or ecological emphasis. The chapters on prosocial behavior and self-esteem reflect the vigorous research in the past several years. The chapter on the behavioral approach has been revised to include a broader overview of this theoretical approach.

Acknowledgments

The second edition reflects feedback I have received from students and colleagues on the first edition over the past six years. Franklin Fox, Sacramento City Community College; Ena Goodrich-Shelly, Butler University; and Carol Seefeldt, University of Maryland, served as reviewers for the first edition for Merrill. Each of their reviews was thoughtful, specific and helpful. Each reviewer gave positive feedback along with suggestions for change, and many of the changes incorporated herein came about because of their suggestions.

Special thanks go to my students for participating in the learning process with such zest and to my colleagues who have made the past few years a time I will never forget.

M.M.

To Bill, my husband, for his gift of time,
and to Casey and Harvey, for their friendship

UNIT ONE

The Guidance System

For many years people believed in the "social mold" approach to personality and social development. It was thought that a child's personality was like a blob of playdough, ready to be molded by adults. This was a *uni*directional view of development—that the influence flows primarily from an adult to a child. In this view, the child is a passive object of socialization by adults (Hetherington, 1983).

The "social mold" view has been replaced by an *interactive* model (Maccoby & Martin, 1983). A child in this model is viewed as an active partner in the process of development. The child, of course, is influenced by an adult but at the same time influences the adult. This is a *bi*directional or even a *multi*directional perspective on development—that influence in development flows back and forth among participants in an interaction. This view is a major feature of the interactive model.

Another feature of the interactive model of social development is an emphasis on a child's embeddedness in a variety of systems. A *system* is a functioning integrated structure with properties other than those of the components making it up. The University of Wisconsin System, for example, is made up of a large number of individual universities. Your family is another example. It is a functioning system made up of separate parts (people). Your body is also a system made up of several parts that also happen to be systems, like the cardiovascular and digestive systems.

Concepts from systems theory can be used to explain a child's development. An individual child is actually an integrated organized system and exists in higher-level systems of family and peer group. These systems are, in turn, embedded in a community system and a cultural system (Brim, 1975; Bronfenbrenner, 1979; Maccoby & Martin, 1983; Parke & Slaby, 1983; Sameroff, 1982). All of these systems affect a child's development.

The perspective guiding the writing of this book is the interactive model with emphasis on the concept of a child's embeddedness in a *guidance system*. The chapters in this unit focus on some of the systems impinging on a child's social development: the child herself, the adults who live and work with a child, and the physical environment in which the child exists.

In chapter 1, "Adults in the Guidance System," you will read about specific processes through which adults influence children and about characteristics of supportive adults. You will also learn how to set reasonable, fair limits and use socializing techniques that elicit child *compliance* (obedience).

Chapters 2 and 3 focus on another part of the guidance system—the child. Hetherington (1983) points out that the study of social development now examines the effect of a child's cognitive developmental level on other aspects of development. In chapter 2, "The Child in the Guidance System: Guidance and Cognitive Development," you will read about the first two stages of cognitive development identified by Jean Piaget. The cognitive abilities and limitations of each stage affect a child's interactions with others and hence the effectiveness of any guidance strategy.

In chapter 3, "The Child in the Guidance System: Cognition and Social Interaction," you will again see that a child's cognitive capacities affect other areas of development. A child's *social cognition*—ideas about friendship, conflict, and morality or justice—changes as her cognitive development changes. In this chapter you will also read about *metacognition*. An important function of metacognition is the shift from control by others to self-control. Self-control becomes possible as cognitive skills develop during early childhood.

In chapter 4, "The Physical Environment: Its Role in the Guidance System," you will read about how adults guide children indirectly by structuring and managing the physical environment. An early childhood classroom is used as an example of how the design and management of space, materials, and activities affect a child's behavior.

1

Adults in the
Guidance System

Chapter Overview

After reading and studying this chapter, you will be able to:

☐ *List and discuss* six specific techniques used by adults to influence children.

☐ *Describe* several characteristics of "supportive" adults.

☐ *Explain* why child compliance is a developmental issue for both adults and children.

☐ *Identify and discuss* criteria for good limits.

☐ *Analyze* a limit and *say* whether the limit meets criteria for good limits.

☐ *Describe* several specific strategies adults can use to help children comply with good limits.

TECHNIQUES USED BY ADULTS TO INFLUENCE CHILDREN

Adults are an important part of the guidance system. It is through your "personal style" that you establish the general emotional climate in your home, your classroom, or any setting in which you and children live and work together. Some children exist in a warm, nurturant, and supportive atmosphere and are likely to develop positive personality traits and good interactional skills. Other children are guided by adults who are cold, nonnurturant, and nonsupportive, and these children have a more difficult time learning to live and work with others.

Radin (1982) urges us to examine the specific processes we use when we socialize childen. All adults, whether they are warm and supportive or cold and nonsupportive, influence children both directly and indirectly. Their *direct influence* is exerted through six different processes.

STUDY HINT: When memorizing a list of items it is helpful to use a *mnemonic* (the first *m* is silent)—a memory aid or strategy. Take the first letter of the most significant word in each item and put all first letters together to make an easily remembered word. For the list of methods of adult influence the mnemonic is *MIRPEC*.

Modeling "M"

Modeling involves learning from observation or imitation. Children usually imitate models who are powerful, nurturant, and skillful. Many adults are powerful, prestigious, and nurturant and therefore influence children through modeling. Note here that children learn both positive and negative behaviors by observing and imitating models. They can learn generosity, cooperation, kindness, and helpfulness, or they can learn to hurt or abuse others or to be uncooperative through modeling. (Modeling is discussed in connection with other topics in this text, so you will be encountering the concept again.)

Modeling "M"

Direct Instruction "I"

Adults influence children by *instructing* them. Adults teach academic subjects like math, reading, and other cognitive skills. They instruct children in physical safety: traffic safety, safe use of toys, how to protect oneself from unwanted touches. Children can be directly instructed in the social sphere as well. We can teach them how to control anger, how to resolve conflicts, how to make friends. (You will read more about instructing children in social skills as you go through this text).

Modeling "M"
Direct Instruction "I"

Use of Rewards and Punishment "R"

Adults influence children by reinforcing, rewarding, and punishing them. Approved behavior, such as saying "please" and "thank you," receives reinforcement, while inappropriate behavior, such as cursing, results in punishment or no reinforcement. Note here that adults do not agree on what constitutes "appropriate" behavior. For example, some adults reward their children for fighting and hurting. The point is that reward and punishment are used by many adults to influence children's behavior. What the adult rewards depends on the adult's value system.

Modeling "M"

Instruction "I"

Reinforcement "R"

Providing Physical Materials and Settings "P"

Example   Pete, 7 years old, watches a lot of television in which people hurt or kill others, reads violent comic books, goes to see violent movies, and plays video games like "Bloody Murder." The parents of 7-year-old Tim keep television viewing to a minimum, have enrolled their son in a couple of sports programs and the library reading program, look for interesting planetarium and museum programs to attend, and make an effort to find video games that do not focus on violence.

Because of the different materials to which they have access, Pete and Tim have learned different things about how to deal with conflict and are likely to differ in their levels of aggression. Pete will very likely show higher levels of aggression and will more easily accept aggression toward others. (Throughout this text you will read about how a child's physical setting and the materials he uses influence his behavior).

Modeling "M"

Instruction "I"

Rewards "R"

Physical Materials and Settings "P"

Stating Expectations of Desired Behaviors "E"

Some adults are adept at developing good rules or limits, communicating them clearly to children, and then maintaining the limits firmly and kindly. Other adults do not realize how important it is for them to state expectations clearly. A child's behavior is influenced by an adult's ability and willingness to define what behavior is considered appropriate.

Modeling "M"

Instruction "I"

Reinforcement "R"

Physical Materials and Settings "P"

Expectations "E"

Using Cognitive Modification Strategies "C"

Example   Ten-year-old Bill has not fed his dog Duffy for the third time this week. You have had to feed the dog as well as get dinner for the family and do the taxes. How can you remedy this situation without swooping down on Bill and using all your power?

You can influence Bill's behavior by using one of several *cognitive modification strategies*. Remember that humans, including childen, have large brains and therefore are thinking creatures. Children can modify their own behavior when someone takes the time to confront them with something to think about. There are three things you can try if you decide to use this approach.

Arouse the Child's Empathy

The goal here is to make the child think about how his actions have affected the victim. You want to make Bill feel empathy for the dog's plight, to imagine how Duffy might feel when he does not get his food. A good way to arouse empathy is to describe the victim's situation in a nonaccusatory way.

Example   "Duffy is hungry, Bill. He depends on you to feed him and doesn't understand when you forget."

Arousing a child's empathy, i.e., having him "walk a mile in Duffy's tracks," is a powerful technique because it encourages a child to look at how a situation makes another creature feel. It forces a child to see things from someone else's perspective and, most important, does not threaten or accuse the child.

Help a Child Alter His Self-Perception

Did Bill not feed Duffy because of lack of effort, or because he is incapable of doing the job? Dweck (1978) notes that children who are told that they have failed at a task because of lack of effort, i.e., because they just did not try hard enough, often show increased effort and a better performance. According to this finding, Bill would be more likely to feed Duffy willingly if you said,

Example   "Bill, you've always done a good job of taking care of Duffy. I think that you just haven't made an effort to remember to feed him this week."

Dweck's research also demonstrates that children who are told that they have failed at a task because of things over which they had little control actually show a worse performance. If you told Bill,

Example   "Well, I guess I was right! You just can't handle the job of taking care of a dog. You aren't smart enough. I told you what would happen if we got that dog, didn't I?" then he would be *less* likely to take care of Duffy in the future.

Responsible adults help children identify a lack of effort. Effort is a factor that an individual can control, and when people are in control, they are more likely to perform better, whether in feeding a pet, practicing music, studying for an exam, controlling the urge to hit someone, or eating more nutritious snacks.

Focus on the Child's Values and Actions

As Bill's parent, you know that he loves his dog. He pets him gently, lets him sleep on his bed, and likes playing with him. You are pleased that Bill is developing a set of values that keeps him from hurting others. His action, *not* feeding Duffy, and his value of fair treatment of others do not match. You can change Bill's behavior by focusing on the mismatch or discrepancy between his actions and his values.

Example   "One of the things I like about you, Bill, is that you treat people well. You have never hurt Duffy. So I guess I'm really surprised that you haven't fed your buddy Duffy."

STUDY HINT: Review what you have read. Before reading the next section, *list and briefly discuss* six ways in which adults influence children's behavior. Try it without referring to the text. Try using the mnemonic—*MIRPEC*—but if you forget any of the six techniques, review this section before proceeding to the next section.

SPECIAL FOCUS: Characteristics of Sensitive, Supportive Adults

Some adults really like children; others do not. Some adults treat children with dignity, even when they discipline them; others do not. Some adults understand how childen develop; others do not. Some adults know what to expect from children at different stages; others do not. The point? As a professional, when you work with parents and other professionals you will be astonished at how different adults are in their "personal style" of working with children. Specifically, a sensitive, supportive, responsible adult (Stayton, Hogan & Ainsworth, 1971):

☐ understands child development.
☐ sees things from a child's perspective.
☐ is tuned in to signals from the child.
☐ responds to signals quickly and appropriately.
☐ makes expectations for desired behavior clear, but avoids imposing his own will.
☐ is adept at arranging the physical and temporal environments so he is not always interrupting a child.
☐ knows how to get children to accept control willingly when control is necessary by "setting the mood" for control.

ADULTS HELP CHILDREN DEAL WITH DEVELOPMENTAL ISSUES

Child Compliance: A Developmental Issue
One of the most notable changes of early childhood is the emergence of the capacity

for voluntary self-control (Flavell, 1977) During toddlerhood, in particular, autonomy, compliance, and impulse control are cardinal issues (Sroufe & Ward, 1980). Certain developmental phenomena—a child's new locomotor and linguistic abilities as well as cognitive and emotional developments—challenge caregivers by making *non*compliant (some people refer to this as disobedient) behavior possible. The struggle for autonomy (independence) is brought about, for example, by the child's understanding of the meaning of the word "no" as well as by his becoming aware of himself as a separate person with a will of his own (Haswell, Hock, & Wenar, 1981; Marion, 1983).

The developmental issue of child compliance is a significant one for all members of the guidance system, adults as well as children. During early and middle childhood a child has to learn to comply and cooperate with others as a part of the larger process of learning effective social interaction. Adults are faced with a dilemma when dealing with young children—how to encourage autonomy and at the same time elicit the compliance necessary to keep children safe and to teach them what the society *prohibits* (forbids). Adults must communicate rules of conduct to children so that excessive conflict can be avoided (Maccoby & Martin, 1983; Marion, 1983; Toepfer, Reuter, & Maurer, 1972).

Do you believe that young children are generally obedient or naturally disobedient? If you think that children *are* generally compliant or obedient, then you agree with the *ethological-evolutionary* viewpoint. Two major assumptions of this view are that a child's willingness to comply is an important step in the socialization process and that children are predisposed to be obedient. Several studies have supported this view by documenting a high level of compliance among preschool children (Green, Forehand, & MacMahon, 1979; Lytton, 1979; Lytton & Zwirner, 1975; Minton, Kagan, & Levine, 1971).

Adults who believe that children are naturally inclined to obey emphasize the link between the attachment process and a child's willingness to comply. They believe that children who trust adults, who have a harmonious relationship with an adult, and who do not fear loss of the adult's love are the most likely to comply with adult suggestions or commands. For example, Stayton et al. (1971) found that 1-year-old children whose mothers were cooperative and sensitive to their child's signals complied with commands and prohibitions more consistently than did children whose parents were insensitive and interfering.

ADULTS' ROLE IN CHILD COMPLIANCE

Child compliance is affected by two processes. One is the trust developed between an adult and a child, and the adult's level of sensitivity to the child's abilities and state. The other is the adult's use of socializing techniques that emphasize the child's responsibility and avoid adult power assertion (Maccoby & Martin, 1983). This section focuses on these two mediating processes.

Discipline: Effect on Compliance

Supportive adults use positive discipline effectively and support the development of self-control and compliance (Marion, 1981, 1982). The research reviewed in this section focuses specifically on the effect of different adult control attempts on level of child compliance. In situations where external control is clearly necessary, some adult control attempts contribute to noncompliance while other discipline techniques seem to elicit heightened compliance.

Positive and Negative Discipline
Some adults use negative discipline. They try to force or coerce a child to obey. *Coercion* (force, or the attempt to compel) is when an adult in a clash of wills puts much pressure on the child to behave as the adult wishes. The adult may use force, deprive the child of privileges or material objects, or inflict physical punishment (Rollins & Thomas, 1979). Any of these coercive techniques may be used when a command is first issued or after a child fails to comply.

Greater adult coercion results in less compliance from children. Noncompliant child behavior has been found to be associated with several forms of coercive control: physical control like slapping, restricting, or restraining (Lytton, 1977); negative action like expression of displeasure, criticism, or threat (Lytton & Zwirner, 1975); restrictive commands (Minton et al., 1971); and mother's use of pyschological punishment (Lytton, 1977).

Other adults use positive discipline. They try to avoid clashes of wills like the following interchange:

Adult: "You'd better pick up these toys!"
Child: "Just try and make me!"

Instead, supportive adults try to obtain voluntary compliance with adult suggestions. Positive discipline involves setting fair, reasonable limits, explaining the need for desired behavior, and avoiding threats or force (Becker, 1964). Children tend to be more compliant when adults use positive discipline.

Positive discipline is a powerful method for eliciting compliances because it does not hurt children and because it tells them why they should or should not do something. Giving a reason along with a suggestion or prohibition is effective because it communicates the adult belief that the child can understand the reason; it enhances the child's self-esteem (Freedman, Carlsmith, & Sears, 1970); and it conveys adult trust in the child's willingness to comply.

Verbal Control: Effect on Compliance

Commands are positive or negative direct statements instructing a child to do something, e.g., "Don't pour the sand onto the sidewalk." "Keep the sand in the sandbox." *Suggestions* are statements phrased as requests or as questions, e.g., "How about getting your coat on now and we'll go outside."

The type of verbal control used illustrates an adult's general style of control. Some adults use both commands and suggestions, while others use commands almost exclusively. Each verbal control technique has a different effect on children's willingness to cooperate with an adult's request.

In Lytton's study all types of verbal control yielded compliance from children, but some types were much more effective than others. Suggestions resulted in compliance more frequently than did commands, and this finding has been supported in other studies as well (Forehand, Doleys, Hobbs, & Resick, 1976; Lytton, 1979; Minton et al., 1971; Peele & Routh, 1978). Lytton concluded that suggestions are so effective because adults who use them are sensitive and combine their verbal control with other excellent techniques that elicit compliance.

How do very young children respond to different verbal control techniques? In one interesting study, Schaffer and Crook (1980) found that very young children, 15 to 24 months old, respond to directions given either as commands or as suggestions. They concluded that other factors, especially nonverbal cues, carry crucial communicative meaning for children in an early stage of linguistic development, as very young children are.

Nonverbal Cues: Effect on Compliance

Appropriate physical contact, a source of comfort to a young child, is a part of the style of sensitive, supportive, encouraging adults (Satir, 1976; Sroufe & Ward, 1980). *Appropriate physical contact* reassures a child, is never imposed on a child, and is given in response to the *child's* needs. Examples of appropriate physical contact include physical guidance like an arm around the shoulder used as a matter-of-fact way to guide a child toward compliance, or a hug or reassuring pat or a handshake.

Appropriate physical contact may also be a necessary part of effective communication and an important factor in eliciting compliance. Kramer (1977) found that young children rely heavily on contextual situational cues in their earliest comprehension of adult speech, i.e., they rely on nonlinguistic cues to respond appropriately. Schaffer and Crook (1980) found that mothers who combine a verbal directive with some form of nonverbal reference to an object are two to three times more effective in getting a child's attention focused than are mothers whose verbal statements are unaccompanied by a nonverbal cue.

Clarity of Adult Instructions: Effect on Compliance

Adults rely on verbal instructions with varying degrees of success. To be helpful to a child and effective in eliciting compliance, adult instructions must be easily understood and must communicate enough information to get a child to carry out a suggestion. A child is able to decode statements that are simple, age-appropriate, and specific enough for the child's receptive verbal skills.

Timing and Pacing Instructions: Effect on Compliance

Timing
Proper timing of controls is an important factor in obtaining child compliance (Schaffer & Crook, 1980). *Timing* is the adult's ability to tune in to a child's state or level of awareness before offering a suggestion. The sensitive adult lets a child have enough time to work on one task before giving another hint or another command. However, this adult is able to sense when the child needs a new suggestion to maintain interest.

Instructions which come too late or when a child cannot use them are improperly timed and are likely to result in noncompliance. *Active poor timing* occurs when an adult gives another suggestion before a child has had time to respond to the last suggestion. *Passive poor timing* occurs when the adult does not even realize that his suggestions were not heard or were ignored. An adult with passive poor timing misses signals from the child.

Pacing
Proper *pacing* of instructions and suggestions involves the amount of information offered in one sentence or the speed at which an adult tries to make a child work. *Improper pacing* means that an adult gives too many suggestions at once, often in a "rapid-fire" series of sentences, is insensitive to a child's developmental limitations,

speaks too quickly for the child to comprehend, or does not allow the child to process what has been said before giving another suggestion or before repeating the instruction. When commands are given too rapidly a child can miss many of a series of instructions and become angry because it is simply impossible to comply.

What happens when a command is repeated too rapidly? Forehand et al. (1976) did a pretest before their study began and found that over 50 percent of the childen disobeyed commands. During the study in the experimental group, the adult repeated commands every 8 seconds if a child disobeyed, and found that repeating commands increased *non*compliance. Why did Forehand get this result?

The pacing of the commands could have been the problem. In the study, it was possible for a child to receive up to 80 repeated commands. A child who was non-compliant before the study and who did not have the option of refusing to participate might simply have withdrawn and refused to comply as a form of protest. The volume of commands and the rapidity with which they were given could have exacerbated the problem, arousing anger, frustration, and subsequent refusal to comply.

Rather than simply repeating a command every 8 seconds, a more effective and humane approach would be to tune in to a child's state of readiness to respond to the suggestion or his willingness to stop doing one thing when commanded to do another. Repeated commands in this experimental study were given abruptly by what might have appeared to the child to be an insensitive adult. Improper timing and pacing contribute to noncompliance. Repeated commands, given by a sensitive adult who properly orients the child and paces the commands well, might yield a higher level of compliance.

Reinforcement: Effect on Compliance

Positive Reinforcement

Studies of child compliance demonstrate that compliance is positively related to the use of a variety of positive reinforcement contingencies. They include verbal praise and reinforcement, positive statements, the presence of an adult, and physical expressions of pleasure like applause, hugs, or smiles (Goetz, Holmberg, & Le Blanc, 1975; Lytton, 1977, 1979; Matas, Arend, & Sroufe, 1978; Toepfer et al., 1972).

Reinforcement must be well-timed so that a child makes a connection between his actions and the adult's actions and comments. Verbal praise should also be related to the target behavior because it results in greater compliance.

Example "Thank you for picking up the blocks" is better than "That's a pretty dress" if the target behavior was picking up blocks.

Negative Attention

Some rather disturbing results show that some children are more compliant when they receive negative attention for what they have done. Why did these results occur and, more important, why should responsible adults be concerned about this finding?

Negative attention seems to "work" for several reasons. First, negative adult reactions are more likely to be used contingently, i.e., they are very likely to follow the

Appropriate physical contact is an important factor in eliciting compliance.

child's "misbehavior" rather closely in time. Second, negative reactions are more likely to be backed up by further consequences (Grusec & Kuczynski, 1980), while adults fail to back up positive comments as readily. Third, strength of consequences might have an effect. A child might be punished more severely for doing what adults say they dislike than for not doing what adults say they like (Forehand et al., 1976). Fourth, intensity of adult reaction plays a part. Negative attention in the Forehand study was fairly intensely aversive (the adult stood up quickly, crossed arms and said, "You did *not* do what I said right away, I don't like it when you disobey me!" The experimenter also glared at the child for 56 seconds). How would you feel if your instructor did that to you if you talked in class?

What is the real and long-term effect of using negative, hurtful tactics to get children to obey? Lytton and Zwirner (1975) believe that such power-assertive tactics do occasionally elicit immediate compliance, i.e., if you scare a child he will do what you want. Over a period of time, however, childen who are threatened or scared into obeying, as they were in the Forehand study, do not obey willingly. In fact, Lytton and Zwirner believe that the long-term effect will be greater *non*compliance or disobedience. Supportive adults just do not treat children like this.

Survey: How Adults Reinforce Compliance

With the value of reinforcement of child compliance clearly documented, Lytton (1979) investigated actual parental responses to child compliance. He found that in over 50 percent of the cases a child was given no reinforcement for compliance, especially by fathers. The most common response to obedience from a child was no response at all. The next most common response to a child's compliance was a neutral response, followed in third place by a parent issuing another request or command. Positive responses were only the fourth most common response. In natural encounters between adults and children it seems, then, that adult reinforcement of a child's obedience or compliance is erratic.

SPECIAL FOCUS: What Is A "Good" Limit?

Like most people, you probably see the necessity for placing limits on children's behavior. At the same time, you might have questions about setting limits: "How is this limit going to affect a child's behavior?" "How can I state limits so that a child will listen and cooperate?" "What should I do if a child won't comply with a limit that is clearly necessary?" "Can I ever be flexible about a rule once it is in place?" The following sections focus on what a good limit is and on how adults can help children comply with good limits.

A Good Limit Helps a Child Achieve Self-Control and Develop Positive Interactional Skills

Setting reasonable, fair limits on children's behavior benefits children in several ways: they develop self-esteem (Coopersmith, 1967), become cooperative and helpful (Marcus & Leiserson, 1978), develop independence and self-reliance (Baumrind, 1967), and become competent (White & Watts, 1973). Good rules and limits prohibit unacceptable behavior, like damaging property, disturbing others, or hurting people or animals and help children predict what will happen if they ignore the limits.

Example   You tell children that they can paint only on their painting and not on someone else's, but Jenny insists on splashing paint on Jean's work. The consequences of ignoring this limit might be that she would not be allowed to paint at all the next day. Jenny would soon learn to predict the consequences of her behavior.

Reasonable, fair rules and limits give children a chance to choose their behavior (painting on one's own work or not painting at all). Deciding how to act and experiencing safe consequences of behavior helps children achieve self-control and learn how to work well with others.

A Good Limit Protects a Child's Health and Safety

Adults have often been warned recently about the spread of disease in groups of young children. Responsible adults develop rules and limits for both children and adults that protect children from disease. Examples: following recommendations for diapering babies and toileting young children, a thorough handwashing routine, proper handling of food in cooking projects, washing and sterilizing toys and other equipment, using one's own toothbrush or towel, using tissues when sneezing, washing hands after sneezing, and giving children clothing that protects them from weather.

Supportive adults also develop rules and limits that ensure safety. Children feel safe when they know that they will not be hurt; therefore, a good limit would encourage children to work cooperatively with and not hurt others. Safety rules might govern the safe use of toys and equipment, e.g., drive trikes but no crashing; they might regulate where children could play, e.g., inside the playground fence. Can you think of other limits that focus on safety?

A Good Limit Never Degrades a Child

Good limits are stated and maintained so that the dignity of a child is protected. It is unprofessional and irresponsible to embarrass or humiliate a child when setting rules. Insensitive adults somehow manage to take a perfectly legitimate limit and state it or carry it out in such a way that a child feels degraded.

Example   In a rainy, wet climate a reasonable limit is that children must wear dry clothing inside. When children get clothes wet, Mrs. Johnson makes them take off socks and pants and wear a coat until their clothes dry. She does not bother to ask parents to send extra clothes. She embarrasses the children when maintaining the rule. Mrs. Weaver asks parents to send extra socks, pants, and shoes and merely tells children to change. She carries out the limit humanely.

A Good Limit Has Real Meaning

Some rules are meaningful. They have a purpose that most people recognize and acknowledge. Other rules are arbitrary, imposed with no justification. We have all experienced and have been angry with arbitrarily imposed purposeless rules, and children can feel the same frustration. Adults might ask questions or complain about arbitrary rules, but children usually act out their frustration.

Example   A reasonable rule is that everyone gather in a group before going outside. Mrs. Johnson invites trouble by making children stand in a straight line with their hands on the shoulders of the child in front of them. The children squirm around and start shoving. Mrs. Weaver makes the group gather but allows the children to sit on the floor and talk quietly until everyone is present and then issues a firm, quiet request for careful listening.

A Good Limit Is Developmentally Valid

Remarkable changes occur in a child's development in the first several years of life. Rapid cognitive, linguistic, motor, and social developments set the stage for the development of self-control. As children grow and develop, their new skills lead adults to expect different behavior from them. Adults must be ready and willing to examine limits as children get older to make sure the rules are valid for a child's changing developmental level.

Example   A 2½-year-old might be allowed to climb to the second rung on a rope ladder. When he is 4 he will be allowed to climb higher because he is motorically more skillful and has more self-control.

SPECIAL FOCUS: Helping Children Comply with Limits

Imagine yourself as the teacher of a group of 4-year-old children. It is Friday morning and that makes it 5 days in a row that John has clearly ignored your request to put things away at cleanup time. You have tried blinking the lights for a 5-minute signal and again at cleanup time. You announce cleanup to the entire group and are surprised (and annoyed) to see several children scatter, leaving toys in various areas. Today, for example, John left the play village set in the block corner at the 5-minute warning and went to the book area. He has done something like this every day this week. What can you do?

There is very little that you can do to force John to clean up, but several practical strategies that you can use will set the stage for compliance. These strategies will make it possible for John to obey or comply willingly with a legitimate request to clean up. All of these strategies are rooted in adult sensitivity to a child's abilities and limitations and to the child's state of awareness and needs.

Adults influence children indirectly *by providing physical settings and materials.*

Tune In to the Situation and Orient the Child Properly

☐ *Decrease distance between adult and child.* Walk over to the reading area and then bend or stoop so that you are not towering over John.

☐ *Minimize intense, intruding stimuli if necessary.* Make sure that you are not competing with loud noises when you give a suggestion. Your goal is to have John listen to you and not be distracted.

☐ *Observe what the child is doing.* John is reading. If lights are blinked and cleanup announced to the group, the chances are great that he will not go to the block area to put away the play village.

☐ *Direct the child's visual attention to a specific object or task.* Have John look at the block area.

☐ *Have the child make contact with a specific object or situation.* Have John move to the block area and specifically to the play village setup.

☐ *Finally, make a specific request.* John is much more likely to comply with a specific adult request if he is in the block area and holding some of the play village equipment when you suggest that he put them away than if he is sitting in another area reading when lights are blinked.

Use An Effective and Positive Method of Verbal Control

☐ *Use suggestions whenever possible.*

☐ *Use commands when necessary, but use them wisely.*

Avoid restrictive commands like the following: "John, get over to that block corner and put your things away right now!" Restrictive commands arouse anger because they simply order, and they are frequently disobeyed. Instead, use *nonrestrictive* commands, e.g., "John, I want you to put the play village away because you took it out and because we need the space for group time." Suggestions and nonrestrictive

Children who trust adults and who do not fear loss of the adult's approval are the most likely to comply with the adult's suggestions.

commands are usually obeyed because they are given by a self-responsible adult who does not simply give an order.

Use Appropriate Nonverbal Cues
Compliance with a reasonable rule or limit is more likely when you use an appropriate nonverbal cue along with a verbal suggestion.

Examples *Touch* John on the arm to get his attention, *look* directly but non-threateningly at him, *point* to the block area, *put an arm on his shoulder* as you physically guide him to the block area, *point to or touch* the toys, *demonstrate* to get him started, and *point* to the shelf. The use of nonverbal cues is essential with toddlers and is highly recommended with preschoolers, especially those children who have not been very compliant.

Make Sure Instructions Are Clear and Helpful
Responsible adults do not expect children to guess what the rules are. Instead, they

☐ *make sure rules are overt.* All rules and limits are out in the open. They are not hidden, and all the children know what they are.

☐ *use simple language and concrete terms.* "Put the play village on the bottom shelf" is more concrete than "Put it over there."

☐ *tell a child exactly what to do,* rather than what not to do. It is more helpful to say "Put the village set on the shelf" than "Don't leave the village set on the floor."

Give a Reason Along with the Limit
"Play the piano softly *so that the others are not disturbed.*"

"One person is allowed at a time on the slide *so that you don't crash into one another.*"

"Put all of these toys in the box *so that they don't get lost.*"

Such short, simple, concrete reasons given along with a limit tend to foster compliance. Giving a *rationale* (a reason) is a powerful technique used by supportive adults who think that simply ordering someone around is both uncalled for and ineffective.

Time and Pace Suggestions Well
☐ Speak slowly enough that the child hears everything you have said.

☐ Issue only a few suggestions at a time.

☐ Give the child enough time to process the information.

☐ Allow enough time for the child to complete a task before making another suggestion.

☐ Repeat a limit well, if it is necessary to repeat.

Children do not always obey even the best-stated limits, so you will undoubtedly have to repeat limits occasionally. Avoid simply shouting the limit again. Instead, look for ways to restate the limit more effectively. For example, if John ignores your request then you might try calling his name again, tapping him on the shoulder, picking up or touching one of the toys, looking him in the eye, handing him a toy, and then firmly repeating the request.

Reinforce Compliance

Suppose that John finally complies with your request. You then want him to pick things up in the book area. What should you say as he finishes in the block area?

Recognize obedience/compliance before giving another command. Instead of just issuing another command immediately, use positive verbal or physical reinforcers to let John know you recognize his effort. Give reinforcement soon after he finishes. Connect the reinforcer with the act and do it simply.

Examples "I see that the play village has been put away. Thanks, John." "You've really cleaned this area up, John" (shake his hand). At group time note contributions made by each child at cleanup, "We really cleaned our room today. Sam and Lou cleaned the paintbrushes, John put away the play village . . . . Thank you for working together."

Enforce a Limit Firmly but Gently

Some children forget limits and have only to be reminded that limits exist. Others "test" limits, and others simply refuse to comply. It is with the "testers" and "refusers" that you will have to carry out what may well be the most difficult part of responsible caregiving. If a limit is reasonable and fair, if it protects the child's health or safety, or if it teaches self-control, then your responsibility does not allow you just to shrug it off when a child ignores the limit. Enforcing a limit requires that adults

□ *use positive discipline techniques.* Avoid the urge to become aversive or hurtful. Avoid sarcasm, ridicule, and other hurtful techniques. Getting compliance by arousing the child's fear is not desirable.

□ *be firm but also kind.* Do not act like a dictator. Instead, be real, i.e., match your feeling with facial expression and verbal message. How would you feel if John refused to clean up? Angry? Frustrated? Talk to him alone. Let him know exactly what the problem is without demeaning him. "John, I asked you to put away the village set two times and I see that you did not do it. I get angry when you don't put things away because somebody else has to do your work and that isn't fair. I want you to make a choice: You can either choose to put the toys away now or you can choose not to play in the block corner at all tomorrow."

(See chapter 5 for a more complete description of additional specific positive discipline techniques.)

SUMMARY: KEY CONCEPTS IN THIS CHAPTER

1. All adults, whether they are warm and supportive or cold and nonsupportive, influence children through specific processes: *M*odeling, Direct *I*nstruction, Use of *R*einforcement/*R*eward and Punishment, Providing *P*hysical Materials and Set-

tings, Stating *Expectations for Desired Behavior*, and Use of *Cognitive Modifica-tion Strategies*.

2. Child compliance is a developmental issue because of the convergence of several developmental phenomena. Compliance is an important issue for all members of the guidance system.

3. Adults have a role in helping children comply with reasonable and fair limits. Adults who develop a trusting, harmonious relationship with children and who are sensitive to a child's abilities and state tend to elicit greater levels of compli-ance. Adults who use socializing techniques that avoid power assertion also elicit compliance.

4. Generalizations can be made about "good" rules or limits, wherever the limit is used. Adults can encourage compliance with appropriate rules and limits using several practical techniques. All of the recommended adult techniques center on adult helpfulness; adults must set the situation up so that children will comply, not out of fear, but willingly.

OBSERVE: CHILD GUIDANCE IN ACTION

Observe an adult and a child as the adult attempts to get the child to comply with a limit. Using the information in SPECIAL FOCUS: Helping Children Comply with Limits, briefly describe how helpful the adult's actions are. For example, how well does the adult orient the child? What type of verbal control is used? Does the adult use appropriate nonverbal cues? Are instructions clear and helpful? Does the adult give a reason along with the limit? Are suggestions timed and paced well? What does the adult do if the child *does* obey/comply? If the child *does not* comply? Use the fol-lowing format.

Date: _____

Time: _____

Child's first name: _____

Child's approximate age: _____

Setting: _____

What was the adult? _____(e.g., parent, babysitter, teacher)

EPISODE 1

Describe an interaction between an adult and a child in which the adult attempts to get the child to comply with (obey) a suggestion or a limit.

Briefly describe how helpful the adult's actions were. Be specific by giving examples to back up what you think.

Compare your observations with those of another class member. Disagreement is OK. If you disagreed, say why.

EPISODE 2   Use the same format.

REFERENCES

BAUMRIND, D. (1967). Child care practices anteceding three patterns of preschool behavior. *Genetic Psychology Monographs, 75,* 43–88.

BECKER, W.C. (1964). Consequences of different kinds of parental discipline. In M.L. Hoffman & L.S. Hoffman (Eds.), *Review of child development research,* Vol. 1. New York: Russell Sage Foundation.

COOPERSMITH, S. (1967). *The antecedents of self-esteem.* Princeton, NJ: Princeton University Press.

DWECK, C.S. (1978). Achievement. In M.E. Lamb (Ed.), *Social and personality development.* New York: Holt, Rinehart & Winston.

DWECK, D.S., & ELLIOTT, E.S. (1983). Achievement motivation. In P. Mussen (Ed.), *Handbook of child psychology,* Vol. 4. New York: Wiley.

FLAVELL, J.H. (1977). *Cognitive development.* Englewood Cliffs, NJ: Prentice-Hall.

FOREHAND, R., DOLEYS, D., HOBBS, S., & RESICK, P. (1976). An examination of disciplinary procedures with children. *Journal of Experimental Child Psychology, 21,* 109–120.

FREEDMAN, J.L., CARLSMITH, J.M., & SEARS, D.O. (1970). *Social psychology.* Englewood Cliffs, NJ: Prentice-Hall.

GOETZ, E.M., HOLMBERG, M.C., & LeBLANC, J. (1975). Differential reinforcement of other behavior and noncontingent reinforcement as control procedures during the modification of a preschooler's compliance. *Journal of Applied Behavior Analysis, 8*(1), 77–82.

GREEN, K., FOREHAND, R., & MacMAHON, R. (1979). Parental manipulation of compliance and noncompliance in normal and deviant children. *Behavior Modification, 3*(2), 245–266.

GRUSEC, J., & KUCZYNSKI, L. (1980). Direction of effect in socialization: A comparison of the parent's versus the child's behavior as determinants of disciplinary techniques. *Developmental Psychology, 16,* 1–9.

HASWELL, K., HOCK, E., & WENAR, C. (1981). Oppositional behavior of preschool childen: Theory and intervention. *Family Relations, 30,* 440–446.

HETHERINGTON, E.M. (1983). Preface to volume IV. In P. Mussen (Ed.), *Handbook of child psychology,* Vol. 4, New York: Wiley.

KRAMER, P.E., (1977). Young children's free responses to anomalous commands. *Journal of Experimental Child Psychology, 24,* 219–234.

LYTTON, H. (1977). Correlates of compliance and the rudiments of conscience in two-year-old boys. *Canadian Journal of Behavioral Science, 9,* 242–251.

LYTTON, H. (1979). Disciplinary encounters between young boys and their mothers and fathers: Is there a contingency system? *Developmental Psychology, 15,* 256–258.

LYTTON, H., & ZWIRNER, W. (1975). Compliance and its controlling stimuli obeserved in a natural setting. *Developmental Psychology, 11,* 769–779.

MACCOBY, E.E., & MARTIN, J.A. (1983). Socialization in the context of the family: Parent-child interaction. In P. Mussen (Ed.), *Handbook of child psychology*, Vol. 4. New York: Wiley.

MARCUS, R.F., & LEISERSON, M. (1978). Encouraging helping behavior. *Young Children*, *33*(6), 24–34.

MARION, M. (1981). *Guidance of young children*. St. Louis: Mosby.

MARION, M. (1982). Primary prevention of child abuse: The role of the family life educator. *Family Relations, 31*, 575–582.

MARION, M. (1983). Child compliance: A review of the literature with implications for family life education. *Family Relations, 32*, 545–555.

MATAS, L., AREND, R., & SROUFE, L. (1978). Continuity of adaptation in the second year: The relationship between quality of attachment and later competence. *Child Development, 49*, 547–556.

MINTON, D., KAGAN, J., & LEVINE, J. (1971). Maternal control and obedience in the two-year-old. *Child Development, 42*, 1873–1894.

PEELE, R.A., & ROUTH, D.K. (1978). Maternal control and self-control in the three-year-old child. *Bulletin of the Psychonomic Society, 11*(6), 349–352.

RADIN, N. (1982). The unique contribution of parents to childrearing: The preschool years. In S. Moore and C. Cooper (Eds.), *The young child: Reviews of Research*, Vol. 3. Washington, DC: NAEYC.

REDD, W.H. (1976). The effects of adult presence and stated preference on the reinforcement control of children's behavior. *Merrill-Palmer Quarterly, 22*, 93–97.

ROLLINS, B., & THOMAS, D. (1979). Parental support, power, and control techniques in the socialization of children. In W. Burr, R. Hill, F. Nye, & R. Reiss (Eds.), *Contemporary theories about the family*, Vol. 1. New York: Free Press.

SAMEROFF, A.J. (1982). Development and the dialectic: The need for a systems approach. In W.A. Collins (Ed.), *The concept of development: Minnesota Symposium on Child Psychology*, Vol. 15, Hillsdale, NJ: Erlbaum.

SATIR, V. (1976). *Making contact*. Millebrae, CA: Celestial Arts.

SCHAFFER, H.R., & CROOK, C.K. (1980). Child compliance and maternal control techniques. *Developmental Psychology, 16*, 54–61.

SROUFE, L.A., & WARD, M.J. (1980). Seductive behavior of mothers of toddlers: Occurrence, correlates and family origins. *Child Development, 51*, 1222–1229.

STAYTON, D.J. HOGAN, R., & AINSWORTH, M.D.S. (1971). Infant obedience and maternal behavior: The orgins of socialization reconsidered. *Child Development, 42*, 1057–1069.

TOEPFER, D., REUTER, J., & MAURER, C. (1972). Design and evaluation of an obedience training program for mothers of preschool children. *Journal of Consulting and Clinical Psychology, 39*(2), 194–198.

WHITE, B.L., & WATTS, J.C. (1973). *Experience and environment: Major influences on the development of the young child*, Vol. 1. Englewood Cliffs, NJ: Prentice-Hall.

2

The Child in the
Guidance System:
Guidance and Cognitive
Development

Chapter Overview

EFFECT OF A CHILD'S DEVELOPMENTAL LEVEL ON AN ADULT'S GUIDANCE TECHNIQUES
PIAGET: COGNITIVE DEVELOPMENT
    Infancy: The Sensorimotor Stage
    Ages 2 to 5: The Preoperational Stage
MEMORY
SPECIAL FOCUS: "FFLS RAN:" Setting the Stage for Memory Development
PERCEPTION
SPECIAL FOCUS: Preschool Perceptual Limitations: Implications for Guidance

---

After reading and studying this chapter, you will be able to:

☐ *Name and describe* the positive cognitive accomplishments and cognitive limitations of the first two Piagetian stages.

☐ *Explain* how cognitive abilities and limitations affect adult guidance techniques.

☐ *List and describe* specific guidance techniques for helping children remember things and for dealing with preschool perceptual limitations.

EFFECT OF A CHILD'S DEVELOPMENTAL LEVEL ON AN ADULT'S GUIDANCE TECHNIQUES

Examples Ross, 8 years old, ran over his sister's sandcastle. When questioned by his father, Ross lied, "No, Dad. I was down near the water. I saw somebody run over it, though." Ross is becoming an accomplished liar and has also been accused of cheating in school.

Pete and Amanda, 4 years old, worked at the watertable. Pete was using a large pitcher to transfer water from one container to another. Amanda grabbed the pitcher and when Pete claimed ownership, she hit him.

Seven-year-old Jenny's parents had been recently divorced and Jenny thought her mom had left because Jenny was a "bad girl." Her father did not know how to help her.

Five-year-old Courtney went to a funeral. "What *is* this, Mama?" she asked as they entered the viewing room. "Oh, no!" thought her mother, "I thought Grandma told her about funerals." "Tell me, Mama, tell me!" "Aunt Blanche died, Courtney." "What is that—*died*?" Courtney's mother thought, "What do I say now?"

Cris's father stormed into Cris's teacher's office and shouted, "Let me tell you what Cris said yesterday! '@@@@@ you.' How do you like that? Is that what you teach in this school?"

"If she asks one more question, I'm going to scream," said the leader of the 7- and 8-year-old campers. "Judy asks a question about every three minutes." Just then Judy approached and said, "Is this the way I should write my name, Mr. Hoffman?" Mr. Hoffman pasted a smile on his face and said through clenched teeth, "Yes, Judy." Then he sat down, put his head in his hands, and said, "Help!"

How should these situations be handled? Some adults guide children effectively and help them become honest, cooperative, kind, and assertive people who like themselves. These adults guide children effectively, not because of any magic answers, but because of their attitudes about children, knowledge of child development, and general style of behavior toward children. Adults who guide children effectively tend to view other people, including children, as basically good. They genuinely like most other people, including children, and believe that every person, including a child, deserves respectful treatment.

Effective adults understand child development. They realize that children influence adults just as adults influence children (Bell, 1968) and that children have a unique temperament or behavioral style from infancy (Thomas, Chess, & Birch, 1968). Some adults guide children effectively because they know that age-related capabilities and limitations determine the nature of a child's relationship with others and set limits on a child's ability to understand and comply with an adult's guidance.

How do we help children like Courtney, Amanda, Ross, and the others? First, we can help them best by always remembering that these children are just as much an active part of the guidance system as we adults are—that regardless of a child's age, her behavior is part of an interaction and does not exist in isolation (Maccoby & Martin, 1983). Second, whenever a problem presents itself, focus on the child and what she is like. How old is she? What stage of thinking is she in? How does she perceive things? What is her memory capacity?

This section focuses on cognitive development. Piaget's theory tells us much about the cognitive abilities and limitations of each stage. Effective guidance techniques during childhood take into account both the abilities and the limitations of a child.

PIAGET: COGNITIVE DEVELOPMENT

Infancy: The Sensorimotor Stage

Piaget called the first stage of cognitive development (birth to approximately 24 months) the *sensorimotor* stage because infants are equipped with *sensory* (looking, listening, and touching) and *motor* abilities (grasping, head turning, hitting, etc.) and use the sensorimotor schemes to acquire information about their world. Infants do not "think" or reflect on problems or contemplate as older children or adults do.

Piaget divided the sensorimotor stage into six substages to describe the transformation in cognitive skills during a child's first 2 years. In the first few months of life infants practice sensorimotor schemes. By 24 months they show evidence of the emerging ability to use symbols. Progress through the six substages occurs partly because of an infant's ability to imitate, which improves as the infant gets older. Infants also acquire knowledge about object permanence as they progress through the sensorimotor stage (Harris, 1983).

In spite of relatively poor motor skills, the human infant is a competent, active, information-processing person. A baby's perceptual skills are good enough, even at birth, to allow her to explore and discover her world, but perceptual skills change in several ways as infants grow older (Gibson & Spelke, 1983). Infants seem to prefer some patterns over others and are able to use color to perceive their world. They also become able to perceive depth. The visual and nervous systems undergo continual development during a child's first year, making more sophisticated perception possible.

An infant's sensorimotor and perceptual skills affect learning and memory during infancy. During an infant's earliest months, motor and neurological immaturity limit her ability to process information. Sensory, perceptual, and attentional skills develop rapidly from birth to 12 months. From about 6 to 12 months, infants use all of their skills to acquire and retain a knowledge base.

The second year of life (12 to 24 months) is a time of profound cognitive changes, all of which converge in the development of symbolic thought. By age 2, children can picture things in their minds, can imitate something seen earlier, and can use and understand language. Language is considered to be one of the most important ways in which a child shows us that she can, at age 2, use symbols.

Ages 2 to 5: The Preoperational Stage

Children aged 2 to 5 are usually in the second of Piaget's stages of cognitive development, the *preoperational* stage. The preschool years are a time of intellectual accomplishment, but preoperational thinkers also have some major limitations on their ability to think. This section focuses on the positive features and also describes some of the cognitive limitations of preoperational thinking. These cognitive abilities and limitations influence the child's interactions with adults and the child's capacity for self-control.

Symbolic Function: The Major Cognitive Ability of Preoperational Thinking
The major cognitive accomplishment of the preoperational stage is the attainment of the *symbolic function*. Two- to 5-year-old children can "hold pictures in their mind" and use symbols to represent or "stand for" their experiences (Flavell, 1977; Piaget, 1952, 1976, 1983). Given a bucket of water and a brush, a preschool child will happily paint the nearest brick wall. She uses the water to "stand for" or represent paint because she is now capable of using symbols.

Several indicators tell us when a child has attained the symbolic function—the use of language, deferred imitation, and the use of art media. Mr. Moore's class, for example, took a field trip to an apple orchard and the children used all of these methods to represent the experience.

Language   Words are symbols that are agreed on by many members of a social group and give the children in Mr. Moore's group an excellent way to represent their experience. After the trip the children dictated a story about the field trip. At group time Mr. Moore taught the children a rhyme about an apple tree. Three of the children reenacted apple picking by doing a puppet story with each puppet having a part.

Deferred Imitation   *Deferred imitation* is a good sign that a child has acquired the ability to use symbols. It refers to the ability to observe an event, form and hold a visual image of the event, and then imitate the action at a later time. While on the field trip to the orchard, the children observed an adult picking apples and loading them into a container. The next day, Tim climbed onto a ladder and pretended to pick apples. He reached, plucked an imaginary apple, and dumped it into a basket. Tim spontaneously reproduced the apple picker's actions at a later time—hence the term *deferred imitation*. This ability appears now because he can hold pictures of events (apple picking) in his mind and can recall the events at some later time, something that was not possible during infancy.

Use of art media   "I'm making apples, just like the ones we picked!" Tony rolled chunks of red playdough into apple-like shapes. Over at the fingerpainting table, Sandy smoothed the red paint onto her paper and then began making circles. "Look, Mr. Moore. Apples." Some of the children were busy bending red pipe cleaners into apple shapes and placing them on a big branch stuck in a bucket—their own version of an apple tree.

What does the symbolic function have to do with child guidance? The preoperational thinker, because of her ability to use symbols, is no longer locked in the private world of infancy. She experiences events and can now represent them in several ways. She can now symbolically represent her own private experiences, whether good or bad. For example, if the adults in a child's life use harsh discipline, then this is what a child experiences. Some of the pictures in her mind are of harsh

John is engaging in deferred imitation. *He observed a baker, formed and held a picture of the event, and is imitating the action at a later time.*

discipline. Another child experiences more humane, loving treatment and sees adults dealing with others fairly. The pictures in this child's mind are different from the first child's. A child's new cognitive skill allows her to reproduce her experiences, whether they are good or bad.

Limitations of Preoperational Thinking

On the one hand, if you compare the thinking of a 4-year-old with that of an 18-month-old you will quickly note how much more "grownup" the 4-year-old's cognitive skills are. Being able to represent experiences is a significant cognitive event in a human's life. On the other hand, if you compare the thinking of this 4-year-old with that of his 10-year-old sister you will see that the abilities of the 4-year-old are balanced by some equally significant limitations on his ability to think logically. A preoperational child's cognitive limitations determine how effective an adult's guidance techniques will be. (See figure 2.1.)

Sandy's use of paint shows that she has the ability to use symbols to represent her experience.

Preoperational thinkers tend to be egocentric. Listen to a preschool child for a short time. You will smile at some of the funny things she says and the charm with which she says them. You will also be slightly puzzled. The author had the following conversation with her 5½-year-old niece about how to get to a store:

Adult: "Lisa, tell me how to get to the ice cream store."
Lisa: "You go to the corner and then turn."
Adult: "Which corner?"
Lisa: "You know, the one with the trees."

Lisa, at that time, was *egocentric.* She did not give all the necessary information, largely because she did not understand exactly what the listener had to know. She probably also thought that the listener had the same information as she.

Children who are *egocentric* tend to be centered on their *selves.* This is not the same thing as being selfish. It does mean that the distinction between their own perspective or point of view and that of another person is blurred (Piaget, 1968, 1976). A preoperational thinker like Lisa believes that everyone thinks the same way she does (Jackson, Robinson, & Dale, 1977).

One of the significant themes in cognitive development is the gradual movement away from egocentricity. This shift takes place slowly and not automatically. Children become less egocentric through *social interaction* (Piaget, 1968, 1976).

Example Kathy and Jane were making tunnels in wet sand. Their tunnels met and the girls argued loudly about which direction the tunnel should take. Mr. Moore

FIGURE 2.1   **Step (a):** The child agrees that each container holds an equivalent volume of water. **Step (b):** The child watches the teacher pour the liquid from "B" into "C." The preoperational thinker will say that "C" contains more than "A." When asked for a reason, she will indicate that it simply looks like more.

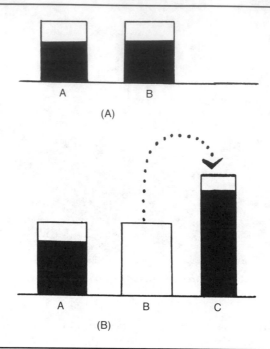

watched but decided not to step in because he had helped them work through many similar disagreements. The girls finally compromised and dug a long wide tunnel together.

As children get older they interact socially with other children and are frequently confronted with others' viewpoints. Adults can help children become less egocentric by pointing out that another person does have rights and does have a different viewpoint. Adults who guide young children through situations when viewpoints clash by teaching children how to negotiate, to be assertive, and to use problem-solving skills help children become less egocentric.

Some researchers have begun to question whether young children are as egocentric as Piaget originally thought they were (Gelman & Baillargeon, 1983). These recent questions are based on research that seems to show that the original tests of egocentricity were too abstract and complicated (Flavell, Green, & Wilcox, 1981). In spite of this research, adults who work and live with children realize that young children are not very skillful in dealing with confrontations or different viewpoints and need adult guidance.

Preoperational thinkers tend to judge things by how they look.   Preoperational thinkers say that the tall container has more water in it "because it looks like it has more." (See figure 2.1.) Young children frequently judge things not on the basis

FIGURE 2.2 The *pouring* of the liquid is the transformation.

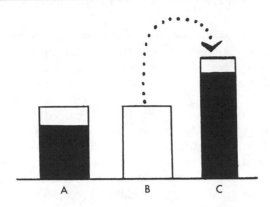

of logic but by how they appear on a surface level. Children are often deceived by appearances.

Adults can use their understanding of this aspect of preoperational thinking to guide children effectively. Suppose, for example, that 3-year-old Jack pinches other children. Two adults in his life deal with his pinching quite differently.

Babysitter: Pulls Jack away from the other child, pinches him, and hisses, "Now you know how it feels when you pinch other people."
Jack's dad: "Oh, no, Jack! Ouch! Pinching *hurts* Sara. If you want her to move, tell her. No pinching."

Some adults, like Jack's babysitter, think that pinching a child who pinches someone else will teach her not to pinch. These adults think, mistakenly, that pinching a child will help her understand how the other person felt. An egocentric child, deceived by appearances, does not benefit from the adult's retaliatory pinch. In spite of what an adult says along with the pinch, the intense stimulus is the pinch and that is the target of the child's attention.

Jack's father seems to have a better understanding of his egocentric child and uses a more effective, humane way of dealing with the problem. He is firm and makes it clear that pinching is not allowed, but he does it in a way that does not hurt Jack.

Preoperational thinkers focus on the here-and-now and ignore transformations. Preoperational thinkers tend to look at things as they currently exist and to ignore the process or transformation that resulted in the perceived change. In the conservation task, a preoperational thinker focuses first on water in the two short glasses. Then she focuses on water in one short and one tall glass. She ignores the transformation, the pouring of water from *B* to *C* (figure 2.2). An older child, adolescent, or adult would notice the pouring and would say, "All you did was to pour the water."

What impact does this particular limitation have on how adults guide children? It is not very fruitful to try to explain a *transformation* (like pouring water) to a child.

The child in a conservation experiment actually watches the water being poured but simply ignores it. This inability to see how things change affects a young child's social world.

Example Three-year-old Jeff watched his older brother disguise himself as a monster for Halloween. Putting on the costume and makeup was the transformation. When his brother was finished Jeff looked startled, screamed in terror, and ran to his father. "Oh, Jeff. You know he is just Erik," his father explained, but Jeff was not convinced.

Jeff focused on his brother before makeup, ignored the putting on of makeup (the transformation), and then focused on the monster. Jeff's father then tried a different approach. He let Jeff put on some of the makeup to create his own disguise, thus having Jeff actually perform the transformation. Many early childhood teachers who set up watertable activities in which children pour water from one container to another also encourage the children to focus on a transformation, the process of pouring.

Preoperational thinkers have difficulty reversing a process You realize that you could quickly show that the amount of liquid in *C* is equivalent to that in *A* by simply pouring the contents of *C* back into *B* (figure 2.3). Young children would not think so logically. How would this limitation affect how adults guide children? Adults often forget that children do not automatically know how to reverse an action.

Example Alex took all of the french fries he was supposed to share with his sister. His mother noticed and said, "I'm going to get more napkins and you'd better be sharing when I get back." Alex is not likely to know how to remedy the problem, largely because he is not able to reverse a process. His mom is justified in expecting him to share, and she probably would have been more effective if she had simply stated her instructions more clearly, "Alex, your sister needs some french fries, too. I want you to give some to her. Here are two napkins. Put some french fries on each."

FIGURE 2.3 Preoperational thinkers have difficulty reversing their thought.

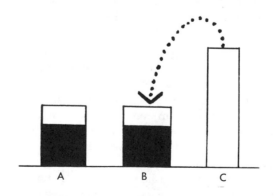

Memory

As children move through the preschool years their memory capacity and memory skills improve, but the memory of a preschool child, like all of her other cognitive skills, is limited. Limited memory capacity and skills have an impact on how well a child remembers suggestions or limits. This section focuses on the memory of a preschool child. Practical techniques for helping children remember things are suggested.

Types of Memory: Recognition, Long-term, Short-term

Recognition memory is the ability to recognize something seen previously (Perlmutter & Myers, 1979). Infants have good recognition memory, and young children do, too. However, preschool children are not as good with recognition memory when the thing to be recognized is complex or if they have to scan and compare stimuli systematically for a sustained period of time.

Example Marty watched her teacher write her name and birthdate on a tagboard "birthday cake." The teacher then showed Marty her "cake" and one other. Marty recognized hers easily (good recognition memory). The next day, however, Marty's cake was on the wall with 20 others. Marty looked for a long time but this time could not recognize her "cake."

Long-term memory is a process used to store or keep a permanent record of events (Jackson et al., 1977). People can remember things that happened years and years before. They often forget specific details but remember strong sensory images: the strong odor of disinfectant present in hospitals, the aroma of chocolate as the family car rolled into Hershey, Pennsylvania, the flames and sirens of fire engines that followed an explosion, the "clickety-click" of a teacher's metal signal used to line children up. Children who have been hospitalized or sexually abused will often reenact their experience long after the event by talking about it, using puppets, or even drawing pictures.

Short-term memory is the process used for temporary storage of new information.

Example The first time that fingerpainting was made available, Peter observed the procedure—put on apron, wet the paper, blob paint on the paper, paint, hang up painting, wash the table and hands. He stored the instructions and when it was his turn he remembered each step except wetting the paper and washing the table.

Short-term memory is also used for temporary storage of well-known information. Information is pulled out of long-term memory because the child needs access to it for something that is happening. For example, a small group in Mr. Moore's class was preparing to make cupcakes. Mr. Moore encouraged them to access their long-term memory and call up some information to be placed temporarily in short-term memory by reminding them of a similar baking activity about 6 weeks earlier.

Example "We made a heart-shaped cake for Valentine's Day. Tell me what things we used—a bowl, a mixer, and a _____. What sorts of things went into the cake? Flour, sugar, butter, _____, _____, _____. What went into the bowl first? Second? When everything was in the bowl, what did each of you do? Well, today

SPECIAL FOCUS: "FFLS RAN": Setting the Stage for Memory Development

It is grouptime in Ms. Alvarez's class of 4-year-olds. She will be showing a film about a veterinarian examining a dog but is first reviewing another day's activity—a visit from a dog groomer. "Last week Janet's dad brought their dog Max for a visit and showed us how he grooms Max. I am going to show you some pictures I took of Max being groomed, and I want you to remember and tell me what is happening in each slide." Ms. Alvarez, in addition to planning lessons about animals and community helpers, is using one of several strategies that contribute to a child's memory development (Jackson et al., 1977). An early childhood classroom is replete with opportunities, during routines and more structured learning activities, to focus on memory development.

Suggestion Use a mnemonic, pronounced by omitting the first *m,* a memory device or strategy to help you remember the following list of suggestions. This mnemonic consists of the string of letters *FFLS RAN;* each letter is a cue for one of the suggestions.

---

1. *F* *Use familiar pictures, sounds, and objects.* Ms. Alvarez knows that recognition memory is easy for preschoolers and shows the slides to help children pull information from their long-term memory. After a visit to the zoo she plays a tape of sounds made by the animals the children saw.

2. *F* *Plan activities and lessons with fewer steps.* Ms. Alvarez plans an obstacle course with the limited memory capacity of preschoolers in mind. She arranges four parts to the course so that the children can easily remember "over the rope, through the tire, up the ladder, and down the slide."

3. *L* *Learn thoroughly and do not overload.* Young children remember better when they are asked to retain relatively few pieces of information. When the children have trouble remembering the names of all six shapes introduced in one lesson, Ms. Alvarez realizes that she has simply given too much information. Focusing on four instead of six new shapes results in better recall.

4. *S* *Encourage children to use memory strategies.* Preschool children remember better when they use memory strategies, but they tend to use them only when prompted by adults. One memory strategy is *verbal rehearsal,* e.g., repeating the names of the bones in the skull until they are memorized. Ms. Alvarez encourages the children to use verbal rehearsal when they sing a "name song" at the beginning of the year to learn each child's name.

5. *R* *Repeat things to be remembered.* Watching slides of the dog grooming session secures the memory of that event. Remembering that a square is a rectangle with four equal sides is easier when the information is repeated in several creative

ways on different days — using transparencies, styrofoam models, a construction paper mural, and square cookie cutters.

6. **A** *Actively involve children with things to be remembered.* Active involvement enhances memory. Learning and remembering the emergency fire escape route is easier when the class practices walking it a number of times and talking about it with the firefighter who visits the class.

The length of time spent on an activity depends, in part, on how attractive the activity is to the child.

7. **N** *Name things and experiences.* Labeling things helps children remember them. Before the trip to the zoo, Ms. Alvarez shows pictures of animals she thinks might be unfamiliar and names them for the children. At the zoo she repeats the names. When making pizza crust she labels the process of dough "rising" and many of the children remember the name of the process when they make yeast bread two weeks later.

FFLS RAN. Name as many of the ways adults can set the stage for children's memory development as you can — by using the mnemonic. Refer to the list only when your memory fails!

we're going to use exactly the same things but we will pour the batter into small cupcake pans instead of one large cakepan."

Perception

Preschool Children: Problems with Perception

Two- to 5-year-old children bring with them perceptual abilities acquired during infancy, but they still have problems with directing their attention. These problems fall into four categories (Jackson et al., 1977).

Searching and Scanning Skills   One of the major problems affecting perception in preschool children is their inability to plan and execute a well-coordinated search for information. Young children, for example, do search for something they have lost, but are not systematic in their search. Their search is not very accurate, it is less efficient than an older child's, and they do not seem to realize that they should stop searching at some point. Just watch a preschool child search for a detail in the picture on the back of a cereal box in which a person is asked to find something specific in an array. A 2- to 5-year-old has great difficulty finding a specific detail in a picture or in a printed word.

Tuning Out Irrelevant Information   Another perceptual problem is caused by a preschooler's incomplete ability to control attention. Young children have difficulty "tuning out" or ignoring meaningless information or stimulation. Their attention is captured by stimuli that are intense or novel. Anyone who has read a story to a group of preschool children can usually recall moments when the children stopped listening to the story upon hearing squeaky wheels in the parking lot or seeing the lights flash on and off. Older children might notice the light or noise but are better able to maintain attention to a lesson.

Attending Simultaneously to Several Aspects of a Problem   Suppose you were searching for a specific puzzle piece. It should be straight on two sides to fit into a corner and should have an inward curve on the third side. You could quickly distinguish the correct piece, but a young child might focus only on the straight sides and ignore the curved side. As a result she is quite likely to pick out the wrong corner piece. She has focused on only one aspect of the problem, and her perception is thus affected.

Degree of Reflectivity/Impulsivity   Children who are *reflective* work slowly and tend to be accurate. *Impulsive* children tend to work so quickly that they miss important information and therefore make unnecessary mistakes. Younger children tend to be more impulsive and thus create additional perceptual problems for themselves.

How Perception Will Change as Preschool Children Get Older

As children get older their perceptual abilities change, and these changes are related to advances in cognitive development. Children develop more mature reasoning skills, memory becomes more efficient, and they are better able to organize information using language and abstract concepts. Changes in perceptual abilities are also related to a broader base of experience (Jackson et al., 1977).

Selective Attention becomes Refined Even infants *select* patterns at which they look. A 2-year-old can attend selectively to stimuli, and this ability becomes even better during the childhood years as the child gradually learns to "tune out" or ignore distracting stimuli.

Time Spent "On-Task" Increases with Age Older children tend to stay with a task for a longer time than do younger children. The length of time spent on an activity, whatever a child's age, depends in part on how attractive the activity is to the child. Vincent, for example, merely glanced at a book about flowers but spent nearly 1½ hours with a family album at his grandmother's house. Looking at pictures of his father as a child seemed to fascinate him.

Redirecting Attention Becomes More Efficient with Age Older children can redirect their attention faster than younger children, When a task has a number of parts, the older child has an advantage because she is able to shift her focus quickly from one aspect to another. A child who can shift focus quickly and accurately is better able to pick out relationships between two parts of a task.

SPECIAL FOCUS: Preschool Perceptual Limitations: Implications for Guidance

Screen for Sensory Impairments
"Kathy is really getting to me. She just kept playing when I announced that it was cleanup time. She has done this several times before."

Kathy's teacher was unaware that Kathy had a mild hearing problem until she was screened. Children with a sensory handicapping condition are limited in how they function in their environments. This limitation can pose problems for the adult-child relationship (Levitt & Cohen, 1977).

Minimize Intense Intruding Stimuli
"Children have short attention spans" is a phrase that most adults have heard at one time or another. A young child's attention *is* captured by sudden or intense stimuli, but adults can help children concentrate on activities and learn self-control if they minimize intense intruding stimuli.

Example Mr. Moore's group took place just before lunch in the same room where lunch was served. The children were distracted by the noise of the food cart and of the aide as he cleaned and set tables. Mr. Moore and his aide brainstormed and came up with a number of ideas:

☐ Change the seating arrangement during group time so children face away from the lunch area.

☐ Bring in the food cart before group time.

☐ Wash and set table before group time or as children wash hands, or set the table quietly.

Teach Children to Scan Systematically
Peter could easily recognize his printed name. Mr. Moore noticed, however, that Peter, like almost every other child in the class, could not pick out his nametag when

all nametags were on a table. Peter looked at every nametag, even those whose first letter was not *P*. He failed to scan one row or column and then go to another. Peter's search was random and not systematic. Mr. Moore decided to teach some scanning skills.

Example   "Peter, look at this row. Touch each nametag as you look at it."

or

"Your name begins with *P*. Look for the first letter. Look for *P*." He encouraged Peter to ignore cards without a *P* as the first letter.

Encourage Impulsive Children to Slow Their Reaction Time

Impulsive children work very quickly and are frequently less accurate in their responses. They search even less efficiently than age-mates (Hartley, 1976). They get themselves into trouble because they are so impulsive.

Example   Tina ran into the classroom and zoomed into the crowded block area with only a brief glance around the room. The area was filled to capacity. Mr. Moore called Tina aside and said, "Tina, look at the sign. It says *4*. Now, count the children. There are four children here already. Let's find something else for you to do until you can play with blocks."

SUMMARY: KEY CONCEPTS IN THIS CHAPTER

1. Lying, grabbing things, questions about death, poor self-esteem, cursing. The manner in which adults react to typical developmental problems depends on their knowledge about child development, their attitude toward children, and the skills they possess for working with children. Adults who use positive guidance techniques realize that a child's level of development is largely responsible for the effectiveness of any technique. Piaget described stages of cognitive development. A child's ability to think changes with each new stage, but a child at each stage also has limitations on the ability to think.

2. Children from birth to approximately 24 months are in the first of Piaget's stages of cognitive development, the *sensorimotor* stage. Perceptual skills are refined, children acquire language, motor skills improve, and cognitive skills evolve.

3. Two- to 5-year-old children are usually in the second of Piaget's stages of cognitive development, the *preoperational* stage. The preschool years are a time of positive intellectual accomplishment, but preoperational thinkers also have some major limitations on their ability to think. Their cognitive abilities and limitations suggest implications for guidance.

OBSERVE: CHILD GUIDANCE IN ACTION

Observe a preschool child or a group of preschool children. Determine whether each child has acquired the *symbolic function;* i.e., is the child able to represent her experiences? Make this determination by observing whether the child engages in *de-*

ferred imitation and whether she *uses art media* to represent experience. Use the following format to record your observations.

Date: _____

Time: _____

Setting: _____

Child's first name: _____

Your name: _____

Give an example of deferred imitation. Describe what the child did.

Observe a child as he works with art media. Give an example of this child using art media to represent some experience he has had.

Share your observations with a classmate or with your class.

REFERENCES

BELL, R.Q. (1968). A reinterpretation of the direction of effect in studies of socialization. *Psychological Review, 75,* 81–95.

FLAVELL, J.H. (1977). *Cognitive development.* Englewood Cliffs, NJ: Prentice-Hall.

FLAVELL, J.H., FLAVELL, E.R., GREEN, F.L., & WILCOX, S.A. (1981). The development of three spatial perspective-taking rules. *Child Development, 52,* 356–358.

GELMAN, R., & BAILLARGEON, R. (1983). A review of some Piagetian concepts. In P. Mussen (Ed.), *Handbook of child psychology,* Vol. 3. New York: Wiley.

GIBSON, E.J., & SPELKE, E.S. (1983). The development of perception. In P. Mussen (Ed.), *Handbook of child psychology,* Vol. 3. New York: Wiley.

HARRIS, P.L. (1983). Infant cognition. In P. Mussen (Ed.), *Handbook of child psychology,* Vol. 2. New York: Wiley.

HARTLEY, D.G. (1976). The effect of perceptual salience on reflective-impulsive performance differences. *Developmental Psychology, 12,* 218–225.

JACKSON, N.E., ROBINSON, H.B., & DALE, P.S. (1977). *Cognitive development in young children.* Monterey, CA: Brooks/Cole.

LEVITT, E., & COHEN, S. (1977). Parents as teachers: A rationale for involving parents in the education of their young handicapped children. In L.G. Katz (Ed.), *Current topics in early childhood education,* Vol. 1. Norwood, NJ: Ablex.

MACCOBY, E.E., & MARTIN, J.A. (1983). Socialization in the context of the family: Parent-child interaction. In P. Mussen (Ed.), *Handbook of child psychology*, Vol. 4. New York: Wiley.

MEICHENBAUM, G., & GOODMAN, J. (1971). Training impulsive children to talk to themselves: A means of developing self-control. *Journal of Abnormal Psychology*, 77, 115–126.

PERLMUTTER, M., & MYERS, N.A. (1979). Development of recall in 2- to 4-year-old children. *Developmental Psychology*, 12, 271–272.

PIAGET, J. (1952). *The origins of intelligence in children.* New York: Norton.

PIAGET, J. (1968). *Six psychological studies.* New York: Random House.

PIAGET, J. (1976). The stages of intellectual development of the child. In N. Endler, L. Boulter, & H. Osser (Eds.), *Contemporary issues in developmental psychology* (2nd ed.). New York: Holt, Rinehart, & Winston.

PIAGET, J. (1983). Piaget's theory. In P. Mussen (Ed.), *Handbook of child psychology*, Vol. 1. New York: Wiley.

THOMAS, A., CHESS, S., & BIRCH, H. (1968). *Temperament and behavior disorders in children.* New York: New York University Press.

3

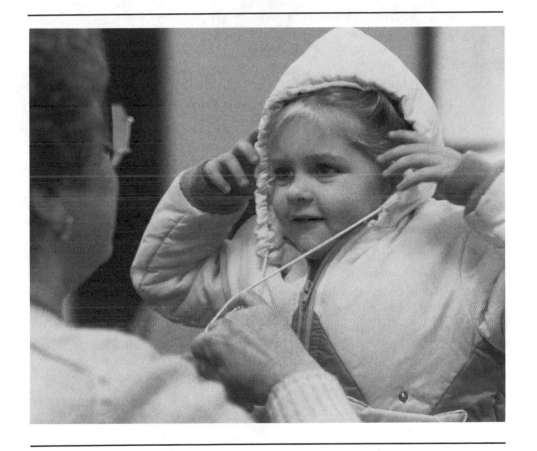

The Child in the Guidance System: Cognition and Social Interaction

Chapter Overview

After reading and studying this chapter, you will be able to:

☐ *Trace* the development of self-control.

☐ *Discuss* the relationship between cognitive development and social development.

☐ *Describe and discuss* how young children conceptualize the behavior of others, friendship, conflict relations, and morality or justice.

☐ *List and describe* specific guidance techniques for teaching the social skills of conflict resolution and the art of developing a friendship.

METACOGNITION:
FROM OTHER-REGULATION TO SELF-REGULATION

Other-Regulation

Michael and his brother helped their father make chocolate chip cookies. Michael popped several chocolate chips into his mouth as they worked. "Hey, Mike. Remember the ad on TV where that man sings 'Please don't eat all the morsels — or your cookies will look like this' [a chipless chocolate chip cookie]? How about putting the chips into the mix and later into your mouth?" Mike sang the jingle a few times as he added the chips to the batter and not to his mouth.

One of your long-term goals as an adult who guides children, and perhaps the most important, is to help children become humane people who can control *themselves*. Self-control or self-regulation is a long-term goal because it takes several years to develop. You, as an adult, act as a *supportive other* in the lives of children and have an impact on their development of self-control. Adults control a very young child's behavior and actually perform most of an infant's or toddler's ego functions. Gradually, as a child interacts with supportive others in social settings, the adult transfers executive control to the child and begins to expect him to control himself.

Just as a master carpenter guides an apprentice to mastery of professional skills, so do supportive adults guide children in the development of self-control. Brown, Bransford, Ferrara & Campione (1983) note that the process of teaching children how to control themselves is a gradual one. At first an adult controls or guides a child's actions. Gradually, when the adult thinks the child is ready, the child is expected to try solving a problem with the adult maintaining control and correcting when necessary. Finally, the adult gives control to the child (Brown & French, 1979).

Responsible adults regulate the behavior of very young children but understand that a child can and should take on more responsibility for controlling himself as he grows older and acquires different cognitive skills. Effective adults gradually transfer control to a child. The child actually assumes the role of supportive other.

Self-Control or Self-Regulation

Self-control or self-regulation may well be one of the most significant changes during the preschool years (Flavell, 1977). It is a central issue in the field of metacognition (Brown & DeLoache, 1978) and is important in the research of Genevan (Piagetian) psychology. Self-regulatory functions are an integral part of the learning process and are also important mechanisms in a child's growth and development (Brown et al., 1983). Piaget (1976) described a developmental progression from unconscious to active regulation.

The "self" has many facets (Harter, 1983). First, it is a cognitive construction that changes with age. Second, the self is the object of scrutiny and evaluation. A child decides whether he likes the self that he sees, and develops self-esteem, either positive or negative. Third, the self must learn to control its own behavior. Self-control is an essential part of preserving social and moral order (Harter, 1983).

Larry shows self-control because he is examining a situation before he acts.

What is Self-Control?

Self-control is a voluntary and internal regulation of behavior. Internalization is a central process in the development of self-control (Flavell, 1977; Harter, 1983). Internalizing control over one's actions is a slow process. When children are very young, other people control them either verbally or nonverbally. Control is external. Children learn what control is. This knowledge is internalized and is eventually manifested as internal control. Children show self-control when they exhibit any of the following behaviors:

1. *Control impulses—wait and suspend action.* Self-control is shown when children resist their first impulse—when they step back, examine the situation, and then decide how to act.

Example In the block corner things went smoothly until Kyle joined the group and took a block from Jenny's structure. In similar situations in the past Jenny had responded by slugging the other child, but this time she did not hit. She looked surprised when the block was taken, but instead of hitting and grabbing, she took her teacher's advice and used words to say what she felt and wanted: "Kyle, *I* was using that block. Give it back."

2. *Tolerate frustration.* Children demonstrate self-control when they can refrain from doing something that is either forbidden or inappropriate to the situation.

Example   While on a Christmas shopping trip, Joel was attracted to the huge tree with hundreds of crystal ornaments. He stood and looked, raised his hand to touch one, and then withdrew, showing self-control.

3. *Postpone immediate gratification.* Delaying gratification is often difficult for adults who already know how important it is to be able to impose delays of reward. Going out for coffee and "chit-chat" (gratification) the night before a major exam is probably not the smartest thing to do, and it sometimes takes enormous self-control to delay the gratification. It might be good to remember how difficult it is for you to delay gratification when dealing with people far younger than you. Very young children will not automatically delay gratification and therefore need an adult's help in this area. Children need help in putting off until later something that they want "right now." The example of Mike and the chocolate chips at the chapter opening is such an example. Mike's dad helped him control himself.

4. *Initiate a plan and carry it out over a period of time.*

Example   Suzanne decided to build a structure in the sand when she went to the beach with her family. She lugged water to the dry sand, mixed sand and water, and patiently patted and pushed the sand into place. She worked on her sandscape for 3 days, and her mother took pictures of the work in progress.

How Does Self-Control Evolve?

Self-control develops slowly. Babies are not born with self-control but begin to develop it around the age of 2 and it takes several more years before this emerging ability is fully in place. Self-control evolves haltingly. Preschool children often astonish adults with remarkable self-control, only to demonstrate a surprising lack of control at other times. Jenny controls herself in the block corner but on the same day shoves someone out of the way in her rush to the slidingboard. Young children have to practice self-regulation just as musicians or skaters have to practice their skills. It is reasonable to expect some measure of self-control in young children, but it is probably a mistake to expect total and perfect control.

Self-control seems to develop in stages (Kopp, 1981). These stages are associated with changes in perception, attention, and cognition during infancy and early childhood. Self-control would be impossible if certain cognitive and attentional mechanisms did not develop. The sequence of development is described below.

Birth to approximately 12 months   Reflex movements shown early in the first year yield to voluntary motor acts like reaching and grasping. Infants can mediate these motor acts, but the modulation is not conscious.

12 months to about 24 months   Children *begin* to be able to start, stop, change, or maintain motor acts or emotional signals. They also demonstrate an emerging awareness of the demands made on them by caregivers. Communication skills become more sophisticated, enabling a child to understand another person's instructions and modeling. Children between ages 1 and 2 are susceptible to control by others.

Example   Bea ran down the corridor of the airport. Her dad called, "Bea, stop." Bea turned and looked at her father who held out his arms, "Come on, Bea." Bea understood what her father said and also had control over walking and running to some extent. This made it possible for her father to control her.

Self-control begins at approximately 24 months   Children are now able to recall what someone has said or done and they are also able to engage in representational thinking. These new abilities help them make the transition to beginning self-control. At this stage, however, children have a very limited ability to control themselves, i.e., to delay gratification or to wait for things.

Advanced self-control emerges at around 36 months   Children are now able to use certain strategies that help them delay, and this sets the stage for better self-control. Kopp (1981) did research with groups of 18-, 24-, and 36-month-old children to find out how children of different ages use strategies to tolerate delay. Raisins were hidden under a cup, and the child being tested was told not to eat them. The older children did things spontaneously to distract themselves, e.g., they sang, talked, sat on their hands, or looked away.

SOCIAL COGNITION

Social cognitive development is a field of study that merges the studies of social and cognitive development. Piaget's theory of cognitive development has been largely responsible for this new field, one assumption of which is that a person's level of cognitive development affects his style of interaction with other people. A child's interactions with adults, siblings, and peers are affected by how he conceptualizes and reasons about them. A child's thinking about his social world *(social cognition)* is affected by and similar to his thinking about the nonsocial world (conservation of liquid, seriation) (Shantz, 1983).

Developments in perception, attention, memory, and language enable children to describe the behavior of others and to understand relations between individuals and groups. A child's conceptualization of the social areas of friendship, conflict resolution, and morality or justice changes as cognitive development occurs.

How Children Describe the Behavior of Others

A child's actions are affected by how he understands the behavior of other people. When children watch someone in real life, on film, or on television, what do they notice, what do they remember, and how do they describe the other person's behavior?

Flapan (1968) used episodes on film to find out how children perceive the behavior of other people. Subjects were 6-, 9-, and 12-year-old girls who watched two segments of a movie. One segment showed a female child's guilt over accidentally killing a squirrel; the other showed interpersonal problems between a girl and her father. The girls were then asked to describe what they had seen. A developmental progression in the ability to describe behavior of others emerged.

Six-year-olds described actions that had occurred. They also described obvious emotional reactions like crying, but they explained the other person's feelings purely on the basis of the situation. The youngest subjects did not try to interpret feelings. Nine-year-olds also described actions, but gave some interpretations of the feelings and intentions of the person. Twelve-year-old subjects, making the transition to Piaget's highest level of cognitive development, offered the greatest number of inferred feelings and intentions.

How accurate are children in perceiving behavior? Here, too, a developmental progression is evident. Children's ability to recall information necessary or central to the plot improves as they get older and acquire different cognitive skills. Second and third graders recall about 66 percent, while children in eighth and ninth grades recall up to 90 percent of central information. The ability to view motives accurately improves with age and parallels changes in cognition (Shantz, 1983).

Distinguishing Intentional from Accidental Behavior

Children must be able to distinguish between accidental and intentional acts before they can understand or predict another person's behavior. Shantz (1983) notes that a person's judgments of responsibility and morality or justice rest on whether another person is thought to have *intended* to do something. Again, a developmental trend seems to exist in the ability to distinguish accidental from intentional behavior. King (1971) found that 4-year-olds tend not to differentiate between intentional and accidental behavior. By 5½ years, however, many children can make the distinction, and they are even more accurate by age 9.

Friendship

Five-year-old Frank proudly says to his mom, "That's Pat. He's my *friend!*" Friends play an important part in Frank's social development now and will continue to do so throughout his life. *Friendship* is a reciprocal relationship between two individuals. As a child's cognitive development proceeds, his conception of friendship also changes (Damon, 1977; Youniss & Volpe, 1978).

Young children tend to define friendship in terms of giving things or playing together. Friendship to a young child is a concrete relationship. In contrast, adolescents view a friendship as an internal abstract relationship in which two people comfort each other, share thoughts, and care about each other.

Young children's egocentrism affects friendship just as it affects other areas of their life. At 5 years, Frank views his friend Pat as someone who can satisfy his

Young children tend to define friendship in terms of playing together or giving things.

(Frank's) needs. Frank's adolescent brother views his friendships as relationships in which needs of both parties are met. Young children tend to see friendship as a fleeting thing, based on momentary "good acts"; adolescents view friendships as relationships that survive conflict and separation and endure over time.

Conflict Relations

The PIPS (Preschool Interpersonal Problem Solving) is used to measure the number and types of strategies a child uses to solve a conflict. The child is presented with a hypothetical conflict situation and is asked to generate some ways to solve the conflict.

Example Five-year-olds Sue and Jill were asked, "How can you get a toy that another child has?" Sue generated several nonaggressive suggestions, while Jill generated only a few suggestions, all aggressive.

Both Sue's and Jill's methods of resolving conflict are likely to affect their social adjustment. Conflict is an inevitable part of social life between children, adults, or adults and children, and a person's method of solving conflict will have an effect on how he interacts with others and how they view him. Successful conflict resolution requires that a child be able to use cognitive skills like

1. thinking of alternative ways of solving problems.
2. knowing how another person is likely to respond to different solutions.
3. using means-and-ends problem solving (Shure & Spivack, 1978; Spivack & Shure, 1974).

By age 5 children realize that they can defend their rights, e.g., not to have somebody take a toy they are playing with. As we saw with Sue and Jill, however, children's knowledge of how to solve conflicts varies considerably.

Asher and Renshaw (1981) found that popular and unpopular children suggested different strategies for solving conflict. Unpopular children are more likely to suggest aggressive strategies. Jill, for example, said, "You could hit him or you could grab the truck." Popular children like Sue suggest any of several nonaggressive strategies. Sue said, "Well, say 'I want the truck back' and then take it [a direct nonaggressive action], or say, 'You're supposed to ask first!' " [an appeal to social convention]. Sue suggested two other strategies, turn-taking [a compromise] or appealing to an authority figure.

SPECIAL FOCUS: Social Skills Training: Helping Children Learn to Solve Conflicts and to Make Friends

Many children have poor social skills. They do not know how to make friends or play cooperatively; they tend to be aggressive. Aggressive children are likely to be unpopular and to be rejected by their peers (Moore, 1967). Children who have poor relationships with peers have often had poor social skills training. Adults have a significant role in teaching social skills to children and can help unpopular, aggressive children develop better relationships with peers. Asher, Renshaw, and Hymel (1982) suggest a three-step method of teaching social skills.

Modeling

Modeling is an effective method for teaching social skills to children. It is most effective when a child thinks that a model is similar to him, when the model's presence is pointed out to the child, or when the child's attention is focused on the model's behavior, purposes, and consequences by a narrator (O'Conner, 1969).

Coaching

Modeling involves showing. *Coaching* involves explicitly verbalizing or telling a child how to perform a social skill. For example a child might be coached on how to enter a group and how to participate. The child would then rehearse the new skill. Renee, for example, plays a game with a classmate, rehearsing skills explained earlier by an adult. A review of the rehearsal is then held in which the adult and Renee talk about the rehearsal session. Oden and Asher (1977) found that coaching resulted in peer acceptance for third and fourth grade children. Zahavi and Asher (1978) modified social skills training for younger children. They did not ask the younger children to evaluate themselves.

Positive Reinforcement

Positive social skills are encouraged when desired behavior is reinforced (Asher et al., 1982). Positive peer interaction increased in a preschool child, and aggressive behavior decreased as cooperative behavior increased, when cooperation was praised and aggression ignored (Brown & Elliott, 1965).

Morality/Justice

If you, as a professional, work with 4- or 5-year-olds you will discover that their ideas about friendship and conflict resolution depend on their level of cognition. If you work with adolescents you will find that their ideas in these two areas are far more sophisticated and rely on different cognitive skills. The same is true for children's ideas at different ages about morality or sense of justice. Concepts of morality and justice change as cognition changes.

Piaget

Piaget's greatest influence has been on how we now view changes in children's cognitive abilities as they grow older. He also wrote about the development of morality in *The Moral Judgment of the Child* (1932/1965). Piaget believed that children develop a better understanding of the social world (social cognition) as their cognitive abilities develop. Children move from a morality based on what others tell them to do or not to do *(morality of constraint)* to a *morality based on cooperation.* Piaget's message, then, was that a person's concept of what constitutes morality changes with age and cognitive development and that not all morality is imposed on one person by another.

Piaget believed that two specific factors account for changes in moral development (Rest, 1983). One of these is *cognitive disequilibrium.* A child is thrown into a state of disequilibrium when he experiences something that cannot be placed easily within an already existing structure. The child strives to reestablish cognitive equilibrium by searching for new cognitive structures.

Piaget maintained that *social/peer interaction* also promotes change in a child's judgment of morality and justice as well as changes in cognitive development. As children interact they often have conflicting ideas or different needs. Social/peer interaction encourages children to acknowledge the ideas and needs of another person and to negotiate or bargain and make agreements that ultimately benefit both people.

Peer interaction does two important things that ultimately result in higher levels of moral development: it encourages equality among peers and also encourages role-taking.

Example   Jenna and Diane were decorating a cake, each using a different color of icing. When it was time to draw a happy face on the cake, each girl insisted on using her color of icing. They finally decided to draw the face in Jenna's color and the eyes, nose, and mouth in Diane's color.

Jenna and Diane were each confronted with an idea of the other person and had to figure out how the other viewed the situation. Piaget believed that humans learn about a morality based on cooperation from thousands of similar opportunities to take someone else's perspective.

Kohlberg

Lawrence Kohlberg's research (Kohlberg & Kramer, 1969) is also a cognitive developmental account of how children develop ideas of morality and justice. Kohl-

TABLE 3.1   Kohlberg's Definition of Moral Stages

Stage 1: Punishment and Obedience Orientation

When deciding on how to act in a situation the child obeys rules "to the letter" simply to avoid punishment.
The child obeys authority figures unquestioningly.
The child does not consider the interests of others when deciding how to act.

Stage 2: Instrumental Relativist Orientation

The child realizes that he cannot make others angry if he is to get his needs met.
He is pragmatic and learns to "make deals" so that everyone's needs are met.
He obeys rules when it is in his immediate interest.

Stage 3: Good Boy/Nice Girl Orientation

The child believes that pleasing members of his group or getting the group's approval is the criterion for whether behavior is "good" or "bad."
The child believes that he has to be "nice" to get the approval of others.

Stage 4: Law and Order Orientation

The social order or "system" becomes important and defines rules and laws.
Good behavior is viewed as doing one's duty and showing respect for authority.
Maintaining the "system" for its own sake is important.
The person is oriented toward fixed rules and authority.
(*Note:* Stages 5 and 6 represent a major shift in moral reasoning. A person operating at this level defines moral principles on his own).

Stage 5: Social Contract and Individual Rights

This stage is possible because of cognitive abilities that emerge during adolescence.
Not many people reach this stage. Most operate at stage 3 or stage 4.
The person values and participates in the social system and obeys laws, but not without question.
This is often labeled a *law creating* stage because a person tries to change existing rules and laws if they conflict with his principles.
Protecting rights and liberty is important.

Stage 6: Universal Ethical Principle Orientation

Even fewer people reach this stage than reach stage 5.
This orientation seems to crystallize in the early 20s *if* it is reached; there are twice as many stage 6's at age 26 as at age 16.
Moral principles are valued at this stage, e.g., justice, reciprocity, equality, human rights, respect for human dignity.
A person at stage 6 respects the social order *except* when it violates human rights, and believes that one has an obligation to ignore social order when rights are violated.

Source: Kohlberg & Kramer, 1969.

berg based his original research on Piaget's but has extended Piaget's work in several important ways (Rest, 1983).

Both emphasize that basic cognitive structures serve as a base for reasoning about morality. Changes in moral reasoning, from this perspective, are made possible by changes in cognitive development during the first 20 years of a person's life. As children move to higher levels of cognitive development they acquire powerful new skills for thinking about moral issues.

Like Piaget, Kohlberg believes that the central concept in moral development is *justice*. Changes in moral development, then, represent changes in how a child thinks about justice or increasing social equilibrium between people as they interact.

Kohlberg's method differs from Piaget's. To identify changes in moral development Kohlberg interviewed adolescent males. Subjects were presented with several stories or "moral dilemmas" and were asked what should be done. Dilemmas chosen dealt with human moral issues: the importance of contractual agreements, the value of human life, the value of honesty, and the meaning of social rules and laws. For example, the subject might be asked what a man should do if his wife needed a medicine developed by someone who was selling it at an exceedingly high price. Kohlberg wanted to know how a person would reason about this moral dilemma. Would the subject say that the man had a right to take the medicine if he was unable to buy it, or would the subject say the man should not take the medicine even though his wife would surely die without it? What would you do?

One important outcome of Kohlberg's research was his description of stages in moral development. He defined three levels of moral development, each level having two stages (Table 3.1). Kohlberg considered the six stages to be sequential; to get to stage 5, for example, a person must have gone through the first four stages. Each stage describes how a person is oriented to a moral dilemma and includes the reasons used when making a decision about a dilemma. Each stage defines a person's view or perspective on moral values — the base from which an adult eventually makes moral judgments about issues like capital punishment, abortion, and euthanasia.

Like Piaget, Kohlberg views social interaction as an important avenue for developing mature reasoning on moral dilemmas. Social interaction affords a child opportunities to discuss another person's point of view and to participate in a group's decision-making. Social interaction gives children a chance to take on different roles and yields information from which children construct ideas about justice, cooperation, and equality.

SUMMARY: KEY CONCEPTS IN THIS CHAPTER

1. As children develop *metacognition* they progress from control by others to self-control. Responsible adults regulate the behavior of very young children but understand that a child can and should be expected to take on increased responsibility for controlling himself as he grows older and acquires cognitive

skills. Effective adults act as "supportive others" and gradually transfer control to a child.

2. *Social cognition* is a child's ability to conceptualize and reason about his social world. This thinking is directly affected by and similar to his level of cognitive development. A child's conceptions of the social areas of friendship, conflict, and morality or justice change with the changes of cognitive development.

OBSERVE: CHILD GUIDANCE IN ACTION

Observe an adult as he interacts with an infant under 1 year old. Look for evidence that the adult actually performs the infant's ego functions for the infant, i.e., that he does not expect the infant to control himself. Record your observation using the following format.

Date: _____

Setting: _____

Infant's approximate age: _____

Describe specific things an adult does for the infant: rocks him to sleep, calms him down, burps him, wipes the baby's mouth, changes his diaper.

Observe an adult as he interacts with a preschool child (ages 2 to 5). Look for evidence that the adult expects a child of this age to begin to control himself.

Does the adult expect the child to listen to instructions? To obey? To remember to wash hands? To go to the bathroom? To put toys away? To say "thank you"? To use a tissue? To put his coat away? To be quiet when necessary? Other? If your answer to any of these is yes, *then record several specific examples.*

REFERENCES

ASHER, S.R., & RENSHAW, P.D. (1981). Children without friends: Social knowledge and social skill training. In S.R. Asher & J.M. Gottman (Eds.), *The development of children's friendships.* New York: Cambridge University Press.

ASHER, S.R., RENSHAW, P., & HYMEL, S. (1982). Peer relations and the development of social skills. In S. Moore & C. Cooper (Eds.), *The young child: Reviews of research*, Vol. 3. Washington, D.C.: NAEYC.

BROWN, A.L., BRANSFORD, J.D., FERRARA, R.A., & CAMPIONE, J.C. (1983). Learning, remembering and understanding. In P. Mussen (Ed.), *Handbook of child psychology*, Vol. 3. New York: Wiley.

BROWN, A.L., & DeLOACHE, J.S. (1978). Skills, plans, and self-regulation. In R.S. Siegler (Ed.), *Children's thinking: What develops?* Hillsdale, NJ: Erlbaum.

BROWN, A.L., & FRENCH, L.A. (1979). The zone of potential development: Implications for intelligence testing in the year 2000. *Intelligence, 3,* 255–277.

BROWN, P., & ELLIOTT, R. (1965). Control of aggression in a nursery school class. *Journal of Experimental Child Psychology, 2,* 103–107.

DAMON, W. (1977). *The social world of the child.* San Francisco: Jossey-Bass.

FLAPAN, D. (1968). *Children's understanding of social interaction.* New York: Teacher's College Press.

FLAVELL, J.H. (1977). *Cognitive development.* Englewood Cliffs, NJ: Prentice-Hall.

HARTER, S. (1983). Developmental perspectives on the self-system. In P. Mussen (Ed.), *Handbook of child psychology,* Vol. 4., New York: Wiley.

KING, M. (1971). The development of some intention concepts in young children. *Child Development, 42,* 1145–1152.

KOHLBERG, L. (1958). *The development of modes of moral thinking and choice in the years 10 to 16.* Unpublished doctoral dissertation, University of Chicago.

KOHLBERG, L., & KRAMER, R. (1969). Continuities and discontinuities in childhood moral development. *Human Development, 12,* 93–120.

KOPP, C.B. (1981). *The antecedents of self-regulation: A developmental perspective.* Unpublished manuscript, University of California, Los Angeles.

MOORE, S.G. (1967). Correlates of peer acceptance in nursery school children. In W.W. Hartup & N.L. Smothergill (Eds.), *The young child,* Washington, D.C.: NAEYC.

O'CONNER, R. (1969). Modification of social withdrawal through symbolic modeling. *Journal of Applied Behavior Analysis, 2,* 15–22.

ODEN, S., & ASHER, S.R. (1977). Coaching children in social skills for friendship making. *Child Development, 48,* 495–506.

PIAGET, J. (1965). *The moral judgment of the child* (M. Gabain, Trans.). New York: Free Press. (Original work published 1932)

PIAGET, J. (1976). *The grasp of consciousness: Action and concept in the young child.* Cambridge: Harvard University Press.

REST, J.R. (1983). Morality. In P. Mussen (Ed.), *Handbook of child psychology,* Vol. 3. New York: Wiley.

SHANTZ, C.V. (1983). Social cognition. In P. Mussen (Ed.), *Handbook of child psychology,* Vol. 3. New York: Wiley.

SHURE, M.B., & SPIVACK, G. (1978). *Problem-solving techniques in childrearing.* San Francisco: Jossey-Bass.

SPIVACK, B., & SHURE, M.B. (1974). *Social adjustment of young children: A cognitive approach to solving real-life problems.* San Francisco: Jossey-Bass.

YOUNISS, J., & VOLPE, J. (1978). A relational analysis of children's friendships. In W. Damon (Ed.), *New directions for child development: Social cognition.* San Francisco: Jossey-Bass.

ZAHAVI, S., & ASHER, S.R. (1978). The effect of verbal instructions on preschool children's aggressive behavior. *Journal of School Psychology, 16,* 146–153.

4

The Physical
Environment:
Its Role in the Guidance
System

Chapter Overview

After reading and studying this chapter, you will be able to:

☐ *List and describe* characteristics of nonsupportive physical environments.

☐ *Identify* characteristics of a supportive physical environment.

☐ *Describe and give a rationale for* each type of classroom activity area.

☐ *Analyze* a small group area.

☐ *Explain* how to create an attractive, sensory-rich activity area.

☐ *Discuss* the role of developmentally appropriate activities and materials in supportive environments.

☐ *Analyze* the physical setup of an early childhood classroom.

LOOKING AT TWO DIFFERENT CLASSROOMS

Imagine yourself observing two different classrooms. Ms. Hanley and Mr. Fox teach groups of 4-year-old children in preschool classrooms in the same building.

Ms. Hanley's Classroom

The first thing you notice is the noise. Its intensity is disturbing. Several children are running in the classroom, and others appear to wander aimlessly. Then you are struck by how unattractive the room is. It looks like an institution—ugly green cement block walls, bare lightbulbs, curtainless windows, and every area cluttered.

You zero in on specific areas. There is a block corner, but the indoor slide is placed so that a child who uses the slide ends up in the middle of the block area. There is a good set of blocks of various sizes and shapes, but they are mixed together on the shelves. No attempt seems to have been made to organize them. Crayons, magic markers, and chalk are jumbled together in one plastic container. In one basket, drawing paper of different sizes is piled up with paper scraps mixed in. It looks more like a trash pile than drawing paper. Library books are piled up on a table so that it is difficult for children to get one without knocking all of them over. Puzzles have pieces missing and are piled one on top of one another.

The easel is set up on a carpet far from the sink. The result is that paint spills cannot be cleaned easily, and the adults frequently reprimand a child whose paint drips. Because the games, toys, and other equipment are stored in high, closed cabinets, children have to ask Ms. Hanley to get needed equipment. A child who feels like being alone really has no private place for retreat.

The adults in this classroom complain about a number of things: the children's running around and seeming lack of ability to concentrate on any one task during the "free play" period, the pushing and shoving while waiting for a turn in the toilet, the high noise level, the children's lack of respect for library books, and their constant nagging for teachers to get something from cabinets. The adults also frequently mention that they have no time to do individual work with children or even think about working with parents. Much time in staff meetings is taken talking about problem children and how to "handle" the problems.

Mr. Fox's Classroom

You find the contrast with Ms. Hanley's room astonishing. These classrooms are the same size, constructed of the same materials, have the same furniture, and have the same number of children and teachers. Mr. Fox's classroom, however, is attractive, with children's work displayed, green and healthy plants arranged throughout the room, posters on the walls, and curtains on the windows. The room is orderly and is arranged in distinct activity areas. There is a hum of talking and laughing, but no yelling and screaming. Children are working at any one of several activity centers arranged by the teachers. Materials are stored on low, open shelves, and children can get them whenever needed. One teacher aide is supervising fingerpainting. The sink is nearby, and a bucket of water and large sponge have been strategically placed next to the table. The children actually seem to enjoy cleaning up the paints as much as they enjoy the process of painting. Another adult (a parent volunteer) is moving quietly from area to area to warn children of an impending change of activity and the need to clean up. The parent aide has already set up snack trays.

Teachers in this classroom spend their staff meeting time planning activities for the children and ways to involve the parents. They discuss individual children, but the focus is more positive than in Ms. Hanley's classroom. Little time is given to complaining about problem behavior. Instead, the teachers spend time evaluating children's developmental level and planning specific activities to optimize development.

As you leave the school you wonder what the magic ingredient is in the classroom of quietly active and involved children and relatively calm adults, and puzzle over the classroom of rowdy, noisy children and frenzied adults. Of course, several factors go into making a supportive classroom atmosphere: the adults' knowledge of child development and degree of supportiveness, the use of positive discipline, the setting of good limits, and the ability to communicate well with children. But another crucial factor is the physical environment itself (Phyfe-Perkins, 1980).

Professionals in architecture, environmental psychology, and early childhood education are concerned about the impact of the environment on people who live or work there. Their theorizing and research tell us that a well-designed environment creates a positive adaptive setting for the group using it (Marcu, 1977). A poorly-

In a supportive physical environment, children are encouraged to move. Reasonable, fair limits control their movement.

designed physical environment, on the other hand, sets the stage for discipline problems (Heimstra & McFarling, 1974; Marcu, 1977; Mehrabian, 1976; Olds, 1977; Phyfe-Perkins, 1980).

This chapter discusses the effect of the built environment on the behavior of young children and makes practical suggestions for classroom design.

CHARACTERISTICS OF A NONSUPPORTIVE PHYSICAL ENVIRONMENT

A classroom in which movement is rigidly controlled, arbitrary rules are imposed, disorganization of materials is commonplace, and little thought is given to enhancing the room's comfort and attractiveness is a nonsupportive, hostile environment. This type of space does not support the growth of mastery and self-control.

In a boring, restrictive classroom, adults do not seem to understand the children's need to move around in order to develop positive interaction skills. As a result, the adults usually do two things. First, they try to control the movement by stopping it. Children are forced to wait in groups to do things, to sit at tables for long periods of time to eat or do other activities, to sit a certain way during group time. It is certainly reasonable that a teacher responsible for 20 to 25 children who seem predisposed toward movement should want to keep the movement within reasonable limits. A distinction needs to be made, however, between restrictive control that squelches movement and the reasonable organization of movement in a well-designed classroom (Olds, 1977). Squelched movement often leads to discipline problems—moving around at the table, running away from the line waiting at the toilet, squirming and wiggling while trying to sit a certain way at group time. These disruptive behaviors should signal adults that something is wrong.

The second strategy often used by adults who are confronted with the "discipline problems" of running and squirming is to escalate efforts at control by increasing the use of arbitrary rules. For example, if children squirm in their seats while waiting for everyone to finish the snack, the teacher might respond by making the children be quiet and put their heads down on the table until their friends finish (an arbitrary limit). As was noted in chapter 1, the establishment of arbitrary rules usually elicits resentment rather than cooperation. In the snacktime example, the children would very likely escalate their "disruptive" behavior. Adults who create a boring, restrictive classroom (or any other setting for children) make things difficult not only for the children but also for themselves. In such an atmosphere, adults spend an inordinately large amount of time controlling movement and trying, but failing, to maintain the arbitrary rules and limits.

Adults who are confronted with disruptive behavior from children should probably examine the physical setup of the classroom (or other setting) as a possible source of the problems. It is much easier to rearrange space and equipment than to keep piling more and more arbitrary rules on children, rules that actually keep them from controlling their space and themselves.

CHARACTERISTICS OF A SUPPORTIVE
PHYSICAL ENVIRONMENT

Recall that one of the major ways in which adults influence children is by providing physical settings and materials (see chapter 1). A supportive physical environment fosters positive adaptive behavior and promotes the development of self-control and mastery. Such a setting allows children to control their surroundings when appropriate. It permits and by its very structure encourages the movement needed by young children. Children in a supportive physical environment are encouraged to interact with the things and people in that environment. Adults in a supportive physical environment set reasonable, fair limits on movement to protect the safety of the children.

This section will help you learn to recognize a supportive physical environment, whether in a home, a camp, or a classroom. An early childhood classroom will be used to illustrate general characteristics of a supportive physical environment. You will see that it is possible to transform a nonsupportive space into a more responsive or "soft" environment. When you focus on how a space is organized for children, you can encourage desirable behavior and at the same time prevent or eliminate less desirable behavior.

Division into Activity Areas

As a teacher, you will be confronted with a large classroom space containing an assortment of furniture: tables, chairs, bookshelves. It will be largely up to you to arrange this space. As a competent teacher and a sensitive supportive adult you realize that a well-arranged physical space with clear limits helps children regulate their own behavior. You decide to divide the space into a number of different "areas." Each of the classroom areas will have different general characteristics; some will be small, some large, some will have seating, others will not. Each area will be used for different activities. Your classroom will contain a private area, several learning centers or small group areas, and a large group area.

Types of Classroom Activity Areas

Private Area

Description of private area   A *private area* is a small enclosed space with room for one or at most two children. It is isolated visually from the rest of the children in the room, even though the adults can easily check on the occupant of the space. There are no special materials stored in the private area. There are no chairs or tables in the private area. Figure 4.1 shows one example of a private area.

Rationale for having a private area   Classrooms are, in spite of all of our efforts to soften them, still institutional settings, and children are essentially a captive audience. Few adults can withstand the pressure of working in large groups for several hours. Adults usually have ways of pacing their interactions, but children do not.

FIGURE 4.1 The private area allows a child to retreat from a busy classroom.

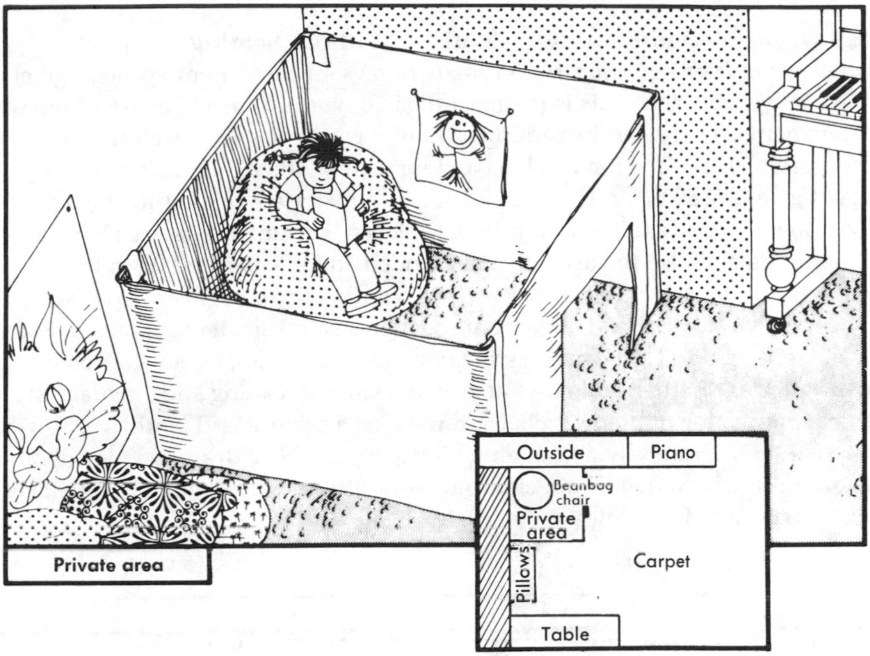

Private area

Outside	Piano

Beanbag chair

Private area

Pillows

Carpet

Table

(Source: Alward, K.R.: *Arranging the classroom for children.* San Francisco: Far West Laboratory for Educational Research and Development, 1973.)

Children who live and work in a group with 20 to 30 other children have a right to some type of privacy and a right to choose or limit contact with others in the group. No child should be expected to work with other children for several hours at a time. Thus, it is important that adults provide for the privacy of children, and an early childhood classroom should include a place to be alone without being disturbed—a private area.

A private area allows a child to control her interactions with others, to be present in the classroom but to be separated from activities when privacy is necessary. Stallings (1975) found that first grade children who were allowed to select their own seating and groups for part of the day and who could choose to talk or get together with others were more independent and cooperative and initiated more verbal interactions. These children were allowed to pace their interactions and to control the degree of their contact with others.

Limits on using the private area There should be very clearly defined limits on the use of this space. Each child knows that it is a place where she and others can go to be alone and that the person using the space is not to be disturbed. This space is not for group play. Adults, too, must be careful about how they use the private space. The private area should never be used as a "time-out" or punishment area. It will quickly lose its appeal as an area of quiet retreat if it is also used as a punishment spot.

Small Group Learning Center—With or Without Seating

A *small group learning center* is a permanent or semipermanent space large enough for five or six children. This is the most flexible type of space because of the seating arrangements. There can be seating around a work surface for all the children, or there can be no surface for working and no seating other than carpeting or pillows. A small group area has a specific purpose, so materials related to the activity are stored on low, open shelves in the area. Children working in the area have access to the materials. Because the area is semibounded and is separated from the other sections of the room, the children are reminded indirectly of the area's special function.

Many early childhood classrooms contain several small group areas. Examples of well-defined small group areas include: an area arranged so that children can choose puzzles or other table toys and sit at a table; a reading and language arts area with a combination of pillows, chairs, and table; a science and math area in which a group can comfortably work; a family living area where dramatic play abounds; a block corner where five or six children work at one time; and a creative arts area where a myriad of activities are available (Figure 4.2).

FIGURE 4.2   A manipulative area.

Source: Alward, K.R.: *Arranging the classroom for children*. San Francisco: Far West Laboratory for Educational Research and Development, 1973.)

The small group learning center. A block corner is one example of the variety of small group areas in early childhood classrooms.

SPECIAL FOCUS: Analyze a Small Group Area

Mr. Fox wanted to create a permanent small group activity area for dramatic play. He wanted the children to have access to a wide variety of props but to be able to get at them and put them away easily. He wanted to keep this noisy area well separated from quieter areas and out of the line of traffic. Figure 4.3 shows the area he arranged.

Description of the Small Group Area

Mr. Fox used a carpeted area of the classroom for the dramatic play area. He supplied the area with a kitchen set, including a sink, stove, refrigerator, and storage space for utensils. Storage cabinets similar to those used in the manipulative play area were also provided in the dramatic play area. Props and materials were placed on the lower shelves. Additional props and materials that could be used in other dramatic play themes were stored above the shelves.

Analyze the Small Group Area by Answering the Following Questions

1. How did the children know where to return the props or materials when they finished playing with them?
2. How did Mr. Fox limit the traffic going through the area?
3. What was done to insure that the noise made by children playing in the area would not distract others?

4. Next to what other area might you locate this area in order to provide "house building" opportunities in the area?

FIGURE 4.3   A dramatic play area

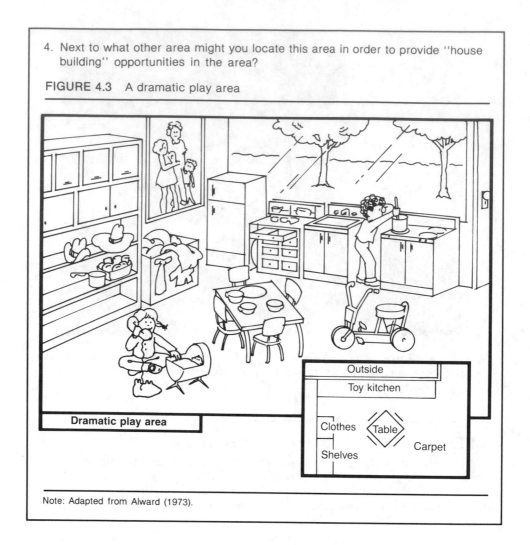

Dramatic play area

Outside
Toy kitchen
Clothes | Table
Shelves | Carpet

Note: Adapted from Alward (1973).

Large Group Area

An early childhood classroom needs a space large enough to accommodate most or all of the children for large group activities (Alward, 1973). This area should be a large open space. It is a fairly flexible space because it can accommodate group participation in any of several activities: music, language arts, creative dramatics, stories, nutrition education, dance, and other activities that fit in with a school's goals. Therefore, specific materials are usually not stored in it but are brought to the *large group area* by the teacher. For example, for a flannel board story the teacher would bring the flannel board and figures to the large group area (Figure 4.4).

FIGURE 4.4 The large group area. On this particular day, materials for large-muscle activity have been brought to the area.

Source: Alward, K.R.: *Arranging the classroom for children.* San Francisco: Far West Laboratory for Educational Research and Development, 1973.)

Develop Enough Activity Areas

Consider the age of the children and the number of children in the classroom when deciding how many of each type of area to include in the room. Suppose that there are 20 5-year-olds in your class. It is recommended that there be one-third more spaces than children so that children can change activities without having to wait. Thus, for 20 5-year-old children, you would have about 27 work spaces in the classroom. These 27 spaces might be in the form of two private spaces, four small group areas, and a large group area. Table 4.1 shows how many of each type of space is needed, depending on the ages and number of children. Generally, the older the children and the more children in the class, the more small group areas are needed.

Arrange Activity Areas Logically

Movement and Traffic Flow
If movement within a physical space and interaction with other children in a space

SPECIAL FOCUS: Develop Enough Activity Areas

Use this chart to answer the following questions on the number of activity areas needed in each classroom.

TABLE 4.1 Number of Activity Areas Needed Based on Ages and Numbers of Children in Class

Type of Area	Ages	Number of Children in Class			
		up to 9	10–14	15–24	25–29
Private Area	3–4	1	1	1	2
	5–6	1	1	1	1
Small Group Area (with or without seating)	3–4	1	3	4	5
	5–6	2	3	4	6
Large Group Area	3–4	1	1	1	1
	5–6	1	1	1	1

Note: Adapted from Alward (1973): 31.

1. How many small group areas are needed for a class of 14 5-year-olds?

2. How many private spaces are needed for a group of 14 5-year-olds? For a class of 25 4-year-olds?

3. How many small group areas are needed for a class of 20 5-year-olds?

are important for developing positive interaction skills in young children, then the activity areas should be arranged to encourage movement and interaction (Mehrabian, 1976; Olds, 1977; Sommer, 1974). A classroom containing the activity areas already described will, of course, encourage interaction among the children using a particular area. For example, children in the block corner (a small group area for five to six children) will play with or next to each other. In addition, activity areas should be so placed in the room that it is easy to move from the block area to the housekeeping area to the reading area to the creative arts area. The idea is that there should be easy access to any of the activity areas and a good flow of traffic between the areas.

Noisy and Quiet Areas

Some areas house relatively quiet activities: private spaces and some small group areas like those for language arts and reading, science and math, classroom pets, and puzzles and other small table toys. These quiet areas should be well separated from areas encouraging more active play. It is difficult to listen to or speak into a tape recorder or read a library book if the reading area is adjacent to the block area.

Placing the private space next to the indoor climbing area is not advisable, but placing the private space near the language arts center is appropriate. Other good combinations include language arts next to science and math or puzzles and small table toys next to the creative arts area.

Some areas in the classroom contain more active and vigorous activities. Active areas include small group areas for family living, blocks, climbing, music, creative dramatics, and creative arts, and the large group area. Children who choose to work in these areas usually move and talk more than in the quieter areas. It would make sense to place the housekeeping or family living area near the block area because they are both high activity areas and because dramatic play can flow so easily from one to the other.

Creating Boundaries for Areas

The activity areas should be very clearly defined and properly separated from one another. Olds (1977) believes that, even when activity areas are fairly well developed, disruptive behavior might occur if the areas lack clear division and children have difficulty knowing where one area ends and the next begins. There are a variety of methods for separating the areas—shelves, moveable or permanent dividers, bulletin boards, pegboards, cloth hanging from ceiling to floor. Can you think of other ways to divide one area from another? By clearly defining the areas with visible boundaries, adults can help children understand that some activities need to be separated from others. Clear boundaries also help children know where each piece of equipment belongs and encourage them to put things away in their proper areas (Figure 4.5).

Create Attractive, Sensory-Rich Areas

Sommer (1974) argues for the use of "soft" architecture, environments responsive to the users. He urges the design of spaces that reflect the presence of humans. The concept of a space serving the needs of users has also been applied to animals. You have seen this concept in action if you have ever visited a zoo like the one in Apple Valley, Minnesota, where developers have replaced traditional cages with each animal's natural habitat.

Even a seemingly hard, cold classroom with tile floors, formica tables, concrete walls, curtainless windows, and harsh lighting can be "softened" and made more responsive to the young children who spend a large part of their day there. It is possible to take such a sterile environment and create a refuge from "hard" surroundings. The changes you make to soften and enliven a dull room need not be expensive.

There are two general ways to alter a classroom environment to make it sensory-rich. You can add things to or subtract things from the environment and children can be helped to learn to observe the changes.

Many early childhood teachers do a good job of adding interesting items to the classroom, but it is also important to weed out items that have served their purpose and are no longer needed. Uncluttering an area or a room can actually help children

FIGURE 4.5 Boundaries help define activity areas.

Source: Alward, 1973.

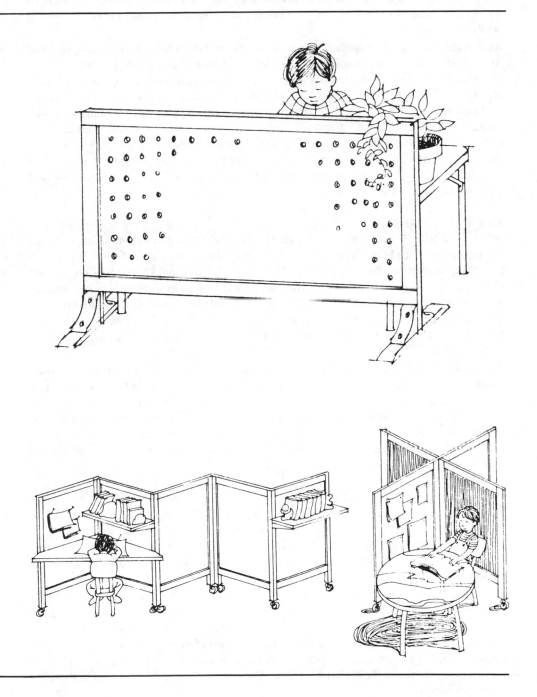

focus on the novel sensory material available by decreasing the number of stimuli to which they must attend. A cluttered room is not necessarily pleasant and might even be distracting.

Example   Ms. Hanley planned a unit on insects and decided to focus on butterflies. After adding a beautiful book on butterflies, two large color photographs, and several real butterfly models to the science area, she was puzzled at the children's lack of interest in the subject. A close look at the science corner showed that the butterfly book was on the table with the cups of seeds, the rock collection, magnets, and a magnifying glass. The pictures had been pinned to a similarly cluttered bulletin board, and the butterflies had been dwarfed by a large green plant. After clearing the science table, Ms. Hanley put back only the items dealing with butterflies. The bulletin board was also cleared and the pictures of butterflies attractively arranged so that they were the central focus.

Modify the Lighting

Add to, subtract from, or simply change the type of lighting in a room. Many schools are equipped with bright lights, and while adequate lighting is desirable, it can also be boring and overstimulating to be in a harshly lighted room for extended periods of time. Classrooms are often equipped with only one or at most two light switches so that the adults have only two options—all harsh lights off or all lights on.

Teachers can control the intensity of the lighting by installing dimmer switches and then use them to control the intensity of lighting in different sections of the room.

Example   Mr. Fox noticed that the children did more looking around the room during large group time than he wanted them to. He and the aides discussed this problem and decided to try to guide the children *indirectly* by changing the lighting. There were three banks of lights in his classroom. During group time the children really only needed the lights on in the section where they sat, so Mr. Fox turned the lights in the other two sections down. The children's attention was focused on the lighted area in which group time took place.

Lower the Ceiling or Add Platforms

Many schools build inexpensive platforms in parts of the room. The children use the platforms for activities like reading or dramatic play. A high ceiling can be made to appear lower in parts of the room with wide strips of cloth suspended between dowel rods. This method is especially useful when a private, quiet, semienclosed activity area is desired.

Example   Ms. Hanley's reading area was a disaster. She had placed one shelf against the climbing gym, leaving only the hard, cold tile floor to sit on for reading. The children rarely read books. She asked Mr. Fox for advice, and together they changed the area. They created a separate, well-bounded area for reading. In it they placed a fluffy carpet and big soft cushions to lean against. They also suspended cloth across two dowel rods hanging from the ceiling. The children loved it! Reading activity soared.

FIGURE 4.6   A platform set in a corner against the wall.

(Source: Alward, K.R.: *Arranging the classroom for children.* San Francisco: Far West Laboratory for Educational Research and Development, 1973).

Modify the Sensory Environment

The classroom can be made more pleasant and attractive by changing its sensory aspects, within the whole room or individual areas.

Create visual interest   Sommer and Davis (cited in Sommer, 1974) found that decorations in a college classroom were judged by students and faculty to make the room pleasant, comfortable, relaxing, and cheerful. The aesthetic appeal of an early childhood classroom can also be enhanced by adding well-chosen, inexpensive decorations like paintings, posters, green plants, large and small photographs of the children, cloth hangings, and examples of children's artwork.

Create auditory interest   A certain sound level in the form of talking is to be expected and is even desirable in a classroom, but yelling and screaming are not. If yelling and screaming are commonplace then the adults should examine both the physical setup of the room and the classroom limits they have set. A teacher and children not plagued by a constantly high noise level, working in a room where quiet, purposeful interactions are the norm, will enjoy modification of the auditory environment.

How pleasant and relaxing it is for children to enter a classroom and hear their favorite composer's music. Other sounds—new musical instruments, a gerbil gnawing a box or scratching around in her bedding, a mobile tinkling, or the hum of the computer—can help create a pleasant relaxing atmosphere, if the children are tuned in to the sounds and if they are not distracted by unnecessary noise.

Create olfactory interest   Some of our fondest childhood memories are triggered by aromas—bread baking, fresh flowers, luscious strawberries picked right from the plant, the garden after a rainfall. In a pleasant, relaxing classroom, the air is often filled with good smells.

It is easy to add a pleasant aroma to a room. Add peppermint extract to play-dough, place inexpensive scented soap in the bathroom, place safe flowering plants in the room, bake bread or muffins. Can you think of other things to do to add safe, inexpensive, pleasant aromas to the classroom?

Create textural interest   Think of all the ways in which you could add texture to an uninteresting classroom: carpeting on floors or walls, bulletin boards of cork or burlap-covered styrofoam, a collage of fur and cloth scraps, a "touch" wall created with an expanse of corrugated paper and other materials, or fabric wall hangings.

Plan Developmentally Valid Activities

Mr. Fox's preschool classroom had been divided into the appropriate number of activity areas. He developed six different small group areas. When the children arrived in the morning, they found each area ready for play, with at least one new activity emphasized. On Monday there were four new library books on the rack plus a flannelboard with figures for retelling a story heard the previous week. The tape recorder was on the language arts table along with a set of pictures that illustrated a story. In the science and math center, Mr. Fox placed a set of homemade counting and numeral recognition games on the table. On shelves were several seriation games. The science table held a butterfly display introduced on the previous Thursday. A basin of soapy water, towels, aprons, and two dolls were set out on a large rug in the family living area. To follow up a visit to the fire station, the block corner contained large pictures of fire engines, a real firefighter's hat, and a steering wheel set in a large wooden block. In the creative arts area, the teacher had set out egg cartons, clay, pipe cleaners, and crackly paper for making stabiles. In the puzzle and table toy area, three new puzzles were displayed on the table, and familiar small interlocking blocks were divided among three small tubs and were placed on the table in front of individual chairs.

Monday turned out to be a good day in Mr. Fox's classroom, with children busy at developmentally valid activities in well-organized activity centers. Children moved from activity to activity and did a lot of talking while they worked, but there was no running or screaming.

The children in Mr. Fox's class are likely to develop self-control, independence, competence, and prosocial behavior. These characteristics are found in children when their classrooms

1. contain a wide variety of activities that occur throughout the day.
2. contain a wide variety of activities that occur at the same time.
3. contain activities requiring active involvement of the children.
4. encourage them to choose their own activities.

Mr. Fox, aware of these factors, planned an activity for each small group area each day and let the children choose an area in which they wanted to work. Specific

activities in any classroom depend on the goals of the school and the developmental level of each child.

Supply Appropriate Materials

Adults influence children by providing materials and equipment (see chapter 1). Specific materials chosen should, of course, reflect the developmental level of the children, the goals of the school, and the learning centers in use, but there are general criteria for organizing any type of material chosen (Olds, 1977). White and Watts (1973) and Stallings (1975) found that competent, independent behavior is encouraged when adults provide a moderately rich assortment of exploratory materials.

Provide All Materials for a Task
It is extremely frustrating for a child to begin a project and not have the materials to carry it out. To complete a cut-and-paste collage a child needs scissors and paste and materials to be cut. It is the adult's responsibility to gather materials that will be needed by children for specific projects.

Organize Materials Well

Materials should be organized logically; items for creative arts should be stored in the creative arts area, language arts materials in the language arts center. Children will not have to try to figure out where things are kept and can better spend their energy and time on learning activities.

Display Materials Well

Books should be displayed with the front cover visible, puzzles should be kept in puzzle racks and not stacked on top of each other, blocks should be classified according to size and stacked neatly on shelves. Crayons, paper, paste, and scissors can be stored in attractive convenient containers and can be placed on low, open shelves in the art area.

Make Some Materials Available and Others Inaccessible

Independence is fostered if children can easily reach materials needed for a certain task. Things with which children are allowed to work should be displayed on low, open shelves or in other logical ways. Things that children are not allowed to use should not be available to them. For example, teacher supplies and scissors should be out of reach of the children.

Provide Properly Sized Items That Work Well

Early childhood teachers know that children's small hands can best use small scissors, a child's short body needs small paint aprons and scaled-down dress-up clothes. Items used by children should also work well so that children can use them easily. The ability to control the environment comes in part from the ability to use equipment and materials without a lot of adult help.

Let Children Personalize the Areas

An important ingredient in soft architecture is personalization of space, the ability to put one's imprint on the surroundings. In an early childhood classroom with a supportive physical environment, this means that the children are able to personalize their space and that they have an individual personalized space in which to store their belongings. A child can put her imprint on a room by displaying her work, which is one reason that so many schools display children's art. It is more difficult but still possible to display a child's work in blockbuilding or language arts.

Examples   Photographs of a child building with blocks or of the finished construction, stories dictated by a child and printed on newsprint, and pictures of the children themselves.

SUMMARY: KEY CONCEPTS IN THIS CHAPTER

1. The adult's role in guiding children is to help them develop internal controls on

their behavior—self-control. Adults guide children *directly* by setting reasonable limits on behavior and by communicating well with children. Adults also guide children *indirectly* when they manage and structure the physical environment.

2. Adults often unwittingly foster disruptive behavior by providing a poorly designed classroom. In such a classroom materials are disorganized, furniture is poorly arranged, the room is uncomfortable and unattractive, movement is rigidly controlled, and arbitrary rules are imposed.

3. A supportive physical environment helps to foster positive behavior. Such an environment has an adequate number of well-designed and well-arranged activity areas, is pleasant, attractive, sensory-rich but not excessively stimulating, and contains developmentally valid activities. It also contains materials arranged and displayed well. Adults allow and encourage children to personalize the room.

OBSERVE: CHILD GUIDANCE IN ACTION

Use the following form to observe and recommend change for a classroom for young children. Look around the room and determine whether the room has each of the areas indicated. Then make recommendations for changes if necessary.

Name: _____

Setting: _____

Date: _____   _____

Number of children: _____

Age of children: _____

PRIVATE AREA:

A small enclosed area large enough for one to two children at most. No materials are normally stored in the area and there is no indication that the area is set up for a specific type of classroom activity. No tables or chairs are kept in the private area.

Present: _____ Not present: _____

Present but changes needed: _____

LEARNING CENTER WITH SEATING:

A partially closed area with surfaces for seating. Tables and chairs are usually present. The area is set up for specific activities, and child-accessible materials used in the activities are stored in the area.

Present: _____ Not present: _____

Present but changes needed: _____

LEARNING CENTER WITHOUT SEATING:

A partially enclosed area with space for children to work while standing up or sitting on the floor. The area is big enough for three to no more than six children and is set up for specific types of activities. Child-accessible materials used in the activities are stored in the area.

Present: _____ Not present: _____

Present but changes needed: _____

How many of these centers are there?_____

LARGE GROUP AREA:

An area where all or most of the class could meet at the same time. It is a large open area in the classroom that already exists or is made by easily pushing furniture aside. There are no or few tables and chairs in the area.

Present: _____ Not present: _____

Present but changes needed: _____

RECOMMENDED CHANGE FOR THE CLASSROOM

If you checked "not present" or "present but changes needed," *describe* how you would add the area to the classroom or *describe* changes needed to make the area meet criteria in the definition. Make drawings to illustrate your ideas.

Private Area:

Small Group Area with Seating:

Small Group Area without Seating:

Large Group Area:

REFERENCES

ALWARD, K.R. (1973). *Arranging the classroom for children.* San Francisco: Far West Laboratory for Educational Research and Development.

HEIMSTRA, N.W., & McFARLING, L.H. (1974). *Environmental psychology.* Monterey, CA: Brooks/Cole.

MARCU, M. (1977). Environmental design and architecture: The friendly environment versus the hostile environment. *Children in Contemporary Society, Special Issue, 11* (1), 3–5.

MEHRABIAN, A. (1976). *Public places and private spaces: The psychology of work, play, and living environments.* New York: Basic Books.

OLDS, A.R. (1977). Why is environmental design important to young children? *Children in Contemporary Society, Special Issue, 11* (1), 5–8.

PHYFE-PERKINS, E. (1980). Children's behavior in preschool settings: The influence of the physical environment. In L.G. Katz (Ed.), *Current topics in early childhood education,* Vol. 3. Norwood, NJ: Ablex.

SOMMER, R. (1974). *Tight spaces: Hard architecture and how to humanize it.* Englewood Cliffs, NJ: Prentice-Hall.

STALLINGS, J. (1975). Implementation and child effects of teaching practices in follow-through classrooms. *Monographs of the Society for Research in Child Development, 40* (7–8, Serial No. 163).

WHITE, B.L., & WATTS, J.C. (1973). *Experience and environment: Major influences on the development of the young child,* Vol. 1. Englewood Cliffs, NJ: Prentice-Hall.

UNIT TWO

Special Topics
in Child Guidance

The chapters in this unit focus on special topics in child guidance—discipline, aggression, prosocial behavior, and self-esteem. These topics were chosen because of their fruitfulness as research areas. Each topic is also of interest to adults who work with children in a variety of settings.

In chapter 5, *Discipline: The Continuing Debate*, you will learn that discipline can be either positive or negative and will read about specific discipline strategies. Positive discipline is used by supportive adults and has positive effects on children's behavior and development. Nonsupportive adults tend to rely on negative discipline strategies, and you will note that there are several undesirable consequences of hurtful discipline.

Chapter 6, *Children's Aggression: Its Origin and Control*, presents a "systems" or ecological perspective on how children become aggressive and on how aggression can be modified or controlled. You will discover that children's families, peer groups, and television viewing all affect their level of aggression and that several practical strategies help control or modify children's aggression.

In addition to controlling aggression, you will need to know how to help childen develop more positive behavior. In chapter 7, *Prosocial Behavior: Its Nature and Nurture*, you will learn how to encourage children to be cooperative, generous, and helpful.

Chapter 8 is called *Helping Children Develop Positive Self-Esteem*. In it you will learn how the "self" develops. You will also discover how supportive adults help childen build positive self-esteem. In this chapter, as well as in the chapters on aggression and prosocial behavior, you will note the powerful effect of an adult's discipline style on a child's development.

5

Discipline:
The Continuing Debate

Chapter Overview

After reading and studying this chapter, you will be able to:

☐ *Define* discipline.

☐ *Differentiate* between positive and negative discipline.

☐ *List* several negative discipline strategies and *describe* the effect of negative discipline on children's behavior and development.

☐ *List* several positive discipline strategies and *describe* the effect of positive discipline on children's behavior and development.

"Every child-rearing practice and technique
of discipline may potentially affect children's behavior . . ."

(Mussen & Eisenberg-Berg, 1977, p. 75)

CONCEPT OF DISCIPLINE

"Should I hit Connie when she pulls the cat's tail?"

"How can I get Toby to come to dinner on time?"

"Is it good to ignore Michael when he curses? My mother told me that I should wash his mouth out with soap. What do you think?"

"I saw somebody bite her toddler after the little girl bit a friend. She said it would 'teach her not to bite.' Is that true?"

These are typical questions about discipline. Discipline is a topic about which it is difficult to be neutral; it arouses the strongest of feelings. All of us have experienced some form of discipline in the process of growing up. Some adults remember the discipline style of their parents and other adults with great anger, while others view their parents' style of discipline as fair and just.

Adults tend to want to do the very best thing for the children with whom they interact, and this includes using appropriate discipline techniques. Just listen to a group of adults who live or work with children in some capacity. You will hear them eventually get around to the topic of discipline. Concern about discipline shows up in popular magazines containing advice columns and childrearing information. Books about discipline abound. It is easy to be confused after reading several articles or books, because each usually reflects the particular bias of the author, who may be advocating one specific method or technique without placing that technique in a broader framework.

This chapter examines some of the questions many adults have about discipline. It focuses on both positive and negative discipline strategies and the effects of each type of discipline on children.

What is Discipline?

Discipline is any attempt by an adult to control or change a child's behavior (Brown, 1979; Mead, 1976; Rollins & Thomas, 1979). *Any* attempt. Think of the numerous ways different adults attempt to control children—ignoring, hitting, isolation, explanation of rules, taking something away, denial of privileges. Adults, then, use a variety of strategies in the effort to control children or to change their behavior.

Is Discipline Positive or Negative?

There is much confusion about this issue. Some nonsupportive adults attempt to change children's behavior with harsh and negative strategies that actually hurt children physically or psychologically. In the minds of these adults, discipline is negative. In a word-association game they would very likely link *discipline* with *punishment*.

Other more supportive adults attempt to change unacceptable behavior with more humane and positive strategies. They believe that children have the right to be treated with dignity even when they have behaved inappropriately. They believe that positive discipline can control children's daily behavior and can help children eventually learn to control themselves. To these adults, discipline is positive. In a word-association game they would probably link the word *discipline* with *teaching.*

Discipline, then, is an umbrella term. In itself, it is neither positive nor negative. Specific strategies subsumed under the umbrella term can be either positive and humane or negative and hurtful. The word *discipline* itself is derived from the root *disciple,* a follower of the teachings or example of another person. Children will follow the example of an adult who uses either positive or negative control attempts or discipline.

Which Discipline Technique Is Best?

Adults are often bewildered by the array of discipline strategies available to them. A parent reads one book that advises using natural consequences, sees an article that urges her to use "time out," and watches a television special advocating a "get tough" attitude. This parent is puzzled and wonders what to do when her three children misbehave. She wants them to develop self-control and realizes that this takes a long time. She is also worried about how to control their behavior on a daily basis. What, she wonders, is the best way to keep them from hurting each other, breaking toys, or running into the street?

This parent needs to know the effects that both positive and negative discipline techniques have on behavior and development. She should be aware of a variety of positive discipline techniques that can help her to stop misbehavior and to teach self-control and responsibility. She should be aware that there is no "best" technique, that each positive technique is effective, and that it is probably wise to choose a combination of techniques.

How Should a Discipline Technique Be Chosen?

Mrs. Sanchez has three children, 10, 6, and 2 years old. She decides that she would like to use positive discipline. She discovers that the age of each child affects her choice of discipline technique. She and her husband tend to set more limits for their 2- and 6-year-olds and exercise more direct control over them than with the oldest child. For example, she removes her youngest child from situations he cannot handle. She frequently uses logical consequences and reasoning with her 10-year-old.

Mrs. Sanchez realizes that some techniques should not be used in some situations. It would be foolish to let any of her children experience the natural consequences of running in front of a moving car. She has also found that she feels extremely uncomfortable about using some techniques like hitting, so she avoids these strategies even though one magazine article said they were a good idea. She has found that she has greater success with any discipline technique when she feels comfortable with her choice.

NEGATIVE DISCIPLINE

Negative, Hurtful Discipline Strategies

Example Two-year-old Sam's father shook Sam violently after Sam ran out into the busy street.

Judy pinched her sister on the arm. Judy's babysitter then pinched Judy and said, "How does *that* feel?"

Ten-year-old Bernie left the gate open and his puppy escaped. Bernie found the puppy next door, but when Bernie's dad heard about the incident he exploded with anger at the dinner table. "You sure are a stupid kid. You can't be trusted to do anything right, can you? That dog is going back to the pound and you can just forget about the movie on Saturday!"

Three-year-old Caitlin pulled cereal boxes off the shelf as she sat near them in the grocery cart. Her mother slapped her on the face and said, "Cut it out now, Caitlin!"

Jim was 8 years old. His father hit his bare buttocks and legs repeatedly with a leather belt to punish him. Jim had bruises from buttocks to ankles and it hurt for him to sit down.

Marie was late in coming home for dinner. Her father glared at her but said nothing.

These are all examples of negative hurtful discipline. Many nonsupportive adults rely almost exclusively on harsh discipline like hitting, shouting, ridiculing, and threatening when dealing with children. There are many reasons why a person, like Jim's father, might hurt a child when "disciplining" him. An adult who uses harsh discipline may himself have been disciplined harshly—he had a model of negative discipline and learned how to discipline from his parents. His culture may view violence as an acceptable way to resolve conflicts. He has seen other parents hit their children. His church says that hitting is a good method of discipline. In addition, Jim's father never learned about positive discipline, so he does not know a better way.

Hitting, threatening, ridicule, sarcasm. A common theme unites different forms of negative discipline—the use of force or *coercion* to change behavior. Some adults do not understand that they do not have a right to hurt children. Some adults use raw power when disciplining children. Adults are obviously larger than children and use their superior physical power to try to force children to behave appropriately. Sam was shaken, Judy pinched, Caitlin slapped, and Jim beaten. Adults also control material goods (Hoffman, 1960), and some adults use this control unfairly. Bernie's dad disciplined harshly by sending the puppy away. Marie's dad used a special form of negative discipline called *love withdrawal*. Even though there is no hitting, slapping, shouting, or ridicule used in love withdrawal, it is a negative or punitive discipline technique.

An adult can withdraw love in a variety of ways (Hoffman, 1970). He can re-

fuse to talk to the child, refuse to listen to the child, threaten to leave or abandon the child, or glare at the child, as Marie's father did.

Love withdrawal is negative and has some of the same negative side effects as hitting or sarcasm. The adult does not tell the child why he is upset and therefore does not help the child understand how his behavior caused a problem for others. Love withdrawal does not help a child develop empathy, and it diminishes interaction between adult and child.

Adults who use harsh discipline usually have good intentions. They want their children to comply with necessary rules, to respect other people and property, to learn "right from wrong." They want their children to be good people, and they use the only method of discipline they know to achieve these ends. Often, however, harsh discipline has an effect opposite to what adults thought it would have.

Effects of Negative Discipline

Negative Discipline Does Not Foster Self-Control

Children who are hit, slapped, threatened, and ridiculed tend to be less self-controlled than children who experience positive discipline (Rollins & Thomas, 1979). An adult who uses harsh discipline relies on a child's fear and not on the child's emerging sensitivity and empathy. Jim's father frequently uses physical punishment —slapping, hitting, and "using the belt"—to force Jim to behave. He fully realizes that Jim is afraid of being hurt and uses that fear to "keep Jim in line."

Adults using harsh discipline do not give children information about what behavior is considered more acceptable or about how their behavior affects others. To avoid the harsh punishment, the child has to figure out what the adult wants. Control for this child is external. He does not get a chance to practice self-control, and a skill not practiced tends not to develop very well.

Negative Discipline Does Not Suppress Unacceptable Behavior

Example "Self-control. Ha! I guess it's OK for some professor to talk about, but I have problems now. I want Jim to listen to me when I tell him not to do something now. I can't be thinking about 5 or 10 years from now. Jim shapes up in a hurry when I get the belt down or when he gets one across the face!"

Jim's dad, like a lot of adults, has legitimate concerns about how a child is acting now. Jim's dad is convinced that harsh forms of discipline are the best strategies for *suppressing* (stopping) deviant behavior. The question then becomes, Does hurtful discipline work to suppress unacceptable behavior?

Apparently not. Punishment can suppress behavior for a short period but, surprisingly, the harsh punishment may even make the undesired behavior worse (Church, 1963).

Example Miss Gell sees Karen take several pegs from Denise and says, "Karen, give Denise's pegs back to her!" Karen complies, but after the teacher turns away she grabs the whole basket of pegs from Denise.

In a typical home or classroom children are not positively reinforced or punished every time they perform a desired or unacceptable behavior. Adults frequently use a *partial* or *intermittent* schedule of reinforcement. This means that a child like Karen is punished for taking things at certain times but not at other times. Partial reinforcement actually makes a response, whether desirable or undesirable, more resistant to change.

Because Karen's undesirable behavior of taking things from others has been partially reinforced, *response recovery* occurs—Karen seems to obey Miss Gell but goes right back to taking things when the teacher turns away.

Adults are Negatively Reinforced for
Using Negative Discipline

Jim's father hits Jim for unacceptable behavior. As he says, "Jim shapes up when he is hit." To adults like Jim's dad, hurtful discipline *seems* to work. For example, when Jim was a toddler he would swing his feet and kick his highchair. His dad slapped Jim's leg and Jim stopped kicking. Dad had been *negatively reinforced* for using slapping. The sequences goes like this:

☐ Jim kicks his highchair (an annoying behavior to Dad).

☐ Dad slaps Jim's leg (slapping is punishment).

☐ Jim is surprised and stops kicking—for the moment (the annoying behavior is withdrawn).

☐ Dad thinks, "H-m-m, that worked." (Dad is *negatively* reinforced because hitting seems to work to *stop an annoying behavior).*

☐ Jim kicks the highchair the next day (his father merely hit and did not explain why he should not kick the chair).

☐ Dad hits him again (remember, hitting seemed to work yesterday).

The real problem here is that hitting Jim becomes firmly entrenched in his father's repertoire of discipine strategies because he becomes convinced that hitting and slapping are effective—but they are not (Patterson & Cobb, 1971). It becomes easy for adults to rely on ineffective techniques, especially when they do not know more effective strategies and when they tell themselves, "Everybody hits their kids. It doesn't hurt them. It's good for them!" These adults downplay the harm to the victims of their discipline and try to rationalize their harsh behavior.

Negative Discipline Fosters Aggression
in Children

Aggression does tend to breed aggression. Hitting, slapping, sarcasm, and other forms of negative discipline are examples of aggression by adults. One very costly side effect of negative discipline is the all-too-frequent increase in aggression by punished children (Parke, 1977). A child might show aggression directly toward the *punishing agent* (the adult who hurt him).

Example   Seven-year-old Gail's mother slapped her on the face and said, "Shut up, Gail. Don't you *ever* sass me again! Do you hear me?" Gail then knocked the newly decorated cake that her mother had finished for a contest off the counter. "It was an accident, Mom," said Gail as she turned away and smiled.

Example   The wresting coach made Greg do 100 pushups as punishment for talking during practice. Greg later let the air out of the coach's tires.

Aggression can also take a more general form. Children who are harshly disciplined often recycle their anger and use the same type of hurtful or degrading behavior with people or animals who had nothing to do with hurting the child.

Example   Jim's dad used the belt on him on Saturday. On Monday Jim got in a fight with Dominic over art supplies and put a hole through Dominic's painting. He also pushed Laurie and hit Jonathan.

Example Jim was training his dog. When she did not sit on command, Jim tightened Ginger's choke chain until Ginger cried in pain.

One goal that adults usually have is to help children develop constructive ways of interacting with peers. Jim is justifiably angry about his father's harsh treatment, but because he in turn hurts his friends, it is unlikely that Dominic, Laurie, and Jon will want to play with Jim. Herein lies the danger. Children like Jim need friends but will damage relationships by acting aggressively. Jim is only 8. The longer his aggressive behavior continues, the more difficult it will become to help him because the attitudes of his peers will become somewhat fixed (Dodge, 1980).

Children Avoid Adults Who Discipline Harshly
How would you react to someone who ridiculed you or something that you did? Would you try to avoid him, refuse to take phone calls from him, and perhaps skip meetings at which he would be present? Children who are disciplined harshly try to avoid or escape from the punishing agent. This avoidance is called *social disruption* and is considered to be the most serious negative side effect of negative discipline (Azrin &. Holz, 1966; Parke, 1977; Wagonseller et al., 1977). Jim, for example, makes a special effort to avoid contact with his father as much as possible. To have a positive influence on children, adults must have good relationships with them. Positive influence is diminished when children avoid adults.

Negative Discipline Diminishes Self-Esteem
Children value themselves as the adults in their lives value them. Children who are disciplined firmly but kindly and in a positive way tend to develop positive self-esteem. Children who are harshly disciplined, psychologically or physically, often develop a negative view of themselves. They evaluate themselves negatively because the adults who punish them do not value them very highly.

POSITIVE DISCIPLINE

Positive Discipline Strategies

Set Reasonable, Fair Limits
One of the major ways in which adults influence children is by stating expectations for desired behavior. Knowing the limits of acceptable behavior and then communicating these reasonable, fair limits clearly to children is actually the core of positive discipline.

Remove Children from Situations They Cannot Handle
We often think of discipline as something adults do *to* children. Discipline is often

more effective when we do something indirectly to help a child behave well. Changing the situation, instead of expecting a child to figure out miraculously how to "be
good," is often the best discipline technique. For example, 10-month-old Reenah is
too young to understand or remember not to touch dangerous items like lamp cords
or electrical outlets. Her father changes the situation by removing lamp cords, cap-
ping outlets, and taking Reenah away from outlets. Reenah's 3-year-old sister has
trouble sitting still through the entire church service, so her mother takes her to a
quiet room where she can observe the service without disturbing others.

Redirect Children's Behavior

Example Pete strums the rope on the drying rack like a guitar. Ms. LeBlanc asks
Pete to come to the music area to try out the autoharp.

Example Courtney, when eating french fries, uses the grease to "fingerpaint" on
the formica table. Ms. LeBlanc tells Courtney that she can fingerpaint with paint
later.

Positive discipline occasionally means that we resist the urge to swoop down
on children like Pete and Courtney, that we simply redirect their behavior. Often,

adults can find a way to let children do something in a safer, better, more acceptable way.

Ignore Behavior When It Is Appropriate to Do So

Some behavior can be safely ignored and some behavior should not be ignored. Which of the following behaviors can Ms. LeBlanc ignore? Which should she not ignore?

1. Julie squeezes the guinea pig.
2. Ann Marie talks nonstop to Ramon during a filmstrip.
3. Willie bites Ramon.
4. Ray pulls out the crocus plants as they emerge.
5. Leslie smashes her modeling clay structure after she finishes.
6. Julie smiles at Ann Marie during story time.

Adults should not ignore behavior when the child is causing an undue disturbance of an ongoing activity (Ann Marie talking), hurting someone (Julie squeezing the pet and Willie biting Ramon), or damaging or destroying property (Ray's destruction of the plants.) Leslie has not destroyed anything by squashing her clay structure, and Julie has not disturbed the group by smiling; therefore, their behavior can be ignored.

The following suggestions explain how to use *extinction* (ignoring of behavior) successfully:

1. *Realize that effective ignoring takes time.* A child will be surprised when you ignore him for the first time. You have paid attention to, say, his temper tantrums in the past, and have actually reinforced him with attention. The first few times you ignore a tantrum a child will try to recapture your attention and will use a bigger tantrum. Eventually, he will get the point and the tantrum will subside.
2. *Decide to really ignore the behavior.* Pretend that the child does not exist. Do not mutter to yourself under your breath, do not make eye contact or use verbal communications or other gestures.
3. *Reinforce more acceptable behavior.* If a child uses an obscenity and you ignore it, then it would be wise to reinforce him for using more acceptable words.

Time Out

Example Jamie screeches — E-E-E-E-H! — during the self-selected activity period. Ms. LeBlanc says to Jamie quietly, "That's a screech, Jamie. Time out." She walks with him to the time out chair, Jamie sits down, and Ms. LeBlanc sets the timer for two minutes. When the timer goes off Jamie is allowed to resume playing. Later, when he talks in a normal tone without screeching, Ms. LeBlanc says, "You talked without screeching for a whole hour, Jamie."

The adult has used *time out* with Jamie. Time out is a positive discipline technique when it is used properly by a sensitive, supportive adult. A child is removed from a situation in which he is reinforced for undesirable behavior and placed in an area where reinforcers are not available. Another way of looking at it is that a child is placed in a safe but boring place when he misbehaves.

Time out is a form of punishment that is frequently used unwisely. The following steps outline the effective humane use of time out (Patterson, 1977).

1. *Identify a specific behavior that should be changed.* Explain time out to the child and identify the behavior that you have targeted.

2. *Use time out every time the target behavior is displayed.* Use time out as soon after the behavior occurs as possible. Use delayed time out if the unacceptable behavior occurs when another activity precludes an immediate time out. A delayed time out is much more humane than some form of harsh punishment that is frequently meted out in public places (Brown, 1979).

3. *When the target behavior (screeching) occurs, say, "That's a screech. Time out."* Do not lecture. Simply state the need for a time out.

4. *Take the child to the time out spot.* It should be a safe, nonfrightening area with as few toys and people as possible. If the child resists, do not back down. Simply restate the need to do a time out.

5. *Set a timer for only a few minutes.* Avoid the urge to say, "Now you sit there and think about what you've done." Do not let the child decide how much time to spend in time out. You decide. Three to 5 minutes is enough. Much more than that is harsh punishment.

6. *If the child "puts up a fuss" in time out, remind him that he will have to be quiet for 1 minute.* Add 1 minute to the time out. Some adults add a half hour when a noisy child in time out creates a disturbance, and this is more like revenge than a fair punishment.

7. *Reinforce positive behavior when the child returns to an activity after completing time out.*

Response Cost

In Ms. LeBlanc's class, the climbing gym is off limits during naptime. Connie consistently ignores this limit. Ms. LeBlanc takes Connie aside, restates the rule, and says, "The no-climbing-during-nap rule is an important thing to remember. Because you climbed during nap, you will not be allowed to climb today at all after nap."

Ms. Leblanc has used *response cost* with Connie. Like time out, response cost is an effective positive discipline strategy when used properly by a sensitive supportive adult. In response cost an inappropriate behavior "costs" something. A child loses something—tokens or privileges, for example—when he acts inappropriately. Connie's cost is the simple loss of the opportunity to climb. She has not, however, been ridiculed or demeaned.

Response cost is effective when used well. Like any discipline technique, it should not be overused. The cost of the child's misbehavior should be reasonable and fair. A child should have accumulated a store of points or tokens so that taking a token away is not devastating. Suppose, for example, that you are awarded three points each time you attend class: 10 classes give you 30 points. If you choose to be absent you lose four points, but you have accumulated enough points so that a loss of four points does not adversely affect your grade. This is an example of *response cost.*

Natural and Logical Consequences

Another limit in Ms. LeBlanc's classroom is that the children must wash their hands before eating snack. Ann Marie has come to the table with dirty hands. The aide asks Ms. LeBlanc for help, who says to Ann Marie, "You may eat your snack when you are clean," and removes her plate. Ann Marie does not wash her hands by the end of snack, and Ms. LeBlanc says, "You have decided to skip snack today. You may try again at lunch."

Ms. LeBlanc has used *logical consequences* with Ann Marie. Like time out and response cost, letting children experience the consequences of their behavior—*when it is safe to do so*—is an effective positive discipline strategy if used properly.

Logical consequences, if used well, is a positive strategy. First, it expresses an adult's support and respect and does not demean or degrade a child. Second, Ms. LeBlanc has held Ann Marie responsible for her own behavior. Formerly, when she lectured, she, the adult, took responsibility for handwashing. Third, Ann Marie has been allowed to make her own decision about which course of action (handwashing in this case) would be appropriate. In the past, Ms. LeBlanc has made the decision for Ann Marie. Finally, Ann Marie will learn that her choice is followed by a consequence that is logically related to her decision. She chooses not to wash and therefore not to eat. Ann Marie will learn that she also has the power to choose to eat her snack when she chooses to wash her hands.

The following steps in using logical consequences are suggested by Dinkmeyer and McKay (1976).

1. *Give the child a choice.* Do this in a way that conveys your respect along with your message. You are not seeking revenge. It is important that your tone be respectful and that your attitude be friendly (but not false) and not vengeful or harsh when presenting the choice.

SPECIAL FOCUS: Positive Discipline Strategies

Responsible, supportive adults choose not to use harsh negative discipline. Instead, they use a variety of positive discipline strategies which include:

☐ setting reasonable and fair limits.

☐ removing children from situations they cannot handle.

☐ redirecting children's behavior.

☐ ignoring behavior using extinction when it is appropriate to do so.

☐ using time out.

☐ using response cost.

☐ letting children experience the consequences of their behavior.

Example "We are in the gym to do exercises, Jerry. You can exercise with us or you can wait for us by sitting on the sideline. You choose."

2. *Accept the child's choice and communicate your acceptance.*

Example (Jerry continues to be disruptive). "I see that you've decided to wait for us on the sidelines, Jerry. You can try again the next time we have gym."

or

(Jerry settles down and joins the group). "I see that you have decided to exercise with the class."

Effects of Positive Discipline

Adults who use positive discipline help children to become humane, caring, assertive people. Positive discipline has powerful effects on a child's development and on the relationship between adult and child.

Positive Discipline Does Not Instill Fear
Adults who rely on positive discipline usually believe that they have a responsibility to keep children safe and to teach children the "rules of the culture." They also believe that it is possible to fulfill their responsibility without using raw power. They do not use force and they do not threaten children. They understand that using power or instilling fear is actually an ineffective and inhumane way to deal with another person. Threatening children or hurting them is also ineffective in stopping undesirable behavior. Responsible adults believe that children control their own behavior best when they are not afraid of being hurt and when they feel safe and secure.

Positive Discipline Encourages Children
to Be Self-Responsible
Examples: "When you leave toys at the end of the slide, someone can fall on them and get hurt. I want you to keep the toys away from the slide."

"Keep the soapy water in the wash basin, Julie. If you splash it onto the floor someone can slip and get hurt."

This adult refuses to use sarcasm or to degrade these children. She does, however, point out that they are responsible for their actions. She explains the consequences of their behavior in a nonjudgmental way. Positive discipline helps children take responsibility for their own actions.

Positive Discipline Fosters Self-Control
The long-range goal in guiding children is the achievement of self-control; that is, we want children to be able to control themselves 5, 10, or 20 years from now. The ability to control oneself is nurtured through interaction with warm, supportive adults who use positive discipline strategies.

Careful observation of adults using positive discipline shows that they model self-control, tell children that self-control is expected of them, tell children how to control themselves, and then reinforce self-control. It should not surprise us, then, that these children achieve self-control more easily than children who are threatened, hit, or ridiculed.

Positive Discipline Encourages Children to Think and Arouses Empathy

Recall from chapter 1 that one of the major ways in which adults influence children is by using *cognitive modification strategies.* Responsible adults credit children with the ability to think and, with guidance, to figure out how to behave appropriately. Positive discipline is used to help a child become more empathic by pointing out the needs of another person and by helping the child figure out why the other person acted in a certain way.

Piaget (1970) posits four ways in which children gradually become less egocentric and more empathic. One of these *classical factors of development* is *social interaction,* a process by which a child is confronted with the ideas of other people. Only through such a confrontation can a child be exposed to ways of looking at things that differ from his own. Adults who use positive discipline frequently confront children with another point of view.

Positive Discipline Builds Self-Esteem

All discipline techniques convey adult disapproval of a child's behavior and indicate a need to change the behavior. Hitting, ridiculing, sarcasm, and threats use force to change behavior and thus degrade children, resulting in damaged egos and diminished self-esteem. Positive discipline, however, allows children to change behavior with no loss of self-esteem. In fact, positive discipline helps children to feel good about themselves.

Positive Discipline Helps Children Become Competent

Children are motivated by a need for competence (White, 1959). Like all humans, children like feeling that they can do something well, whether it is fingerpainting, making friends, or selling Girl Scout cookies. White, et al. (1976) examined factors related to competence in young children and found that parents of competent children used positive discipline. They set clear limits, and they were not afraid either to prohibit some behavior or to explain the reasons for the rules they set.

STUDY HINT: Join the debate on discipline! You have just joined the debate team. Your topic is "Positive Discipline: Why Use It?" Your team is arguing for using positive discipline. Your main task is to present a convincing argument for using positive discipline strategies. The core of your argument should include a clear statement of how positive discipline affects children. Remember that your opponents will try to convince others that using negative discipline is acceptable. You must be prepared to rebut their argument by saying how negative discipline strategies such as hitting, ridicule, or shouting hurt children.

SPECIAL FOCUS: Discipline Will Be More Effective If . . .

☐ *adults are nurturant and supportive.*

☐ *adults keep expectations for themselves and for children at a reasonable level* (Dinkmeyer & McKay, 1976; May, 1979). Having reasonable expectations of children allows them to have success, but unreasonably high expectations result in failure for the children because they cannot meet the expectations.

   Many adults believe that they have to be perfect when they interact with children, that there is a correct way to do everything. These adults have unrealistically high expectations of themselves. Dinkmeyer and McKay (1976) advise these adults to have the courage to be imperfect. They need to be reassured about what they are doing well and to realize that everyone makes mistakes with discipline. They also need to realize that even the most positive discipline techniques do not always work.

☐ *the discipline is well-timed.* Limits should be well-timed. Time out, response cost, and logical consequences are more effective if they are applied as soon as possible after an inappropriate behavior (Parke, 1977).

☐ *the discipline is applied as consistently as is possible* (Parke & Deur; Stouwie, 1972). Mr. Robinson is consistent in the use of discipline; i.e., he deals with unacceptable behavior in the same way each time it occurs. For example, on the playground, the children have been leaving small trucks on the trike path. He has reminded them of the need to clear the path. When children forget, he quietly but firmly reminds them, makes them stop what they are doing, and brings them back to pick up the toys. His consistent approach eliminates the problem because most of the children seem to internalize the limit and accept responsibility for keeping the path clear.

☐ *reasons for using the discipline are given.* Giving a reason or rationale for punishment is essential to the development of internal control. Children who are not given a rationale along with their punishment deviate more often over an extended period of time than do children whose punishment is accompanied by a reason (Parke, 1977). It is essential that a rationale be given when a delayed time out is used.

Example   Ms. LeBlanc uses time out when Jamie screeches. On a field trip, Jamie screeches and Ms. LeBlanc says, "You will do a time out when we go back to school." They return to school an hour later and the teacher reminds Jamie about the time out. She restates the reason for the time out.

SUMMARY: KEY CONCEPTS IN THIS CHAPTER

1. *Discipline* is any attempt to control or change a child's behavior. Many forms of discipline exist, and each affects behavior differently. Discipline can be either positive or negative and harsh.

2. Nonsupportive adults rely on *negative* and often hurtful *discipline strategies* to try to control children's behavior. They hit, shake, slap, yell at, or ridicule children, use sarcasm, or withdraw their love. All of these techniques use force or an adult's power. Negative discipline has several undesirable consequences.

3. Supportive responsible adults use a variety of *positive discipline techniques.* Their choice of strategy depends on the child and situation. They do not use force and they do not threaten children. Positive discipline has powerful positive effects on a child's behavior and development.

OBSERVE: CHILD GUIDANCE IN ACTION

Observe an adult as he interacts with a group of young children. Using the information in the text, identify some of the discipline techniques used by the adult. Observe at least four interactional episodes between the adult and children. Determine from your observable data whether this adult has used positive or negative discipline. Use the following format to record your observations.

Date: _____

Time: _____

Setting: _____

Approximate age of children: _____

Your name: _____

EPISODE

Describe what the child did or said.

Describe what the adult did or said.

Describe the outcome.

Name the discipline technique.

EPISODES 2, 3, AND 4 Use the same format.

Summarize your findings: From the data you have collected, describe the degree to which this adult uses positive discipline strategies.

REFERENCES

AZRIN, N.H., & HOLZ, W.C. (1966). Punishment. In W.K. Honig (Ed.), *Operant behavior: Areas of research and application.* New York: Appleton-Century-Crofts.

BROWN, B. (1979). Parents' discipline of children in public places. *The Family Coordinator, 28*(1) 67–73.

CHURCH, R.M. (1963). The varied effects of punishment on behavior. *Psychological Review, 70*, 369–402.

DINKMEYER, G., & McKAY, G. (1976). *S.T.E.P.: Parent's handbook.* Circle Pines, MN: American Guidance Service.

DODGE, K.A. (1980). Social cognition and children's aggressive behavior. *Child Development, 51*, 162–170.

HOFFMAN, M.L. (1960). Power assertion by the parent and its impact on the child. *Child Development, 31*, 129–143.

HOFFMAN, M.L. (1970). Moral development. In P. Mussen (Ed.), *Carmichael's manual of child psychology*, Vol. 2. New York: Wiley.

MAY, G. (1979) *Child discipline: Guidelines for parents.* Chicago: NCPCA.

MEAD, D.E. (1976). *Six approaches to childrearing.* Provo, UT: Brigham Young University Press.

MUSSEN, P., & EISENBERG-BERG, N. (1977). *Roots of caring, sharing, and helping: The development of prosocial behavior in children.* San Francisco: W.H. Freeman.

PARKE, R.D. (1977). Some effects of punishment on children's behavior — revisited. In R.D. Parke & E.M. Hetherington (Eds.), *Contemporary readings in child psychology.* New York: McGraw-Hill.

PARKE, R.D., & DEUR, J.L. (1972) Schedule of reinforcement and inhibition of aggression in children. *Developmental Psychology, 7,* 266–269.

PATTERSON, G.R. (1977). *Living with children* (rev. ed.). Champaign, IL: Research Press.

PATTERSON, G.R., & COBB, J.A. (1971). A dyadic analysis of "aggressive" behavior. In J.P. Hill (Ed.), *Minnesota symposia on child psychology*, Vol. 5. Minneapolis: University of Minnesota Press.

PIAGET, J. (1970). Piaget's theory. In P. Mussen (Ed.), *Carmichael's manual of child psychology.* New York: Wiley.

ROLLINS, B.C., & THOMAS, D.L. (1979). Parental support, power, and control techniques in the socialization of children. In W.R. Burr et al. (Eds.), *Contemporary theories about the family*, Vol. 1. New York: Free Press.

STOUWIE, R.J. (1972). An experimental study of adult dominance and warmth, conflicting verbal instructions, and children's moral behavior. *Child Development, 43,* 959–972.

WAGONSELLER, B.R., et al. (1977). *The art of parenting.* Champaign, IL: Research Press.

WHITE, B.L., KABAN, B., SHAPIRO, B., & ATTONUCCI, J. (1976). Competence and experience. In I.C. Uzgiris & F. Weigmann (Eds.), *The structuring of experience.* New York: Plenum Press.

WHITE, R.W. (1959). Motivation reconsidered: The concept of competence. *Psychological Review, 66,* 297–323.

6

Children's Aggression:
Its Origin and Control

Chapter Overview

After reading and studying this chapter, you will be able to:

☐ *define* aggression.

☐ *list and describe* different forms of aggression.

☐ *explain* age and sex differences in aggression.

☐ *discuss* the "systems" or ecological approach to the development of aggression.

☐ *explain* how a child's family, peer group, community, and television viewing habits can each encourage the development of aggression.

☐ *list, discuss, and give examples* of specific practices that prevent or control aggression.

UNDERSTANDING AGGRESSION

Definition

A 4-year-old watches his dad slap his mother several times. The Road Runner drops a boulder on Wile E. Coyote's head. One child smashes another's playdough structure. Susan bites Louis. Susan grabs a basket of pegs from Rita. Jason shoots his cat with a BB gun.

These are all examples of *aggression;* a common element in all of them is the act of inflicting harm on a person, animal, or object. *Aggression is any behavior that results in injury to another person or an animal or in damage to or destruction of property* (Bandura, 1973; Berkowitz, 1973; Caldwell, 1977; Feshbach, 1970; Parke & Slaby, 1983). Commonly acknowledged as aggression are slapping, grabbing, pinching, kicking, and punching. More subtle but equally hurtful forms of aggression include threats, sexual harassment, degrading someone, or undermining someone's plans.

Forms of Aggression

Accidental Aggression

Adam crashed into Mario's block tower as he zoomed down the indoor slide. Mario was furious and shoved Adam out of the way. In the same classroom Lori and Nan played at the crowded workbench. Nan hit Lori's finger with the hammer and Lori screamed at her. Carl, swinging the shovel around in the sandpit, flipped sand into Tom's eyes. These are all examples of *accidental aggression* (Feshbach, 1970). Some researchers do not count these as aggression because one person did not intend to hurt the other.

The real problem with accidental aggression is that the injured child often retaliates in an equally aggressive way. In the examples, Mario shoved Adam, Lori screamed at Nan, and Tom hit Carl with his shovel. Young children have difficulty distinguishing between accidental and intentional acts of aggression. They realize that they have been hurt and do not ask if the other person hurt them deliberately.

Accidental injuries cannot be eliminated completely, but adults can prevent some of them. First, children need to have adequate space for activities. Overcrowding sets the stage for problems like bumping into each other and pushing. Second, adults can help children learn to distinguish between accidental and intentional injury. To Mario, Mr. Keller said, "Mario, I can see that you are angry. Adam crashed into your tower because the slide was too close to the blocks. It was an accident." Children are less likely to retaliate when they understand that the damage was accidental.

Instrumental Aggression

Instrumental aggression is aggression aimed at getting back or obtaining some object, territory, or privilege (Hartup, 1974). The child wants something, a goal, and does something aggressive to achieve this goal.

Example   Janet rode the trike around the playground. Sophie wanted the trike (her goal) and Janet was blocking her from obtaining it, so she pushed Janet off the trike (instrumental aggression). Sophie was not angry with Janet. Janet just happened to be in Sophie's way.

Children should not be allowed to use aggression to get what they need or want. If Sophie is allowed to take the trike, then her aggression is rewarded and she learns that she can get what she wants if she applies enough pain.

Hostile Aggression

Hostile aggression is person-oriented aggression (Hartup, 1974). A person who shows hostile aggression injures someone because she is angry with the person as a person. The aggressor believes that the other person has done something to her on purpose and has threatened her ego (Caldwell, 1977).

Example Suppose that 12-year-old Martha has called Jane "dumb" in front of a group of children (a threat to Jane's ego). Jane retaliates for this insult by breaking Martha's clarinet. This is an act of hostile aggression.

Age Differences in Aggression

Instrumental aggression is more common among preschool children, while hostile aggression increases as children get older (Feshbach, 1970; Hartup, 1974). Older children exhibit retaliatory, personally directed (hostile) aggression. Children 6 years old or younger disagree over toys and personal property (instrumental aggression) more frequently than do older children (Dawe, 1934; Hartup, 1974).

As children move through the preschool years, the change in modes of expressing aggression parallels a more general change in cognitive structures. Preschool children are usually in the second of Piaget's stages of cognitive development, the preoperational stage. (See chapter 2 for a more detailed account of this stage.) One of the characteristics of this stage is the child's egocentricity. A preschool child is less able than older people to understand that someone else has a right, for example, to ride the tricycle. A young child seems to center on wanting a ride herself and as a result might resort to pushing the other child off the trike. It is possible that a more sophisticated cognitive and linguistic system with which to express concepts and feelings is a necessary condition to the expression of aggression in a more abstract, verbal manner (hostile aggression).

Sex Differences in Aggression

Maccoby and Jacklin (1980) analyze several studies of aggression in children younger than 6 years old. They concluded that

1. There are clear sex differences in aggression.
2. Boys show more aggression than girls.
3. Boys are both physically and verbally more aggressive than girls.
4. Older boys are more likely than older girls to counterattack when they have been physically attacked (Darvill & Cheyne, 1981).

5. There are more aggressive interactions between pairs of boys than between a boy and a girl or two girls (Smith & Green, 1974).

We can explain these sex differences in aggression by examining how differently society treats boys and girls. Our culture has clearly-defined ideas about how girls and boys may display aggression. Different childrearing tactics are used with boys and girls. Parents tend to use more physical punishment with boys than

with girls, and boys might adopt these aggressive methods in interaction with others (Block, 1978). Parents choose different toys for girls than for boys. Some "male" sex-typed toys like guns are cues for aggression. Boys seem to be exposed to guns more frequently than girls, and thus to aggression-producing cues.

HOW CHILDREN BECOME AGGRESSIVE: A SYSTEMS APPROACH

Children are not aggressive when they are born, and not all children become aggressive as they get older. Several different socializing forces work together to shape aggression in certain children. The most complete explanation of how children become aggressive seems to be a "systems" or ecological approach, because it acknowledges a child's embeddedness in a variety of social systems—family, peer group, and community (Brim, 1975; Bronfenbrenner, 1979; Parke & Slaby, 1983). This section focuses on how aggression is learned, maintained, and modified in families, peer groups, and communities.

Aggression Develops in a Child's Family

Families play a critical role in the acquisition, maintenance, and modification of children's aggression (Parke & Slaby, 1983). Some children live in violent families, and it is here that children take lessons in how to hurt other people and animals. Violent families become violent because members of the system develop aggressive patterns of interacting with one another. Adults in many aggressive family systems are insensitive and nonsupportive and are poor managers of their children's environment. Adults in many aggressive families also use ineffective, often harsh, discipline techniques. This section describes how aggressive families teach children to be aggressive.

Intrafamilial Violence

Intrafamilial violence is violence within a family system. In families with high rates of violence, children have opportunities to acquire and practice aggressive behaviors. Violence between spouses occurs frequently, according to Straus, Gelles, and Steinmetz (1980). Violence was used as a way to resolve conflict by approximately 12 percent of the couples in their survey.

What does the study of husband-wife violence have to do with children's aggression? Husbands and wives who use violence to resolve conflicts also tend to use violent discipline tactics with their children (Steinmetz, 1977). Pederson, Anderson, and Cain (1977) found that the amount of negative affect between husbands and wives was positively related to a high level of negative affect toward children. The acceptance of physical force as a general pattern of family interaction sets the stage for the use of physical force to discipline children, and this physical force frequently becomes abuse (Gelles & Straus, 1979).

Parents who hurt each other tend to use hurtful aggressive discipline with their children. Their children, in turn, observe their parents and imitate them by using aggression to solve their own conflicts. Straus et al. (1980) observed 733 families with children between 3 and 17 years of age and found that over 80 percent of the children had used aggression on one or more occasions during the previous year. Ninety percent of the children 3 to 4 years old were physically aggressive, while 64 percent of the 15- to 17-year-olds had physically aggressive interactions. Sibling aggression occurs more frequently than other types of family violence, but siblings are far *less* likely to use excessive levels of aggression. Rates of homicide are higher between spouses than between siblings (Straus et al., 1980).

The Cycle of Violence in Family Systems

A family is a system in which members learn to respond to each other by developing specific patterns of behavior. Each member of a family system influences the behavior of all other members during interaction. Patterson (1982) was interested in why some families had aggressive patterns of interaction. After observing family interaction patterns, Patterson identified a specific *coercive* process used by many families, a process through which members of a family learn, maintain, and increase aggressive behavior. This coercive process involves several steps:

1. *One system member presents an aversive stimulus.* Mario pulls his sister's hair.
2. *Second system member is likely to respond with an aversive stimulus.* Mario's sister whirls around and punches him in the face.
3. *The aversive interchange continues and escalates in intensity.* Mario responds by pushing his sister, and she pushes back. Mario slaps her and she cries.
4. *Other system members are drawn into the process.* Dad hears the children fighting, races to the backyard, grabs each child, and slaps them both.
5. *One system member eventually withdraws the aversive stimulus and breaks the cycle of violence for a short time.* Dad retreats to the house, proud of having stopped the fighting. The problem? Dad thinks he has succeeded in stopping the aggressive behavior of his children (actually, Mario's and his sister's aggressive behavior will probably increase). Dad has been *negatively* reinforced for using slapping to end the children's fighting and is highly likely to use more slapping and other hurtful behaviors.
6. *System members reinforced for aggression victimize the same members of the system in future interactions.* Mario continues to aggress against his sister because she "gives in" to his demands. Likewise, Dad directs hurtful discipline methods toward both children because his tactics seem to be effective.

The coercive pattern of interaction teaches children how to imitate aggression and how to be victims of aggression. Children learn how to train adults to use punitive discipline. Mario has learned how to hurt his sister, his sister has learned how to be a victim, and Mario is training Dad to use hurtful discipline to try to stop Mario's behavior.

The coercive process is more common in certain families because of specific characteristics of the children and because parents in these family systems have ineffective parenting skills. Aggressive children show little self-control, have a re-duced responsiveness to threats and to reinforcers, are not very responsive to social stimuli, and are noncompliant and impulsive. These characteristics make aggressive children difficult to control (Parke & Slaby, 1983) and partially explain why the coer-cive process is more evident in some families than in others (Patterson, 1982).

Insensitive, Nonsupportive Adults Foster Aggression

A recurring theme in this book is that sensitive, supportive adults help children be-come competent humane people who like themselves and who treat others with dig-nity. How would an insensitive, rejecting adult affect a child's level of aggression? Adults who reject children, who are cold and nonnurturant, insensitive and nonsup-portive set the stage for increases in children's aggressive behavior (Feshbach, 1970; Martin, 1975; Parke & Slaby, 1983).

There are a number of reasons why insensitive adults foster aggression in chil-dren. First, a child has basic human needs like food, love, affection, nurturance, play, and self-esteem. These basic needs often go unmet when children exist in a sys-tem with rejecting adults. Paul's need for affection is frequently ignored by his dad, who thinks that Paul is a "real pain." Unmet needs result in frustration, and frustrated children frequently act aggressively if other conditions are present.

Second, adults influence children by using reinforcement and rewards. Non-supportive, rejecting adults do not use rewards and reinforcement well and are therefore ineffective teachers of many social behaviors, including control of aggres-sion. They do not help children develop self-restraint, and children who are not self-controlled are likely to react with aggression under many circumstances.

Third, insensitive rejecting adults tend to use discipline strategies that contrib-ute to children's aggression. They use ineffective, negative, often hurtful discipline, they often ignore aggression, and they are poor managers of the child's environ-ment (Martin, 1975).

Adult as Manager

Tony and David are both 7 years old. Tony is allowed unmonitored access to televi-sion and watches much televised violence. He owns several toy guns and frequently plays his brother's video game "Shoot the Rabbit." David's parents monitor the amount of television he watches and eliminate as much televised aggression as they can. After reading an article about aggressive toys, they have decided to search for toys that will be fun but nonaggressive.

Both sets of adults are managing their children's environment, and Parke and Slaby (1983) note that an adult's style of management can affect a child's aggressive behavior.

Parents *indirectly* influence aggression by limiting the types of toys to which their child has access and the amount and type of television she watches. This adult managerial role is probably just as important as the adult's direct role, because chil-dren spend more time interacting with the inanimate environment than they do with people (Parke & Slaby, 1983; White et al., 1976). Some adults, like Tony's parents, provide cues that elicit aggression—lots of televised violence and toy guns. Other adults consciously avoid providing such cues.

Ineffective Discipline Fosters Aggression

Adults in aggressive systems have a part in the coercive process because they use ineffective discipline. These adults do not use just one tactic, like hitting, that fosters aggression. They tend to use a cluster of discipline tactics, and it is this whole group of factors that contributes to aggression. For example, Mario's father hits him, but he also fails to tell Mario not to hurt others. He is inconsistent in punishing, and he is generally nonsupportive. Adults in aggressive systems

☐ *often fail to set limits against aggression.* These adults do not clearly communicate the expectation that hurting others is unacceptable.

☐ *use hurtful, power-assertive discipline.* Many adults use harsh punishment as discipline. Harsh discipline is related to an actual increase of aggression in children (Azrin & Holz, 1966; Baumrind, 1966; Berkowitz, 1973; Feshbach, 1970; Parke, 1977). The most aggressive children in Sears, Maccoby, and Levin's study (1957) had mothers who seemed to permit aggression but who severely punished the child when she was aggressive. The children were placed in a double bind. On the one hand they were told, "It's OK to be aggressive," but on the other hand they were told, "If you *are* aggressive, I'll really let you have it!" The least aggressive children in this study had parents who set limits against aggression and, when these children were aggressive, used nonhurtful punishment to deal with aggression.

Harsh discipline tends to increase aggression for two reasons. First, an adult who uses harsh discipline is a model of aggression. Second, and more important, an adult who uses harsh discipline demonstrates the power of aggression and communicates the message, "When you are as big as I am you may hit whomever you wish."

☐ *Use punishment inconsistently.* Children experience two types of inconsistent punishment. First, one adult can be inconsistent about how she punishes, not treating an unacceptable behavior the same way each time. When Vinnie hits someone on Tuesday, for example, his father punishes him, but he ignores his hitting on Wednesday. This is called *intragent inconsistency* and is ineffective in weakening behavior (Parke & Deur, 1972; Patterson, 1981; Sallows, 1972). Second, two different adults can be inconsistent with each other in how they punish. One adult might punish a child for kicking her cat, and another adult might ignore it or actually reward it. This is called *interagent inconsistency* and is also ineffective in weakening behavior (Sawin & Parke, 1979).

☐ *use ineffective forms of punishment.* Adults in aggressive systems often use harsh punishment like hitting, which is ineffective in stopping aggression. Sawin and Parke (1979) describe another form of ineffective punishment as "nattering," or ineffective scolding and nagging.

Example: "Matthew, put your bike away. Do you hear me? Put it away right now. There'll be no Dairy Queen for you if you don't put your bike away. Are you listening to me? You'd better listen to me. Now, put your bike away."

☐ *permit and ignore aggression.* Ignoring a child when she smashes someone's block tower will not stop the aggression (Caldwell, 1977). Permissiveness is associated with high levels of aggression in young children (Lefkowitz et al., 1977). To find out whether ignoring aggression increased or decreased aggression, Siegel and Kohn (1959/1970) worked with two groups of middle-class preschool boys. Each group participated in two play sessions. Children from one group played aggressively while an adult who was in the room ignored them, and the aggression in this group increased. The other group played but with no adult present, and this group showed less aggression. Why did these results occur?

Adults influence children by stating expectations for their behavior. An adult who watches and ignores children acting aggressively conveys the expectation that she will not interfere with their aggression. Children interpret this ignoring as permission to be aggressive. A nonpermissive adult conveys quite a different expectation, that aggression is not an acceptable way to deal with angry feelings and will not be tolerated.

Aggression Develops in a Child's Peer Group

Aggression has its roots in a child's family, but it is also learned, maintained, and modified in a child's peer group. Peers influence each other's aggression in several ways. They model aggression, teach other children how to avoid being victims, reinforce aggression, set norms regarding aggression, and serve as disinhibiting agents (Parke & Slaby, 1983).

Peers Model Aggression
Jamie watches one child push another off the trike, observes a second child rip another's painting, and later sees the same child hit someone. Jamie's aggressive agemates have *modeled* aggression, and modeling is an effective way to teach someone how to be aggressive (Bandura, Ross, & Ross, 1961). Jamie observes the model and learns how to push people around, rip paintings, and hit other people. Children learn just as effectively from peer models as they do from other models. Hicks (1965) found that the effect of modeling lasts for at least 6 months after observing the model.

Peers Reinforce Aggression
Peers reinforce each other for many kinds of behavior, including aggression. Patterson's research group studied children's reactions to being attacked by another child (Patterson et al., 1967). Some children cried, withdrew from, or gave in to their attackers.

Example Sue gave up her turn on the seesaw when Sam pushed her off. Other children, however, did not give in and tried to get adult help. Lew called the teacher and said, "Sam pushed me!" A child who gives in or cries reinforces an aggressive peer, and the attacker will continue to aggress on this child. When a child refuses to give in, his attacker chooses a new victim.

Peers Teach How to Avoid Being a Victim

Jim is a relatively passive child who has frequently been the victim of Mario's aggression. After being hit several times, pushed out of the way, and having his puzzle dumped, Jim did nothing. One day, when Mario pushed Jim out of place at the slide, Jim counterattacked and shoved Mario. The number of attacks against Jim declined. Jim recognized that he could avoid being a victim by behaving aggressively himself. He had not learned a positive interactional skill, but he had learned that aggression is a powerful tool.

Peers Regulate Aggression by Setting Norms

Peer groups influence the aggression of their members by setting norms for the expression of aggression (Parke & Slaby, 1983). Some peer groups, e.g., gangs, can increase aggression through norms that require aggressive behavior for group membership. Other groups might prohibit aggression through their norms. Some children are inappropriately aggressive, thus violating their peer group norms. Children who are excessively aggressive are less popular than children who abide by their groups' norms.

Asher and Renshaw (1982) discovered that aggressive, unpopular children

solve conflicts with peers through aggressive means and do not seem to know how to resolve conflict in a positive way. Parke and Slaby (1983) note that aggressive children lack certain social skills, such as the ability to resolve conflict. They may never acquire these skills if their peers avoid them.

Television Affects the Development of Aggression

Along with family and peer group, television should be viewed as one of the major socializers of children's aggression. Parke and Slaby (1983) note that any discussion of the development of aggression is incomplete unless the role of television is not only examined but also given status equal to that of family and peer group. Research with over 30,000 individuals, and 630 scholarly papers and books produced in the past 35 years, show that children watch an excessive amount of violent television and that heavy viewing of television violence has major behavioral effects. This section will document the amount of television violence viewed by children and its effects on the development of aggression.

Amount of Television Viewed and How Violence Is Portrayed
The following data show that American children watch a lot of television, observe violence quite frequently, and see a distorted picture of violence.

☐ *Virtually every American household has access to a television (Nielsen Television Index, 1982).* Ninety-eight percent of households have one television and 52 percent have at least one extra television. The extra set is used mainly by children.

☐ *Children watch a lot of television.* Two- to 18-year-olds spend an average of 3 hours each day watching television. Many children spend more time watching television than doing anything else, including exercising, playing, reading, or interacting with friends or family.

☐ *American television programming shows violence as a common form of social interaction.* Gerbner's research team (Gerbner, Gross, Morgan, & Signorielli, 1980; Gerbner, Gross, Signorielli, Morgan, & Jackson-Beeck, 1979) monitored televised violence over a 13-year period from 1967 to 1979. They found violence was portrayed on television consistently and often. Eighty percent of the programs monitored contained violence at a rate of 7.5 incidents per hour.

☐ *Children's television contains an especially high level of violence.* Of weekend daytime programs designed for children, 93 percent contained violence at a rate of 17.6 incidents per hour (Gerbner et al., 1979, 1980). These rates of televised violence have remained stable.

☐ *Few restrictions are placed on children's television viewing.* Many parents express concern about the effects of televised violence on their children. Many of the same adults, however, restrict neither the amount of television nor the content of the programs their children watch.

☐ *Children see a distorted view of violence on television* (Slaby & Quarforth, 1980). Real violence is dirty—people bleed, jaws are broken, people die. Real violence is not funny. Television does not show real violence. Televised violence is distorted because it depicts shootings, fights, knifings, and murder as clean, justified, effective, rewarded, and humorous. Television codes forbid showing real violence, so televised violence is clean and devoid of real suffering. Codes also require that programs show that crime does not pay. As a result, "good guys" are allowed to use violence as a way of punishing "bad guys." "Good guys" are just as violent and break the law just as much as the "bad guys" (Lange, Baker, & Ball, 1969).

☐ *Television violence is shown to be effective in attaining goals* (Larsen, Gray, & Fortis, 1968). Children's television shows violence as an effective way to get things and to get things done. Children see that "good guys" attain goals by hurting others and that they are actually rewarded for being violent. Violence is praised and rewarded as often as it is punished (Stein & Friedrich, 1975).

☐ *Televised violence is depicted as humorous.* Children's television is especially guilty of connecting violence and humor (Parke & Slaby, 1983). Violent cartoons like "The Road Runner" are frequently accompanied by laugh tracks. Linking violence and laughter gives children a cue that tells them, "Violence is a funny thing."

☐ *Certain groups are victimized in televised violence.* Gerbner et al. (1979) note that victimization is especially evident in children's programming on weekends. Victims are most frequently people in minority roles—old, young, noncaucasian, or women. From this sort of irresponsible programming children learn that certain groups who have power and status can force their will on other less powerful people.

Children's Understanding of Television Violence

A young child's understanding of televised violence differs from that of an older child. Collins, Berndt, & Hess (1974) wanted to know what children of different ages would remember about violence on television. They showed a program containing violence to children in kindergarten, second, fifth, and eighth grades. Kindergarten and second-grade children remembered either an aggressive act alone or the aggressive act and its consequences. For example, they would remember that a detective successfully extracted information from a victim by threatening to shoot her (aggressive act). Fifth and eighth graders understood and remembered the motives of an aggressor. Younger children, then, need help in understanding a character's motivation in televised violence.

CONTROLLING AND MODIFYING AGGRESSION

This section describes techniques for controlling aggression at the individual, group, and community levels.

Controlling Aggression: Individual Level

Set and Communicate Limits to Aggression

Anyone who lives or works with children can create a nonpermissive atmosphere

SPECIAL FOCUS: Televised Violence and Children's Aggression: Is There a Connection?

What have we learned about the actual effects of televised violence on children's behavior from decades of research? Two general conclusions have been drawn from research evidence (Parke & Slaby, 1983).

Television Violence Can and Does Increase Subsequent Aggression in Children

This conclusion comes not from just one or two studies but from a variety of studies using different viewing materials, different viewers, different viewing circumstances, and different measures of aggression (Liebert, Spratkin, & Davidson, 1982; Stein & Friedrich, 1975; Watt & Krull, 1977). Aggression portrayed under a variety of conditions will elicit heightened aggression. Specifically, children become more aggressive:

☐ when violence is presented on a television set, a movie screen, or by live models.

☐ whether violent programs are shown as televised or are edited and constructed especially for a research study (Bandura, 1965; Stein & Friedrich, 1972).

☐ whether aggression is portrayed realistically or in cartoons or fantasy (Bandura et al., 1961; Ellis & Sekyra, 1972).

☐ whether or not they have been frustrated before watching violence (Liebert & Baron, 1972).

by establishing limits against hurting others, disturbing others, or damaging toys and equipment. The limits must then be firmly but gently enforced. Even though young children are limited cognitively and are egocentric, adults can begin to help them see that other people have a right not to be hurt. When Mr. Rivera restates a limit, "Mario, I know that you want to sit in that chair but I can't just let you push Pete off. I want you to sit in this chair," he states clearly that he will not tolerate Mario's aggression.

Reduce Exposure to Aggression-Evoking "Cues" and Aggressive Models

Children frequently act aggressively when certain stimuli associated with aggression are available. Turner and Goldsmith (1976) wanted to know if children's aggression would increase if toy guns were available. They observed preschool children during free play. In some of the play sessions toy guns were available, but in other sessions the toy guns were replaced by airplanes. Aggression was much more evident when guns were present.

Modeling is a powerful elicitor of aggression. An effective technique for reducing aggression is to limit the number of models of aggression to which children are exposed and to substitute nonagressive models (Bandura, 1973; Parke & Slaby,

☐ whether or not they have had a history of aggressive behavior (Parke, Berkowitz, Leyens, West, & Sebastian, 1977).

☐ in either a naturalistic or a laboratory setting (Bandura, 1965).

☐ whether they view aggression alone or in a group (Parke, 1977).

☐ whether they are exposed to only one or to several violent programs (Bandura et al., 1963).

☐ whether their response to televised violence is measured immediately following a program or after a longer time span (Lefkowitz, Eron, Walder, & Huesmann, 1972).

To summarize: Watching violence under a variety of conditions increases aggressive behavior in the viewer.

Televised Violence Increases a Child's Passive Acceptance of Aggression by Others

No only do children themselves become more aggressive when they watch televised violence, but they also accept violence by others. Children are most likely to relax their standards if they view violence as effective, justified, reinforced, and commonplace. Televised violence, as noted previously, is presented in precisely this fashion.

Children are also likely to become apathetic toward others' violence when their real world matches television's standards for using violence.

Example   Jim sees people on television hit each other when they are angry. Hitting and punching are television's aggressive method of conflict resolution. Jim's family members, particularly his father, also frequently hit one another when they have a conflict. Jim, then, is highly likely to accept violence toward others.

1983). One of the best ways to do this is to limit the amount of violent television a child watches. Another is to screen and carefully select movies, books, pictures, and other media. Another good way is to model cooperative, nonaggressive behavior for children.

Watch Television with Children and Comment on Aggressive Program Content

Example   (Father to son while watching television). "Why do you think that man punched his neighbor, John? Yes, I think he was mad at him for driving his car over the flowers. That still doesn't make it OK to hit his neighbor. Do you think they can be friends now?" John's friend Pete watched the same show but watched it alone.

Children who watch televised violence with adults and hear negative evaluation of the violence, as John did, are less aggressive than children who watch televised violence without an adult co-viewer (Grusec, 1973; Slaby & Roedell, 1982).

Increase Empathy

Example   "Oh, Susan! You've torn Sarah's painting. I think that she's sad because she is crying."

In the torn painting incident Susan is being encouraged to be empathic. Children who are trained to be more empathic (to see things from someone else's perspective) tend to be more sensitive to others' feelings and to be less aggressive (Feshbach & Feshbach, 1982).

Increase the Child's Awareness of the Harmful Consequences of Aggression for the Victim

Aggression is often decreased when an aggressor is made aware that the victim has experienced pain.

Example Pam's mother saw her hit the puppy when the puppy did not sit on command. "Pam, you *hurt* Fluffy by hitting her. Look at how she is trying to hide from you."

Pam's mother is arousing Pam's empathy for Fluffy by "feeding back" the puppy's pain. Pam's aggressive behavior is likely to decrease because her mom aroused her empathy and empathy is incompatible with aggression.

A word of caution is in order. Not everyone reacts to pain feedback by becoming less aggressive. For highly aggressive children another person's or animal's pain is merely a signal that the aggression "worked," and these children show little or no sorrow for hurting another person or animal.

Teach and Reinforce Behavior Incompatible with Aggression

Teach more positive behavior. Go beyond helping children realize the harmful effects of aggression. Teach and reinforce behaviors like assertiveness, negotiation, cooperation, and sharing. Teach the more positive behavior through modeling and coaching.

Example Mr. Rivera used *modeling* to teach about sharing by showing a filmstrip to his group of 4-year-olds about two children who had an argument about whose turn it was on the trike. Their teacher helped them negotiate turn-taking. Mr. Rivera used *coaching* when he suggested a new behavior to Rita and Mario. Rita hit Mario after Mario had grabbed Rita's trike. Mr. Rivera responded to this act of instrumental aggression by saying, "Rita, I know you had the trike first and Mario took it, but I won't let you hit him. You both have a problem. Tell Mario with words that you are going to finish your ride. Mario, I want you to tell Rita with words that you would like to ride the trike." Both children had been aggressive. The adult has not ridiculed or yelled at Rita for feeling angry, nor has he approved of either child's aggression. He has taught about sharing and has coached the children about alternative positive ways of coping with their frustration. Zahavi and Asher (1978) coached young children on how to resolve conflict without violence and noted a subsequent reduction in aggression.

Reinforce cooperative behavior. When Mario shared his goggles with another child, Mr. Rivera said, "Thank you for sharing, Mario." Mario was considered to be an aggressive child, but his teacher had taken Brown and Elliott's (1965) advice on decreasing aggression. He made an effort to notice and reinforce Mario's helpful behavior and found that both physical and verbal aggression decreased.

Reinforce cooperative verbal responses (Slaby & Crowley, 1977). In this study preschool teachers were instructed to ignore aggressive language ("I'm going to punch you in the nose!") but to pay attention to cooperative statements ("Let's put this puzzle together!"). After hearing a cooperative statement the teacher was instructed to reinforce it by saying something like, "Jake, I heard you ask Sue if you could use some of the flannel pieces." Slaby and Crowley found that verbal aggression decreased and cooperation increased. This was a real classroom in which the adults found that they could notice and reinforce only a small percentage of cooperative statements, but even this was sufficient to decrease aggression.

Step Between Children Involved in an Incident: Ignore the Aggressor and Pay Attention to the Victim

Some children persist in their aggression in spite of well-developed and well-stated limits.

Example Mr. Rivera groaned when he saw Mario grab the funnel away from John. He decided to ignore Mario, the aggressor, and attend only to John, the victim. He suggested that John use an assertive way of dealing with Mario's aggression, "John, you were playing with the funnel. Tell Mario it is *your* turn now."

Why is this method effective? First, Mario was not reinforced for his aggression. His teacher ignored him and did not allow his victim to give in to the aggression. Second, the victim learned how to cope with conflict by being assertive. Third, other children observed the incident and saw that aggression was not tolerated, that aggression is not an effective method of interacting with friends, and that it is good to be sympathetic with a victim (Parke & Slaby, 1983; Pinkston, Reese, LeBlanc, & Baer, 1973).

Teach Children to Control Anger

Children, like other people, become angry and even enraged over some matters. They have a right to feel angry and should not be told not to feel angry. Children must be taught, however, that behavior connected with anger or rage is often maladaptive. Adults control aggression when they help children to control their anger, because anger often goes hand in hand with aggression. Reducing anger also reduces aggression (Novaco, 1978). (See the Special Focus box, "Helping Children Control Anger".)

Use Noncathartic Techniques to Control Aggression: Evaluate Frustrating Situations

☐ Will aggression decrease if children are encouraged to play with guns?

SPECIAL FOCUS: Helping Children Control Anger

Give Children Information about Anger Arousal

Help children pinpoint the specific cues that elicit their anger. Mr. Rivera said to Mario, "You know, Mario, I've noticed that you got angry when John got the paint first and when Mary was first in line."

Help Children Recognize Maladaptive Occurrences of Anger

"I saw you push John away from the easel, Mario, and I saw you grab Mary's arm and put yourself first. John and Mary were both angry with you. If you push children around and hit them, they will probably not want to play with you."

Teach Skills for Coping with Anger

Mr. Rivera realized that Mario did not know how to deal with his anger, so he modeled more positive coping skills. Using a puppet, he said, "You know, Jack [the puppet] gets angry, too. This morning he wanted his turn at pulling the wagon, but Laura wouldn't give it to him. He got very angry and pushed Laura out of the wagon and hurt her. Let's show him a better way to act. First, tell him to stop and think. Then tell Jack not to hit or push. Tell him to use *words:* 'Jack, tell Laura that it is your turn.' " (The puppets acted out the episode.)

Give Children a Chance to Practice Controlling Anger

Mr. Rivera used one puppet and Mario used the other. "Mario, my puppet is going to push your puppet out of the way. (Push!) "Your puppet is very angry. Tell your puppet to stop and think about what to do. Tell him *not* to hit." (Mario did this.) "Good. Make your puppet say something better." Mario's puppet said, "No pushing! I was here first." Mr. Rivera encouraged Mario to apply this new skill with real children in real situations, too.

☐ Will aggression decrease if children watch an aggressive television show?

☐ Will aggression decrease if children punch a punching bag, pound on playdough or cookie dough or bread dough?

Many people would say yes. They believe that watching aggression or acting aggressively is the proper way to "drain aggressive urges" that they believe accumulate in people. Reducing aggression by watching aggression or acting aggressively is called *catharsis* (Parke & Slaby, 1983).

The same researchers note that empirical research shows catharsis to be an ineffective method for controlling aggression. Berkowitz (1966) and Quanty (1976) note that engaging in physical aggression does not reduce aggression and can actually result in higher levels of aggression. A similar finding by Mallick and McCandless (1966) showed that aggression in third graders is not decreased when the children are encouraged to hit an inanimate object like cookie dough or a punching bag.

They did find that a *noncathartic* technique reduced aggression. This means that they explained things to children and helped the children understand and reinterpret a frustrating experience. Children tend not to retaliate against a person who frustrates them if they understand why the frustrator acted as she did.

Example "I think Mary was just in a hurry when she knocked down your blocks," says the teacher, or "Mrs. Sims had to put the paints away before you had a chance to paint. You'll have a chance to paint later today."

SPECIAL FOCUS: Positive Discipline: A Powerful Strategy for Preventing or Controlling Aggression

Example Ross bit his brother. His mother bit Ross and said, "Now that will teach you that biting hurts." This adult used negative discipline, which is likely to increase not decrease, Ross's biting.

Example At school Ross bit another child. His teacher took care of the victim, who cried, and then said to Ross, "*No* biting, Ross. Biting hurts. You hurt Herman and he cried. You should say, 'Herman, give me the cookies.' You will have to do a time out for biting." This adult used positive discipline and is likely to decrease Ross's aggressive behavior.

Positive discipline is a powerful strategy in preventing or decreasing aggression because:

☐ *it helps children figure out more positive ways of acting or reacting.* An adult who bites a child as a form of discipline does not help that child think of a better way to get what she needs or wants. The only thing that biting a child teaches is aggression: that the adult is willing to hurt the child. Positive discipline (setting and maintaining limits, using nonhurtful punishment) teaches children to think about better nonaggressive ways to settle disputes or to get what they want or need.

☐ *it helps children understand how their behavior affects other people.* Piaget (1970) would argue that children can begin to understand how they affect others if adults help them understand. Piaget believed that egocentricity decreases through interaction with other people, adults in this case, who confront the child with a new way of looking at the effect of her behavior as Ross's teacher did.

☐ *it is an important element in creating a safe and secure emotional climate.* When positive discipline is used, children soon learn that aggression will not be tolerated and that adults can be trusted not to hurt anyone. Children who experience positive discipline learn that the adult lets them feel angry but insists on solving problems without aggression—not always the fastest method for solving conflicts, but the most humane.

SPECIAL FOCUS: Prevent or Control Aggression in Young Children

In summary, responsible, supportive adults can control or even prevent aggression in young children when they

☐ use positive discipline.

☐ set limits against aggression and communicate expectations clearly to children.

☐ reduce exposure to aggression-evoking cues and aggressive models.

☐ watch television with children and comment on aggressive program content.

☐ increase empathy.

☐ increase the attacker's awareness of the harmful consequences of aggression for the victim.

☐ teach and reinforce behavior that is incompatible with aggression.

☐ teach more positive strategies like cooperation, sharing, assertiveness, and negotiation.

☐ reinforce cooperative behavior and cooperative verbal responses.

☐ step between children involved in an aggressive interchange, ignore the aggressor, and pay attention to the victim.

☐ teach children to control anger.

☐ use noncathartic techniques: evaluate frustrating situations.

☐ work with a child's family system.

Controlling Aggression: Family Level

Children learn much of their aggression in their family system. We must try to control aggression in the family system as well as in the individual child. Many families have patterns of interaction that result in aggressive behavior. Effective control of *intrafamilial aggression* (aggression within the family itself) focuses on restructuring interaction patterns in aggressive families (Patterson, 1982). Therapists, trained in marriage and family therapy, make parents in aggressive families aware of the connection between their reactions and their child's deviant behavior. These therapists can teach parents different, more effective childrearing techniques.

Controlling Aggression: Community Level

Children are embedded in families. Families are embedded in communities. Families and communities influence each other, and many people believe that families who are strongly connected to their community are automatically influenced in a positive way. This belief is erroneous; a community's influence on a family can be positive or negative. Consider, for example, a family living in a community that advocates hurt-ful punishment of women and children. Aggression directed at women and children in this community will very likely be high. The community's influence is negative.

Garbarino (1976) and Garbarino and Crouter (1978) give clear evidence that child abuse and levels of intrafamilial aggression are largely determined by the avail-ability of community support systems. Aggression within families is lower when families have access to good support systems.

Social networks and support systems for families also affect a family's success with programs intended to teach more effective patterns of interaction in families. Mothers who are successful in learning new childrearing techniques tend to have a network of friends, spend time with them, and judge contacts with friends to be positive.

SUMMARY: KEY CONCEPTS IN THIS CHAPTER

1. *Aggression* is behavior that results in injury to a person or animal or in damage or destruction of property. The various types of aggression include *accidental, instrumental,* and *hostile* aggression. Hostile aggression increases and instru-mental aggression decreases as children grow older. This shift parallels a general change in cognitive development. That boys are more aggressive than girls seems due to different socialization practices for boys and girls.

2. Children are embedded in a variety of social *systems* — family, peer group, and community. Television is also a major socializing element. Children influence and are influenced by each of these systems. The most complete explanation of how aggression develops, then, is a systems or ecological approach in which each sys-tem's contribution to aggression is acknowledged.

3. Responsible, supportive adults use a number of different methods for preventing or controlling aggression. They work with children on an individual level. An ag-gressive child often lives in an aggressive family system, and a therapist can help to modify a family's aggressive patterns of interaction. Responsible adults also at-tempt to decrease the amount of televised violence to which children are ex-posed.

OBSERVE: CHILD GUIDANCE IN ACTION

1. Observe an adult as she interacts with a group of children under 10. Observe by yourself or with a partner. Using the information in the text, determine how this adult deals with aggression from the children. For example, are aggressive cues present in this environment? Does the adult set limits that prohibit aggres-sion? Does the adult use positive discipline?

To record your observations, use 4"×6" index cards. At the top of each card write one of the methods for controlling aggression summarized in the Special Focus box, "Prevent or Control Aggression in Young Children." An example follows:

Adult sets limits against aggression:

Example

Example

Example

2. At your observation site, observe examples of each of these techniques. Write your examples on the appropriate card.

3. Summarize your findings. From the data you have collected, describe the degree to which this adult will be likely to prevent or control aggression.

4. Share your findings. Check the accuracy of your observations by comparing them with those of someone else who observed in the same setting.

REFERENCES

ASHER, S.R., & RENSHAW, P.D. (1982). *Social skills and social knowledge of high and low status kindergarten children.* Unpublished manuscript, University of Illinois.

AZRIN, N.H., & HOLZ, W.C. (1966). Punishment. In W.K. Honig (Ed.), *Operant behaviors: Areas of research and application.* New York: Appleton-Century-Crofts.

BANDURA, A. (1965). Influence of models' reinforcement contingencies on the acquisition of imitative responses. *Journal of Personality and Social Psychology, 1,* 589–595.

BANDURA, A. (1973). *Aggression: A social learning analysis.* New York: Holt.

BANDURA, A., ROSS, D., & ROSS, S.A. (1961). Transmission of aggression through imitation of aggressive models. *Journal of Abnormal and Social Psychology, 63,* 575–582.

BANDURA, A., ROSS, D., & ROSS, S.A. (1963). Imitation of film-mediated aggressive models. *Journal of Abnormal and Social Psychology, 66,* 3–11.

BAUMRIND, D. (1966). Effects of authoritative parental control on child behavior. *Child Development, 37,* 887–907.

BERKOWITZ, L. (1966). On not being able to aggress. *British Journal of Social and Clinical Psychology, 5,* 130–139.

BERKOWITZ, L. (1973). Control of aggression. In B. Caldwell & H. Riccuti (Eds.), *Review of child development research.* Chicago: University of Chicago Press.

BLOCK, J.H. (1978). Another look at sex differentiation in the socialization behaviors of mothers and fathers. In J. Sherman & F.L. Denmark (Eds.), *The future of women: Future directions of research.* New York: Psychological Dimensions.

BRIM, O.G. (1975). Macro-structural influences on child development and the need for childhood social indicators. *American Journal of Orthopsychiatry, 45,* 516–524.

BRONFENBRENNER, U. (1979). *The ecology of human development.* Cambridge: Harvard University Press.

BROWN, P., & ELLIOT, R. (1965). Control of aggression in a nursery school class. *Journal of Experimental Child Psychology, 2,* 103–107.

CALDWELL, B.M. (1977). Aggression and hostility in young children. *Young Children, 32,* 4–13.

COLLINS, W.A., BERNDT, T.V., & HESS, V.L. (1974). Observational learning of motives and consequences for television aggression: A developmental study. *Child Development, 65,* 799–802.

DARVILL, D., & CHEYNE, J.A. (1981, April). *Sequential analysis of responses to aggression: Age and sex effects.* Paper presented at the meeting of the *Society for Research in Child Development, Boston.*

DAWE, H.C. (1934). An analysis of two hundred quarrels of preschool children. *Child Development, 5,* 139–157.

ELLIS, G.T., & SEKYRA, F. (1972). The effect of aggressive cartoons on the behavior of first grade children. *Journal of Psychology, 81,* 37–43.

FESHBACH, N.D., & FESHBACH, S. (1982). Empathy training and the regulation of aggression: Potentialities and limitations. *Academic Psychology Bulletin, 4,* 399–413.

FESHBACH, S. (1970). Aggression. In P. Mussen (Ed.), *Carmichael's manual of child psychology,* Vol. 2. New York: Wiley.

GARBARINO, J. (1976). Some ecological correlates of child abuse: The impact of socioeconomic stress on mothers. *Child Development, 47,* 178–185.

GARBARINO, J., & CROUTER, A. (1978). Defining the community context for parent-child relations: The correlates of child maltreatment. *Child Development, 49,* 604–616.

GELLES, R.J., & STRAUS, M.A. (1979). Determinants of violence in the family: Toward a theoretical integration. In W. Burr, R. Hill, F.I. Nye, & I. Reiss (Eds.), *Contemporary theories about the family.* New York: Free Press.

GERBNER, G., GROSS, L., MORGAN, M., & SIGNORIELLI, N. (1980). The mainstreaming of America. *Journal of Communication, 30,* 12–29.

GERBNER, G., GROSS, L., SIGNORIELLI, N., MORGAN, M., & JACKSON-BEECK, M. (1979). The demonstration of power: Violence profile No. 10. *Journal of Communication, 29,* 177–196.

GRUSEC, J.E. (1973). Effects of co-observer evaluations on imitation: A developmental study. *Developmental Psychology, 8,* 141.

HARTUP, W.W. (1974). Aggression in childhood: Development perspectives. *American Psychologist, 29,* 336–341.

HICKS, D.J. (1965). Imitation and retention of film-mediated aggressive peer and adult models. *Journal of Personality and Social Psychology, 2,* 97–100.

LANGE, D.S., BAKER, R.K., & BALL, S.J. (1969). *Mass media and violence: A report to the National Commission on the Causes and Prevention of Violence.* Washington, DC: U.S. Government Printing Office.

LARSEN, O.N., GRAY, L.N., & FORTIS, J.G. (1968). Achieving goals through violence on television. In O.N. Larsen (Ed.), *Violence and the mass media.* New York: Harper & Row.

LEFKOWITZ, M.M., ERON, L.D., WALDER, L.O., & HUESMANN, L.R. (1972). Television violence and child aggression: A followup study. In G.A. Comstock & E.A. Rubinstein (Eds.), *Television and social behavior: 3. Television and adolescent aggressiveness.* Washington, DC: U.S. Government Printing Office.

LEFKOWITZ, M.M., ERON, L.D., WALDER, L.O., & HUESMANN, L.R. (1977). *Growing up to be violent: A longitudinal study of the development of aggression.* New York: Pergamon Press.

LIEBERT, R.M., & BARON, R.A. (1972). Short-term effects of televised aggression on children's aggressive behavior. In J.P. Murray, E.A. Rubinstein, & G.A. Comstock (Eds.), *Television and social behavior: 2. Television and social learning.* Washington, DC: U.S. Government Printing Office.

LIEBERT, R.M., SPRATKIN, J.N., & DAVIDSON, E.S. (1982). *The early window: Effects of television on children and youth* (2nd ed.). New York: Pergamon Press.

MACCOBY, E.E., & JACKLIN, C.N. (1980). Sex differences in aggression: A rejoinder and reprise. *Child Development, 51,* 964–980.

MALLICK, S.K., & McCANDLESS, B.R. (1966). A study of catharsis of aggression. *Journal of Personality and Social Psychology, 4,* 591–596.

MARTIN, B. (1975). Parent-child relations. In F.D. Horowitz (Ed.), *Review of child development research,* Vol. 4. Chicago: University of Chicago Press.

NIELSEN TELEVISION INDEX. (1982). *National audience demographics report, 1982.* Northbrook, IL: A.C. Nielsen.

NOVACO, R. (1978) Anger and coping with stress. In J. Foreyt & D. Rethjen (Eds.), *Cognitive behavior therapy, theory, research and procedures.* New York, Plenum.

PARKE, R.D. (1977). Some effects of punishment on children's behavior — revisited. In E.M. Hetherington & R.D. Parke (Eds.), *Contemporary readings in child psychology.* New York: McGraw-Hill.

PARKE, R.D., BERKOWITZ, L., LEYENS, J.P., WEST, S.G., & SEBASTIAN, R.J. (1977). Some effects of violent and nonviolent movies on the behavior of juvenile delinquents. In L. Berkowitz (Ed.), *Advances in experimental social psychology,* Vol. 10. (1983). New York: Academic Press.

PARKE, R.D. & DEUR, J.L. (1972). Schedule of reinforcement and inhibition of aggression in children. *Developmental Psychology, 7,* 266–269.

PARKE, R.D., & SLABY, R.G. (1983). The development of aggression. In P. Mussen (Ed.), *Handbook of child psychology,* Vol. 4. New York: Wiley.

PATTERSON, G.R. (1981). Mothers: The unacknowledged victims. *Monographs of the Society of Research in Child Development, 45* (5, Serial No. 186).

PATTERSON, G.R. (1982). *Coercive family processes.* Eugene, OR: Castilia Press.

PATTERSON, G.R., LITTMAN, R.A., & BRICKER, W. (1967). Assertive behavior in children: A step toward a theory of aggression. *Monographs of the Society for Research in Child Development, 32* (Serial No. 113).

PEDERSON, J.A., ANDERSON, B.J., & CAIN, R.L. (1977, March). *An approach to understanding linkages between the parent-infant and spouse relationships.* Paper presented at the meeting of the Society for Research in Child Development, New Orleans.

PIAGET, J. (1970). Piaget's theory. In P. Mussen (Ed.), *Carmichael's manual of child psychology.* New York: Wiley.

PINKSTON, E.M., REESE, N.M., LeBLANC, J.M., & BAER, D.M. (1973). Independent control of a preschool child's aggression and peer interaction by contingent teacher attention. *Journal of Applied Behavior Analysis, 6,* 115–124.

QUANTY, M.B. (1976). Aggression catharsis: experimental investigations and implications. In R.G. Geen & E.C. O'Neal (Eds.), *Perspectives on aggression.* New York: Academic Press.

SALLOWS, G. (1972). *Comparative responsiveness of normal and deviant children to naturally occurring consequences.* Unpublished doctoral dissertation, University of Oregon.

SAWIN, D.B., & PARKE, R.D. (1979). The effects of interagent inconsistent discipline on children's aggressive behavior. *Journal of Experimental Child Psychology, 28,* 525–538.

SEARS, R.R., MACCOBY, E.E., & LEVIN, H. (1957). *Patterns of child rearing.* Evanston, IL: Ron Peterson.

SIEGEL, A.F., & KOHN, L.G. (1970). Permissiveness, permission, and aggression: The effects of adult presence or absence on aggression in children. In F. Rebelsky & L. Dorman (Eds.), *Child development and behavior.* New York: Alfred A. Knopf. (Originally published in 1959)

SLABY, R., & CROWLEY, C.G. (1977). Modification of cooperation and aggression through teacher attention to children's speech. *Journal of Experimental Child Psychology, 23,* 442–458.

SLABY, R.G., & QUARFORTH, G.R. (1980). Effects of television on the developing child. In B.W. Camp (Ed.), *Advances in behavioral pediatrics,* Vol. 1. Greenwich, CT: JAI Press.

SLABY, R.G., & ROEDELL, W.C. (1982). The development and regulation of aggression in young children. In J. Worell (Ed.), *Psychological development in the elementary years.* New York: Academic Press.

SMITH, P.K., & GREEN, M. (1974). Aggressive behavior in English nurseries and playgroups: Sex differences and response of adults. *Child Development, 45,* 211–214.

STEIN, A.H., & FRIEDRICH, L.K. (1972). Television content and young children's behavior. In J.P. Murray & E.A. Comstock (Eds.), *Television and social behavior: 2. Television and social learning.* Washington, DC: U.S. Government Printing Office.

STEIN, A.H., & FRIEDRICH, L.K. (1975). Impact of television on children and youth. In E.M. Hetherington (Ed.), *Review of child development research,* Vol. 5. Chicago: University of Chicago Press.

STEINMETZ, S.K. (1977). *The cycle of violence: Assertive, aggressive and abuse family interaction.* New York: Praeger.

STRAUS, M.A., GELLES, R., & STEINMETZ, S. (1980). *Behind closed doors.* New York: Doubleday.

TURNER, C.W., & GOLDSMITH, D. (1976). Effects of toy guns and airplanes on children's antisocial free play behavior. *Journal of Experimental Child Psychology, 21,* 303–315.

WATT, J.H., & KRULL, R. (1977). An examinatin of three models of television viewing and aggression. *Human Communication Research, 3,* 99–112.

WHITE, B.L., KABAN, B., SHAPIRO, B. & ATTONUCCI, J. (1976). Competence and experience. In I.C. Uzgiris & F. Weizmann (Eds.), *The structuring of experience.* New York: Plenum Press.

ZAHAVI, S., & ASHER, S.R. (1978). The effect of verbal instructions on preschool children's aggressive behavior. *Journal of School Psychology, 16,* 146–153.

7

Prosocial Behavior:
Its Nature and Nurture

Chapter Overview

UNDERSTANDING PROSOCIAL BEHAVIOR
> Definition
> Behaviors Studied in Research
> Risks and Benefits of Acting Prosocially
> Developmental Trends

NURTURING PROSOCIAL BEHAVIOR
> Factors Affecting Prosocial Behavior
> Adult Practices That Foster Prosocial Behavior

SPECIAL FOCUS: Postive Discipline: A Powerful Strategy for Encouraging Prosocial Behavior

SPECIAL FOCUS: Encourage Sharing, Cooperation, and Helpfulness

---

After reading and studying this chapter, you will be able to:

☐ *Define* prosocial behavior.

☐ *Identify, describe, and give an example* of the types of prosocial behavior studied in research.

☐ *Discuss* the benefits from encouraging prosocial behavior in children.

☐ *Describe and explain* developmental trends in prosocial behavior.

☐ *Discuss* several factors affecting the development of prosocial behavior.

☐ *Identify, describe, and observe* several specific techniques used by adults to encourage prosocial behavior.

Humans are capable of committing horrible acts of violence against each other and animals. Humans are also capable of kindness, generosity, helpfulness, sharing, and indignation at cruelty. Think of some of the generous, helpful things people have done for you. Did somebody rescue you after an accident? Do you remember someone defending you? How about the time someone shared something with you, not because he was urged to but because he wanted to? Has anybody ever helped you do something even though he did not have to?

Turn this around. Recall all the times you have been helpful, cooperative, or generous. Now, think about acts of generosity or kindness on a larger scale. Recall the Live Aid concert of 1985, Willie Nelson's Farm Aid concert of 1986, Mohandas Gandhi's actions in India several decades ago. All of us survived infancy because somebody took care of us.

Why are some people so aggressive and others so kind? The roots of both aggression and kindness are present in every human child. Like aggression, kindness develops largely because of a child's embeddedness in a number of social systems— family, peer group, and culture. Children who grow up in violent families, whose peers reward aggression, and who observe a lot of televised violence learn from these experiences and will likely act aggressively. Children whose families teach positive methods of conflict resolution, whose television watching is monitored, and whose peers teach cooperation and helpfulness learn and exhibit prosocial behavior.

As John Steinbeck said in *East of Eden,* the beauty of being human is that humans can make choices. Adults who value the essential goodness that resides in every child choose methods of interaction that nourish the roots of altruism, sharing, cooperation, and helpfulness.

UNDERSTANDING PROSOCIAL BEHAVIOR

Definition

Prosocial behavior includes any action intended to benefit or help another person, animal, or group of people without expectation of external reward (Bryan & London, 1970; Macaulay & Berkowitz, 1970; Mussen & Eisenberg-Berg, 1977; Radke-Yarrow, Zahn-Waxler, & Chapman, 1983). The central concept in this definition is that someone benefits because of the prosocial behavior of another. Under this definition, it seems that children do act prosocially. They share things and work together. Children show sympathy, and they get angry when one person is cruel to another.

Behaviors Studied in Research

Many behaviors are subsumed under prosocial behavior, and some have been investigated more frequently than others. The most frequently investigated have been acts of helping, sharing or donating, and cooperation. These have been examined in studies primarily with children from preschool to age 12 (Radke-Yarrow et al., 1983).

A person acts prosocially if he shares or donates materials, information, or time. Examples:

1. *Sharing or donating time.* Tim shares time at the computer with his friend. Tim's father donates 2 hours of his time each week to the Humane Society.

2. Sharing or donating resources. Christina needs goggles to wear at the work-bench and Kyle says, "Here, see if these fit," as he takes his off. Children in an elementary school donate cans of food to a food bank at Thanksgiving.

3. *Sharing or donating information.* Mary learns how to use the pulley and then shows Jenny how to use it.

Prosocial behavior also includes acts of helping—relieving distress in another person by rescuing, removing the cause of distress, or defending (Marcus & Leiserson, 1978). Examples:

1. *Rescue.* David runs over to Jake just as Jake is about to fall into the swimming pool and grabs Jake's hand. Researchers have examined several aspects of rescue behavior: whether one child will rescue another; how the rescue takes place; and how quickly the rescue is carried out (Bryan, 1975).

2. *Removing the cause of distress.* Jean sees that Yvonne has fallen over the trike and removes the trike.

3. *Defending the other person.* When Tom loses his lunch money, Sid calls him stupid. Jim tells Sid, "Tom only lost his lunch money. That doesn't make him stupid!"

Cooperation is prosocial when people work together to get a job done, to ensure fair treatment of another person, or to help others. The Live Aid concert of 1985 required cooperation. Children who work together to clean a campsite also demonstrate cooperation.

Risks and Benefits of Acting Prosocially

It is often easy to be helpful, and there are few risks in some small acts of generosity like sharing a pair of goggles. In fact, much of the research carried out thus far has tested only small donations and small acts of helping and has rightfully not placed

Sharing things is one aspect of prosocial behavior

FIGURE 7.1   Prosocial behavior.

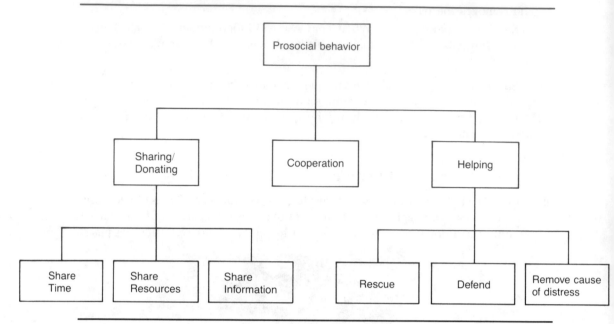

children in situations involving great risk or sacrifice (Radke-Yarrow et al., 1983). Some prosocial behavior, however, does involve great risk (e.g., rescuing someone from a mugger) and a lot of personal investment (e.g., parenting).

Just as there are risks associated with prosocial behavior, there are also benefits from kind, helpful behavior. Interestingly, the benefits go to both the person who acts prosocially and the recipient of his altruism, as well as to the system in which he operates (Marcus & Leiserson, 1978).

Examples   Jeanette helps a new child at camp by showing her where the showers are, how to get to the dining hall, and where her cot is. Jonathon surprises his dad by clearing the sidewalk of snow. Janet gets a sponge when her friend spills milk. Janet helps in the cleanup operation.

All of these children will benefit personally by their prosocial behavior. One personal benefit is the feeling of competence, the belief that "I am capable of helping," that develops from helping someone. The desire for competence is a strong motivational factor (White, 1959).

Another personal benefit accrues to children who act prosocially. They tend to receive help from other children and adults (Marcus, 1977). Marcus looked at the relationship between help given and help received by 19 preschool children. The correlation between giving help to and getting help from other children was .80. Patterson's (1977) idea that people get what they give seems to hold for helping behavior. A child who never gives help willingly to classmates will probably get very little assistance in return.

Encouraging prosocial behavior has two positive side effects on the systems in which children live. First, as members of family and classroom systems, children have an obligation to share in the work of the system, whether the work involves farm or ranch chores, snow shoveling, setting tables, washing paint cups, or putting trikes away.

The second benefit to the entire system centers on the general atmosphere of the home, classroom, or other setting. When children are encouraged to be cooperative and helpful, the atmosphere is friendlier. The home, classroom, camp, or hospital playroom is simply a more pleasant and relaxing place.

Developmental Trends

Under Age 2

Children act prosocially before they are 3 years old. Rheingold, Hay, and West (1976) found that almost all the children 15 to 18 months old in the study shared things with parents or with an unfamiliar person. Rheingold (1979) also examined helping behavior in 2-year-olds and found that all the children in this study helped their mothers in a laboratory study and nearly all helped a stranger. Spontaneous sharing was also observed by Stanjek (1978). Cooperation has also been observed in children under age 2, with cooperation increasing as children approached their third year (Hay, 1979). Children seem to understand distress in others and attempt to relieve the distress.

2 to 6 Years

During the preschool years children act prosocially in a number of ways. Over 50 years ago Murphy (1937) did an observational study of children in nursery school and found that children comforted, helped, defended, and protected others. They showed sympathy. More recent research by Sawin (1980) confirms Murphy's findings. Several researchers have documented increases in cooperation, sharing, donating, and rescue behavior for children during early childhood (Bryan, 1975; Marcus, Telleen, & Roke, 1979; Midlarksy & Bryan, 1967; Rosenhan, 1972; Staub, 1970).

How Can These Trends Be Explained?

As children get older they become better thinkers, their cognitive skills become more sophisticated. Young children tend to be more *egocentric* than older children. As children age, egocentrism fades and they gradually become able to see things from another person's perspective (Piaget, 1983). An older child, then, can be more cooperative and generous because of the ability to take the viewpoint of the other person and understand what the other needs (Buckley, Siegel, & Ness, 1979). Children who are less egocentric tend to be willing to share and help others (Rubin & Schneider, 1973).

Necessary and Sufficient? Acquiring better cognitive skills is *necessary* before someone can be helpful or cooperative, and that is why older children tend to be more prosocial than younger children. But is becoming more sophisticated cognitively a *sufficient* condition for becoming prosocial? No. The ability to think at a higher level does not guarantee that an older child will, in fact, act prosocially.

Some children, as they age, are actually less willing to rescue other people or to cooperate (Madsen, 1971; Staub, 1970). Cruelty toward others is also possible as children get older and more cognitively sophisticated. Cathy, 14 years old, is no longer egocentric. She understands that her friend Ellen needs help with algebra. Cathy uses her ability to understand another's need to say, "I know what you need, Ellen, and you're not going to get it." Whether a person becomes cooperative or unhelpful depends on other factors which will be discussed in the next section.

NURTURING PROSOCIAL BEHAVIOR

Factors Affecting Prosocial Behavior

Several factors determine whether a child will learn and exhibit prosocial behavior. These factors include discipline techniques used by adults, whether adults model and reinforce prosocial behavior, and whether the child has a chance to discuss and practice cooperating and helping through verbal labeling and role playing.

Discipline Techniques: Effect on Prosocial Behavior

Baumrind (1971) identifies styles or patterns of parenting. Each style differs in the discipline techniques it uses and in its effect on prosocial behavior in children. One of these patterns is the *authoritarian* style, another is the *authoritative* style, and a third is the *permissive* style.

Authoritarian Discipline Harsh and degrading punishment or punishment not accompanied by reasons does not foster prosocial behavior. A necessary ingredient in cooperating with and helping others is empathy, which results when one is able to comprehend the needs of others as well as the effect of one's behavior on others. Hurtful physical or psychological discipline does not help a child become empathic.

When Ms. Timmons sees that Pam has left the block corner in a shambles, she says, "Pam, this is the third time you've refused to help Jim clean up the blocks. I don't know what I'm going to do with you!" Pam's ability to show empathy for Jim will not develop if Ms. Timmons consistently uses this method of discipline. Pam will be more likely to understand that Jim needs her help if the teacher explains this need: "Pam, when you play with the blocks and then refuse to put them away, Jim has to do all the work. That is not fair to Jim. I want you to put the blocks away, too."

A child who routinely experiences negative discipline often complies with adult demands to avoid the adult's anger. When John, for example, forgets to rake leaves, his father slaps him and says, "That will teach you not to forget your work." This father is relying on John's fear of physical punishment to get help with chores. Even though John may do the chores, he will do them grudgingly and not because he sees the need to share the family's work.

Permissive Discipline A *permissive* adult, unlike an authoritarian adult, sets few if any limits on a child's behavior and allows the child to make decisions even when it is inappropriate. Some of these decisions are about things on which the child should have no choice, such as hurting others. Some of the decisions are beyond the ability of the child and would be best made by the parent or teacher, like how long the child should be allowed to play outside or whether he should wear protective clothing in winter.

Authoritative (Positive) Discipline Baumrind (1971) found that the *authoritative* discipline style is more likely to produce cooperative children than either the authoritarian or permissive styles. Authoritative adults use positive *prescriptive* discipline. They make their standards known to the child and communicate their expectations for mature behavior. They exercise firm but not repressive control over their child

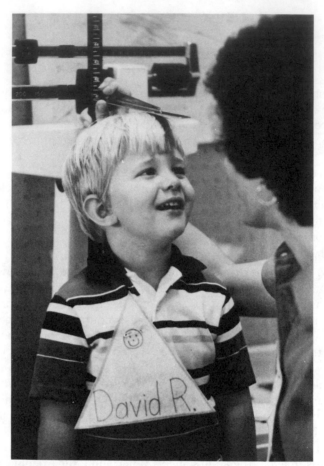

Adults with a prescriptive value orientation tell children what to do; for example, "Stand up straight and keep your hands down by your sides."

by developing humane, reasonable limits on behavior (See the Special Focus box, "Positive Discipline: A Powerful Strategy for Encouraging Prosocial Behavior").

Modeling: Effect on Prosocial Behavior

Modeling is an effective way to teach a variety of behaviors. Several researchers and theorists who study prosocial behavior agree that the modeling of cooperative, helpful, altruistic, generous behavior is a powerful elicitor of the same behavior in children (Bryan, 1975; Bryan & Walbek, 1970; Harris, 1970; Marcus & Leiserson, 1978; Mussen & Eisenberg-Berg, 1977; Rushton, 1975).

The child observing a prosocial model learns a norm of social responsibility. The norm tells the child that helping others or cooperating with others is expected of him (Bryan, 1975). As socializing agents, we adults have the responsibility to help children learn this norm. They do not learn it on their own.

Which Models Have the Greatest Effect on Children? Not all the models to whom a child is exposed have the same effect on his behavior. Certain characteristics of a person affect his efficacy as a model of prosocial behavior:

1. Power
2. Nurturance and support
3. Consistency
4. Attitude about helping or cooperating

Each of these characteristics will now be discussed.

Power of the Model A powerful model is more likely to influence the development of prosocial behavior than is a model with less power (Bryan, 1975; Rushton, 1975, 1976). According to Mussen and Eisenberg-Berg (1977), a powerful model is a person who controls resources and can administer rewards and punishments to the child. Parents and teachers are obviously powerful models because they control resources, rewards, and punishments. Other adults with whom children have contact are powerful models.

Distinguish between the use of raw power and legitimate authority. Even though the use of power facilitates the development of helpfulness and cooperation, some adults are reluctant to use their power. This reluctance stems from the knowledge that power-assertive, hurtful discipline is ineffective in changing behavior. The real problem, and hence the confusion, lies in the distinction between the use of power for hurtful punishment and the exercise of an adult's legitimate authority.

Adults take on a great responsibility when they assume a nurturing role, whether the nurturing is done through parenting, teaching, counseling, nursing, or some other profession. With this responsibility comes a degree of legitimate authority by which adults can and should impose limits on the child for his own safety, the safety of others, or for the development of self-control. An adult who exercises legitimate authority well does so with warmth as well as firmness. He does not use threats or physical punishment but instead sets reasonable limits, enforces those limits, and gives a reason for his actions. There is a real difference between the imposition of raw power by a mean-spirited, spiteful adult and the exercise of legitimate authority by a warm, supportive adult.

Nurturant and Supportive Models Nurturant, supportive models have a positive impact on the development of prosocial behavior, especially helpfulness (Staub, 1971; Yarrow, Scott, & Waxler, 1973). Yarrow et al. investigated the impact of a model's nurturance on imitative prosocial behavior. They wanted to know if a warm, accepting adult who modeled helpful behavior would be imitated more than a nonnurturant model. Subjects were 3½- to 5-year-old preschool children. The method used consisted of several steps:

1. Each child was given a test and was observed to determine his level of helpful behavior.
2. Children were divided into two groups. For 2 weeks the adult model provided

FIGURE 7.2   The methodology of the 1973 Yarrow, Scott, and Waxler study.

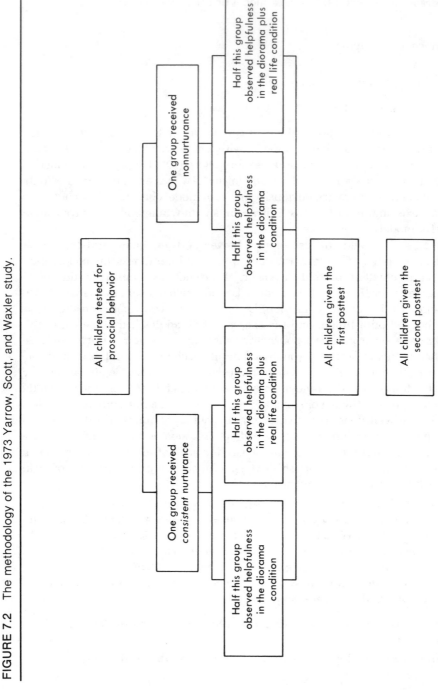

one of two types of treatment—one group received consistent nurturance, and the other group did not receive nurturance.

3. When 2 weeks were up, modeling sessions began. Each child had two individual sessions with the model. A child was exposed to one of two types of modeling, the diorama condition or the diorama plus real life condition. In the *diorama condition* the child observed the adult model working with miniature figures. The model verbalized awareness of and sympathy for the distress of a victim. The model showed pleasure when the victim was helped and used the word "help" to summarize what had been done for the victim. In the *diorama plus real life* condition, the child observed not only the diorama action but also watched the model help a real person. The person bumped her head and the helpful model helped the victim. Again, there was an expression of awareness of the victim's distress and pleasure about helping the injured person.

4. The helping behavior of each child was again measured. The first retest occurred 2 days after the last modeling session. Each child was also tested 2 weeks after the last modeling session. By giving two retests 2 weeks apart, the experimenters could tell not only if their modeling was effective but also if any changed behavior in the child persisted. For the retest each child had the chance to help a mother pick up some buttons she had dropped or help another child retrieve a toy. The results showed that the *modeling plus real life condition* was more effective in increasing helpful behavior. Children who had experienced consistent nurturance prior to the experiment gave the most help in the posttests, even after 2 weeks.

Conclusions from the Yarrow et al. (1973) study were:

1. A helpful model should also be nurturant. Nurturant models elicited more imitation than nonnurturant models.
2. Nurturant helpful models must actually say how they have helped someone.
3. Telling a child to be helpful is not enough. Adults must actually model the behavior they preach about.

What is the main point of this complicated but elegant study? If we want children to be helpful, then we must model helpfulness, must be warm and nurturant, must tell a child about helpfulness, and must express pleasure when we help someone. All of these things seem to work together to produce helpful behavior in children.

Consistency of a Model   Some adults do not practice what they preach to children. They tell children that helping others is important and may even send their children to Sunday school, but they fail to model helpfulness. What is the effect of this failure to practice what is preached on a child's level of prosocial behavior (helpfulness or generosity)?

Bryan and Walbek (1970) found that a model's preaching, or what the model *said* about generosity, determined what the child *said* about giving. A child who hears an adult preach about the virtues of giving to a fund drive, for example, will very likely say that "It's a good thing to give money to our church."

The same researchers discovered that a model who was actually generous and gave to charity had a greater effect on a child's willingness to give. When there is a discrepancy between what is preached and what is practiced, a child is influenced to a much greater degree by the adult's actual behavior (Presbie & Coiteux, 1971). To foster helpful, cooperative, and generous behavior, adults should model the behavior they want to see in children. The research shows that what the child sees is what the child does.

Attitude of the Model   An adult who models helpful behavior is more likely to be imitated if he appears to be pleased about having given help (Midlarsky & Bryan, 1972; Yarrow et al., 1973). Children who watched a happy model were more generous. The mechanism in this case seems to be that children can vicariously experience the same good feeling as the model, and this increases the possibility of the child's helping or cooperating. An adult who gives but grumbles is not likely to be imitated.

Internalizing Behavior That Is Modeled   Most of the studies of prosocial behavior cited in this chapter are laboratory or experimental in nature. Objections and questions have been raised about whether the results obtained in a laboratory study like that of Yarrow et al. can or should be applied to the real world (Rushton, 1976). The main criticism of such studies of prosocial behavior is whether the experimenter has demonstrated that the child has internalized the new behavior.

Two things are necessary to show that a child has internalized a learned behavior (Rushton, 1976). First, the newly acquired behavior must show durability over time—it has to last. The child has to show helpful behavior not only at the time of testing but also well after the testing has stopped. Second, the child must show that he uses the new behavior in situations different from that in the laboratory study. A child who has learned to help someone who is hurt must demonstrate helpfulness in some other way, such as helping someone put toys away.

The Yarrow, et al. (1973) study suggests that laboratory effects do persist over time and across situations. The researchers retested the children twice. In the experiment, the children saw the model help someone who has hurt herself. In the test, however, the children were given a chance to help someone who had dropped something. This experiment was conducted so that children could demonstrate that they had internalized the new, helpful behavior and that this new behavior would generalize beyond the original experimental situation.

Rewards and Reinforcement: Effect on Prosocial Behavior

Prosocial behavior is a learned behavior and as such is subject to the laws of learning. Any behavior followed by a reward is likely to occur again (Patterson, 1977; Sheppard & Willoughby, 1975). Reinforcing or rewarding cooperation and helpfulness increases these behaviors. Group rewards and individual rewards, however, have different effects on the development of prosocial behavior.

Group-administered rewards, according to Bryan (1975) are consistently more effective in fostering cooperative behavior than are rewards given to individuals. He suggests giving rewards on a group basis. Competition among group members decreases, and children are friendlier and more cooperative after they have received a

Small groups that work cooperatively should be reinforced with a brief comment from the teacher.

group reward (Bryan, 1975). An adult working with a group of children might keep a chart on cooperative behavior, not for each individual child, but for the group as a whole.

Rewards given to individuals often foster competitiveness and not cooperation. In our culture, adults sometime make it difficult for children to cooperate by training them to be competitive in situations where cooperation is clearly the goal. For example, a parent or other adult pits one child against another in an effort to get something cleaned: "Let's see who can put away the blocks the fastest." This adult is encouraging someone to win and is not really encouraging cooperation in a cleanup effort.

Adults are sometime puzzled when children are uncooperative. They are puzzled because they know the children, especially the older ones, do have the capacity for prosocial behavior but do not always act prosocially. In addition to learning prosocial behavior, the child has also learned how to be competitive. Competitiveness is desirable in some situations but is not desirable when adults want to teach cooperation.

Role Playing and Verbal Labeling: Effect on Prosocial Behavior

Both role playing and verbal labeling help children learn and perform prosocial behavior. For example, a group of children watches a television program about a child who picks up and disposes of litter on his block. The group discusses this show, and the adult says that picking up the trash makes the neighborhood a prettier place for everyone. Then the adult, a scout leader, plans a "litter walk" and the children get a chance to practice the behavior they observed. Friedrich and Stein

(1975) believe that the discussion (verbal labeling) of a program's prosocial content is important for the learning of the observed content but that the role playing (litter walk) is important for the actual performance of the new behavior.

Certain types of verbal labeling are more effective than others in fostering prosocial behavior. Statements like "It is good to give" or "A person should give" do not encourage helpfulness or cooperation. However, statements that focus the child on how cooperative behavior affects others do seem to foster prosocial behavior (Midlarsky & Bryan, 1972).

Staub (1971) investigated the effect of role playing on helpful (rescue) behavior. He worked with 75 kindergarten children, some of whom had acted out helping another person. These children who had performed the "rescue" role became more willing to rescue another person.

Adult Practices that Foster Prosocial Behavior

Theory, research, and practice show that certain adult practices encourage children to be helpful, cooperative, and generous.

Use Your Personal "Style" to Create an Atmosphere that Encourages Prosocial Behavior

Supportive adults create an atmosphere that fosters a sense of caring about others and a willingness to help them or cooperate with them (Schmuch & Schmuch, 1975). Such an environment is one in which:

1. supportiveness exists between people.
2. power struggles are avoided. A caring adult who cautiously exercises legitimate authority in a positive manner fosters empathy and prosocial behavior in children.
3. open communication exists. Communication is honest and direct but not hurtful. Adults know how to communicate well with children.
4. there is high positive affect. The people in this system actually like each other. Even when it might be necessary to enforce a necessary limit, positive affect would be evident in the firm but gentle, nonhurtful style of enforcement. Children feel safe in such an environment, and these feelings are mirrored in their helpful cooperative interactions.
5. the group examines better ways of working together. When Ms. Timmons finds that her group ignores the rule about putting things away before lunch, she brings them together and they work out the problem. The group also works on a plan to cooperate in cleaning the playground. Tasks are divided, equipment is gathered, and the work is started and completed.

Model Prosocial Behavior

Recall from the previous discussion how powerful modeling is in eliciting prosocial behavior in children. The most effective model is one who is warm, nurturant, and supportive; who uses legitimate authority judiciously; who talks about what he is doing; who is consistent (practices what he preaches); and who seems to be pleased about what he is doing.

Use Positive Discipline

1. *The adult makes his expectations regarding prosocial behavior clear.* Children are aware, for example, that their scout leader expects cooperation in breaking camp, that their parents expect them to help with chores, or that their teachers expect them to help clean up.
2. *The adult usually sets limits well.* The limits are prescriptive, humane, just, well-defined, clearly and positively stated, and firmly but gently enforced.
3. *A child is told how his behavior affects other people.* Mrs. Gonzalez might say to Jerry as he leaves the table, "Jerry, you must clean your part of the table. Michael is going to paint next. If you leave without cleaning then Mike will get paint all over the back of his paper."
4. *The adult often tells a child how to help someone.*

Assign Age-Appropriate Responsibilities

If children are to become aware of their part in a system, then they must be made to feel that they are truly a functioning part of the system. Children of *authoritative* parents (those who use positive discipline) were assigned responsibilities around the house (Baumrind, 1971). This accounted, in part, for the finding that these children were the most cooperative when observed at school.

The responsibilities assigned to children should be based on ability. For example, children can certainly mist plants, feed or water classroom pets, clean up after themselves, and set and clean lunch or snack tables. They should be encouraged to hang up their own coats and to take good care of books, games, and other materials so that the equipment is in good working order for others. Can you think of other responsibilities that children of different ages can handle?

Verbally Label and Discuss Prosocial Behavior

Children learn about helpfulness and cooperation not only by observing models but also by talking about acts of kindness. For instance, after watching a rerun of an episode of "Mr. Rogers' Neighborhood," a group could discuss what Mr. Rogers meant when he talked about being a good neighbor. Stories about people helping others can be read and then discussed. Puppets can be used effectively to discuss prosocial behavior. Do a short puppet story for the children about how one puppet helped the other and then discuss the prosocial behavior.

Practice Prosocial Behavior

Give children a chance to practice the helpful, cooperative behavior they have seen on film and heard about in stories, songs, and discussions by letting them take on the role of the helper. Using puppets is one way not only to discuss prosocial behavior but also to act out situations where help is needed. After the children have used puppets, they might like acting out helpful behavior through creative dramatics (Marcus & Leiserson, 1978). For example, one child plays the role of a father hammering nails into a wall. Another child takes the role of the mother. When "father" drops the whole box of nails, the adult can ask "mother" how she or he could help. Then switch roles to give both children a chance at being the helper.

Reinforce Prosocial Behavior

Children need to be reinforced when they act in an empathic, helpful, cooperative way. Reinforcement for positive behavior at first comes from supportive adults. Appreciation for helpfulness is shown in a quiet comment to the child. A simple "Thank you for clearing the dinner dishes, Jim" combined with a smile is an effective social reinforcer (Patterson, 1977).

Successful attempts by children to work together should be recognized. A teacher, for example, could end the day nicely by gathering the group and saying how well the children worked together. He could sing a short song about all of the children and how each helped or cooperated. For example, Ms. Timmons sang the following song about how the children had cooperated that day (the tune is "Mary Had a Little Lamb"):

Bill and Jim cleaned up the paints,
    Cleaned up the paints, cleaned up the paints,
Bill and Jim cleaned up the paints
    When they came to school.
Anne Marie put away her trike,
    Put away her trike, put away her trike,
Anne Marie put away her trike
    When she came to school.

Singing a song about how each child helped or cooperated during the day.

SPECIAL FOCUS: Positive Discipline: A Powerful Strategy for Encouraging Prosocial Behavior

John's father wants John to help him with the yardwork. He says, "John, there's a lot of work to do again this year in the yard, and I can't handle it alone. You're old enough to help me now. Let's think about some jobs for you to do."

John's dad uses positive discipline. Positive discipline is used by supportive adults and tends to foster prosocial behavior. John's dad is likely to get the help and cooperation he needs for several reasons.

1. *Positive discipline alerts children to the needs of another person.* John's father, by arousing empathy, is making his son aware of his needs ("I can't handle it alone"). This increased awareness of another's needs can lead to empathy, a prerequisite to responding prosocially.

2. *Positive discipline communicates clear expectations about helping, sharing, and cooperating.* This parent makes his expectations of his child's cooperation clear and is more likely to get that cooperation than is the adult who threatens punishment if the child does *not* help.

3. *Positive discipline techniques include suggestions on how to help, cooperate, or share.* John is later told, "The grass has to be raked. You gather the things needed for raking — the bamboo rake and a basket." Telling John how he can help is a natural part of positive discipline and is likely to encourage cooperation because children will help someone more readily if they have the skills to help.

4. *Adults who use positive discipline tell children what to do rather than what not to do.* They usually have a *prescriptive* rather than a *proscriptive* value orientation. John's dad prescribes expected behavior ("There is a lot of work to do — you gather the things for raking").

Olejnik and McKinney (1973) investigated the effect of a parent's value system on generosity of preschool children. Subjects were 4-year-olds and their parents. All of the parents delivered rewards and punishment, but the value orientations differed. Some of the parents had a proscriptive value orientation. They emphasized telling their child what not to do: "Don't throw the towel on the floor." "Don't argue over TV programs." "Don't wiggle around." The other parents had a prescriptive value orientation. They told their children what *to* do: "Hang the towel on the rack." "Stand still so that I can brush your hair." Children whose parents had a prescriptive value orientation were more generous than children whose parents had a proscriptive orientation.

SPECIAL FOCUS: Encourage Sharing, Cooperation, and Helpfulness

In summary, responsible, supportive adults help children act prosocially when they:

☐ use positive discipline.

☐ are nurturant and supportive.
☐ model helpfulness, cooperation, empathy, and sharing.
☐ show pleasure in helping someone else.
☐ provide other models of prosocial behavior.
☐ assign age-appropriate responsibilities to children.
☐ verbally label kindness and cooperation.
☐ discuss examples of prosocial behavior with children.
☐ give children an opportunity to practice prosocial behavior.
☐ reinforce altruistic, prosocial behavior.

SUMMARY: KEY CONCEPTS IN THIS CHAPTER

1. Children learn how to act prosocially. *Prosocial behavior* includes a variety of behaviors—helping, cooperation, generosity.

2. Both immediate and long-range benefits accrue when prosocial behavior is valued and encouraged. These advantages are experienced by the child, the group with whom the child lives or works, and ultimately the society in which the child exists.

3. A developmental shift occurs in the ability to act prosocially. As children get older, they usually achieve more sophisticated levels of thought. These advanced cognitive skills give children the ability to act prosocially. Advanced cognitive skills, however, do not guarantee that the child will act prosocially.

4. The type of discipline experienced by a child affects his level of cooperation, helpfulness, and generosity.

5. *Modeling* has a powerful effect on a child's prosocial behavior. Models holding the greatest appeal to children are those who are powerful, nurturant, who demonstrate prosocial behavior, and who have a positive attitude toward helping and cooperating.

6. Because prosocial behavior is learned, it should be reinforced. Group rewards are more effective than individual rewards in eliciting cooperation from a group of children.

7. *Verbal labeling* or discussion of observed prosocial behavior determines, in part, whether children learn the behavior. A chance to *role play* the learned behavior has been shown to be a determinant of whether a child actually performs the behavior.

OBSERVE: CHILD GUIDANCE IN ACTION

Observe the same adult and group of children you observed for chapter 6. Use the same method used in the observation on aggression to record your observations on prosocial behavior.

Using the information in this chapter and summarized in the Special Focus box, "Encourage Sharing, Cooperation, and Helpfulness," note how this adult encourages prosocial behavior in the children. For example, how can you tell if the children are assigned appropriate responsibilities? Does this adult model helpfulness, cooperation, and sharing? Does the adult reinforce a child's prosocial behavior? How?

REFERENCES

BAUMRIND, D. (1971). Current patterns of parental authority. *Developmental Psychology Monographs, 4*(1, Pt. 2).

BRYAN, J.H. (1975). Children's cooperation and helping behaviors. In E.M. Hetherington (Ed.), *Review of child development research*, Vol. 5. Chicago: University of Chicago Press.

BRYAN, J.H., & LONDON, P. (1970). Altruistic behavior by children. *Psychological Bulletin, 73* 200–211.

BRYAN, J.H. & WALBEK, N.H. (1970). Preaching and practicing generosity: Children's actions and reactions. *Child Development, 41*, 329–353.

BUCKLEY, N., SIEGEL, S., & NESS, S. (1979). Egocentricity, empathy, and altruistic behavior in young children. *Developmental Psychology, 15*, 329–330.

FRIEDRICH, L.K. & STEIN, A.H. (1975). Prosocial television and young children: The effects of verbal labeling and role-playing on learning and behavior. *Child Development, 46*, 27–38.

HARRIS, M.B. (1970). Reciprocity and generosity: Some determinants of sharing in children. *Child Development, 41*, 313–328.

HAY, D.F. (1979). Cooperative interactions and sharing between very young children and their parents. *Developmental Psychology, 15*, 647–653.

MACAULAY, J.R., & BERKOWITZ, L. (Eds.). (1970). *Altruism and helping behavior.* New York: Academic Press.

MADSEN, M.C. (1971). Developmental and cross-cultural differences in the cooperative and competitive behavior of young children. *Journal of Cross-Cultural Psychology, 2*, 365–371.

MARCUS, R.F. (1977, March). *A naturalistic study of reciprocity in the helping behavior of young children.* Paper presented at the biennial meeting of the Society for Research in Child Development, New Orleans.

MARCUS, R.F., & LEISERSON, M. (1978). Encouraging helping behavior. *Young Children, 36*(6), 24–34.

MARCUS, R.F., TELLEEN, S., & ROKE, E.J. (1979). Relation between cooperation and empathy in young children. *Developmental Psychology, 15*, 346–347.

MIDLARSKY, E., & BRYAN, J.H. (1967). Training charity in children. *Journal of Personality and Social Psychology, 5*, 408–415.

MIDLARSKY, E., & BRYAN, J.H. (1972). Affect expressions and children's imitative altruism. *Journal of Experimental Research in Personality, 6*, 195–203.

MURPHY, L.B. (1937). *Social behavior and child personality.* New York: Columbia University Press.

MUSSEN, P.H. & EISENBERG-BERG, N. (1977). *Caring, sharing and helping.* San Francisco: W.H. Freeman.

OLEJNIK, A.B., & McKINNEY, J.P. (1973). Parental value orientation and generosity in children. *Developmental Psychology, 8,* 311.

PATTERSON, G.R. (1977). *Living with children* (rev. ed.). Champaign, IL: Research Press.

PIAGET, J. (1983). Piaget's theory. In P. Mussen (Ed.), *Handbook of child psychology,* Vol. 3. New York: Wiley.

PRESBIE, R.J., & COITEUX, P.F. (1971). Learning to be generous or stingy: Imitation of sharing behavior as a function of model generosity and vicarious reinforcement. *Child Development, 42,* 1033–1038.

RADKE-YARROW, M., ZAHN-WAXLER, C., & CHAPMAN, M. (1983). Children's prosocial dispositions and behavior. In P. Mussen (Ed.), *Handbook of child psychology,* Vol. 4. New York: Wiley.

RHEINGOLD, H.L. (1979, March). *Helping by two-year-old children.* Paper presented at the meeting of the Society for Research in Child Development, San Francisco.

RHEINGOLD, H.L., HAY, D.F., & WEST, M.J. (1976). Sharing in the second year of life. *Child Development, 47,* 1148–1158.

ROSENHAN, D.L. (1972). Prosocial behavior of children. In W.W. Hartup (Ed.), *The young child: Reviews of research,* Vol. 2 (pp. 340–360). Washington, DC: National Association for the Education of Young Children.

RUBIN, K.H., & SCHNEIDER, F.W. (1973). The relationship between moral judgment, egocentrism, and altruistic behavior. *Child Development, 44,* 661–665.

RUSHTON, J.P. (1975). Generosity in children: Immediate and long-term effects of modeling, preaching, and moral judgment. *Journal of Personality and Social Psychology, 31,* 459–466.

RUSHTON, J.P. (1976). Socialization and the altruistic behavior of children. *Psychological Bulletin, 83,* 898–913.

SAWIN, D.B. (1980). *A field study of children's reactions to distress in their peers.* Unpublished manuscript, University of Texas at Austin.

SCHMUCH, R.A., & SCHMUCH, P.A. (1975). *Group processes in the classroom* (2nd ed.). Dubuque, IA: William C. Brown.

SHEPPARD, W.C., & WILLOUGHBY, R.H. (1975). *Child behavior.* Chicago: Rand McNally.

STANJEK, K. (1978). Überreichen von Gaben: Funktion und Entwicklung in den ersten Lebensjahren [The handing over of gifts: Function and development in the first year of life]. *Zeitschrift für Entwicklungspsychologie und Pädagogische Psychologie, 10,* 103–113.

STAUB, E. (1970). A child in distress: The influence of age and number of witnesses on children's attempts to help. *Journal of Personality and Social Psychology, 14,* 130–140.

STAUB, E. (1971). The use of role playing and induction in children's learning of helping and sharing behavior. *Child Development, 42,* 805–816.

WHITE, R.W. (1959). Motivation reconsidered: The concept of competence. *Psychological Review, 66,* 297–323.

YARROW, M.R., SCOTT, P.M., & WAXLER, C.Z. (1973). Learning concern for others. *Developmental Psychology, 8,* 240–260.

8

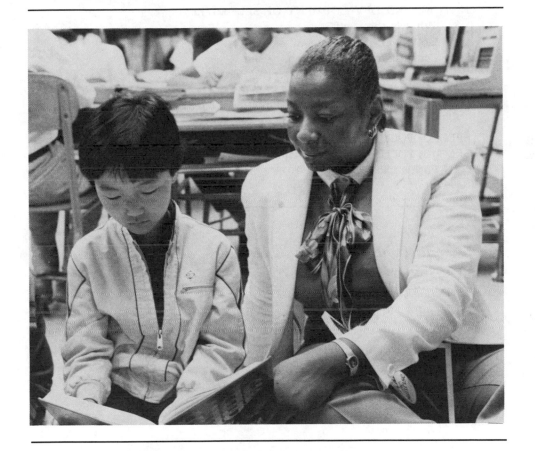

Helping Children
Develop Positive
Self-Esteem

Chapter Overview

After reading and studying this chapter, you will be able to:

- ☐ *Explain* the meaning of *self*.
- ☐ *Define* self-esteem.
- ☐ *Identify, discuss, and give an example* of three dimensions of self-esteem.
- ☐ *Explain* how social interaction affects the development of self-esteem.
- ☐ *Discuss* the importance of adult acceptance and support to a child's self-esteem.
- ☐ *List, discuss, and give examples* of specific adult practices that affect a child's self-esteem.

Children develop self-esteem largely because of the attitudes of adults who are important to them. The process of forming self-esteem is remarkably similar to the process a computer uses to develop information "output." Computer programmers feed or "input" data into the computer. Significant adults feed data to the child. Each adult response tells the child what the adult's attitude toward the child is. The adult data say things like:

"You sure have lots of friends!"
"You seem to enjoy painting."
"I like being with you."
"It's OK to be sad because Henry (the gerbil) died. Henry was our friend."
"You are very good at running and climbing."
"That game was fun. Let's play it again sometime."
"You tell funny jokes."

The adult data can also say things like:

"No wonder nobody plays with you!"
"You never help anybody, do you?"
"Yuck! What muddy colors you've used for painting."
"Don't bother me. Play by yourself."
"It's silly for a big boy to cry over a dead gerbil."
"Why don't you stop cramming food into your face? You're fat enough already."
"What a stupid joke."

A child takes in the "data" over a period of years and uses them to form an opinion of herself. As the cartoon implies, if the input is garbage (demeaning,

FIGURE 8.1   Poor computer programs result from careless programming. Similarly, negative self-esteem in children results from degrading, demeaning adult behavior.

You know the old saying, "garbage in, garbage out."

Source: Stone, M., Ed. Data processing: an introduction by Spencer. Reprinted from INFOSYSTEMS, copyright 1978, Hitchcock Publishing Co.

degrading adult attitudes) then expect the output (child's self-esteem) to be garbage, too. *Garbage in, garbage out.*

This chapter focuses on self-esteem, one part of a child's knowledge of her *self*. The first section defines self-esteem and describes the process by which it develops. The second major section shows that significant adults affect a child's self-esteem. Several specific examples of enhancing and demeaning strategies are included.

NATURE AND DEVELOPMENT OF SELF-ESTEEM

What Is the "Self?"

Humans have been fascinated by the idea of a self and have pondered its meaning for centuries. If newborns know nothing about the self and adolescents think about themselves frequently, then the concept of self must develop sometime in the first several years of life. Does one's concept of self occur suddenly, or does it unfold gradually? What *is* the "self" that humans come to know?

Harter (1983), like Sarbin (1962) believes that the self is a structure that develops gradually. Specifically, they believe that the self is a *cognitive structure*, that humans build or construct a view of the self inside their heads. The cognitive structure of self is built gradually as the result of experience. Infants, for example, must learn that they are separate from other people, and this learning occurs gradually as their perceptual system develops. Young children eventually learn that each of them is a boy or a girl and that their gender will not change even if a boy grows long hair or a girl's long hair is cut short.

Self-knowledge parallels more general changes in cognitive development. In the case of *gender constancy* ("I am a boy and will always be a boy," or "I am a girl and will always be a girl"), children realize their gender will not change at about the same time they understand *conservation*, or the idea that some things remain the same despite apparent surface changes.

A person tends to organize behavior around the cognitive structure of self (Harter, 1983; Sarbin, 1962). This means that a person's set of ideas about herself will affect how she actually behaves. If a 10-year-old boy, for example, believes that washing dishes is "girls' work," then he may refuse his mother's request to wash dishes. If a 10-year-old girl views herself as someone who can run fast, she will more likely enter a race than will her friend who believes she cannot run fast.

Two aspects of self have been identified (Harter, 1983; James 1890/1963; Wylie, 1974, 1979). These two parts are separate from each other but at the same time are also intertwined. One part of your self is an *active observer* and is called the *I*. The other aspect of your self is *observed* by *I* and is called *me*.

To summarize: The *self* is a cognitive construct that is built gradually as a result of experience. A person's view of self affects how she behaves. There are two main aspects of the self, the *I* and *me*. Most research has focused on that part of the self that is observed, the *me*, and this chapter also concentrates on that aspect of self.

Definition of Self-Esteem

Children go through a long process of learning about the self. The observer part of self, *I*, gathers and gives the child information about things like what she looks like, physical abilities, gender, intellectual abilities, and interpersonal skills. Then the child processes this information and decides whether she likes herself. She evaluates and forms an opinion about the self she sees. Self-esteem, then, is only one part of a person's self-system. It is the evaluative part of the self (Coopersmith, 1967; Gecas, 1972; Harter, 1983; Openshaw, 1978; Rosenberg, 1965). Coopersmith's definition reflects this view (1967, pp. 4–5):

By self esteem we refer to the evaluation which an individual makes and customarily maintains with regard to himself; it expresses an attitude of approval or disapproval . . . . self esteem is a personal judgment of worthiness that is expressed in the attitudes the individual holds toward himself.

A child's self-evaluation can be either favorable or unfavorable, positive or negative. Some children like the self that they observe, and form positive self-esteem. Other children do not like the self, and eventually develop *negative* or *low* self-esteem (Gecas, Calonico, & Thomas, 1974).

Dimensions of Self-Esteem

A child observes several different parts of her self in forming an opinion of it (Coopersmith, 1967; Epstein, 1973; Harter, 1983). These parts are called *dimensions* of self-esteem, and include competence, control, and worth or significance to others.

Competence

Competence is success in meeting demands for achievement (Epstein, 1973). Children, like people of all ages, are motivated by a need to feel competent and successful (White, 1959). Children who have positive self-esteem judge themselves as competent in several areas (Gecas, 1971, 1972). They succeed in school—*cognitive competence* (Harter, 1981). They get along well with adults and other children; they can get their parent's or teacher's attention without whining and can make friends easily—*social competence* (Harter, 1982). They are usually fairly successful in playing games or sports requiring coordination or strength, or in other activities like dancing, bike riding, running, or climbing—*physical skills competence.* Children who judge themselves "dumb," lacking friends, or uncoordinated and clumsy often develop negative self-esteem.

Control

Control is the degree to which a child feels responsible for outcomes in life or the degree to which she attributes events to sources beyond her control (Connell, 1980).

Example Jerry wins a race (physical competence) but says, "Sure, I won, but only because Joel wasn't here. I was just lucky." When Jerry gets a B+ on an essay (cognitive competence), he says, "This essay isn't that good." In spite of his abilities, Jerry has negative self-esteem. He believes that the good things he does happen only because of luck or because somebody else is "being nice," and does not believe that he has much control.

Example Christine, on the other hand, works hard in school and gets good grades. When she finally earns a B+ on a math assignment, she says, "Whew! I finally did it. I sure worked hard enough for this." When she has trouble finishing a race she says to her mother, "I know I can do better. I should have practiced more this week." Christine has positive self-esteem, in spite of coming in last in the race. She believes that she has a lot of control over how well she does.

Worth or Significance to Others

Worth or significance to others refers to how much children like themselves, judge themselves to be liked or loved by peers and parents, and think they are accepted by and deserve attention from others. A child who judges herself to be good, valuable, and well-liked will develop positive self-esteem. A child who judges herself to be bad, unloved, and unworthy of attention frequently develops negative self-esteem.

How Self-Esteem Develops: The Social Context

Children exist in a world filled with people and are therefore immersed in a social environment. Children develop social behaviors like aggression, cooperation, and helpfulness because of interaction with other people. So it is with self-esteem. The attitudes that children form about their competence, control, and worth develop as a consequence of social interaction (Felker, 1974).

Many writers have looked at the development of self in relation to others. Early in the 20th century, Cooley (1902) explained the development of self-esteem with a metaphor called the "looking-glass self." The attitudes children hold about themselves are actually reflections of what they imagine others think about them. Mead (1934) also maintained that self-esteem or attitudes toward oneself are much like those held by certain other people in the environment.

That social interaction is a major factor in the development of self-esteem has been an enduring concept. Many modern writers and researchers have relied on this concept (Bandura, 1977; Coopersmith, 1967; Lewis & Brooks-Gunn, 1979). Bandura, for example, believes that a child's sense of competence results from hearing others talk about how well the child does things.

The following sequence of steps describes the general process of the development of self-esteem. It shows that children value themselves as significant others value them (Jimmy) and demean themselves as others do (Frank).

1. Significant adults have opinions and attitudes about a child's competence or significance.

Example Mr. Miles thinks that Jimmy is well-coordinated. Mr. Miles thinks that Frank is uncoordinated.

2. The adult's behavior toward the child shows how he feels.

Example Mr. Miles encourages Jimmy to try the new balance beam unassisted and says, "You did that very well, Jimmy." Mr. Miles does not allow Frank to walk on the beam without assistance and says, "Wait, Frank. You'd better let me help you."

3. The child "tunes in" to the adult's opinion.

Example Jimmy hears favorable comments frequently. He tunes in to Mr. Miles' belief in his physical competence. Frank also tunes in to his teacher's opinion. Mr. Miles is always telling him to be careful.

4. The child's self-evaluations match the adult's attitudes.

Example Jimmy begins to think of himself as competent, just as Mr. Miles does. Frank's attitudes toward his physical skills also match those of his teacher. He hesitates to try new equipment and usually asks for help.

Significant Others Not all adults are "significant" adults to children during each phase of development; the list of those whose attitudes affect a child's self-esteem changes as the child gets older. This is an important concept for caregivers because we must know whose opinion influences children during early and middle childhood. Young children believe that adults possess a superior wisdom, and they rely on the judgments of adult authority to find out what they themselves are like (Harter, 1983; Rosenberg, 1979). This means that both parents and teachers are among the significant others who affect children's self-esteem. As children age, peer evaluations become just as or even more important than those of adults.

ADULTS' ROLE IN CHILDREN'S SELF-ESTEEM

What, specifically, is it in an adult-child relationship that leads a child to think she is competent, worthy, and in control, or the reverse?

Adults affect a child's self-esteem through two main processes. One is the adult's basic support and acceptance of the child. Adults also affect the level of a child's self-esteem by using specific practices as they interact with the child (Hales, 1979a, 1979b). This section focuses on these two mediating processes.

Supportive Adults Help Children Build Positive Self-Esteem

The core of a healthy adult-child relationship is adult *acceptance and support* of a child. Researchers have found that adult acceptance and support are also essential prerequisites to positive self-esteem (Coopersmith, 1967; Hales, 1979a, 1979b; Harter, 1983; Rogers, 1951). Gecas (1971) found that children think of themselves as competent, worthy, happy, good, active, friendly, honest, and confident when adults important to them are supportive. White (1975) found that children are academically and interpersonally competent when significant adults communicate genuine interest in them. Feelings of competence and worth, components of positive self-esteem, come from knowing that one is important and valuable to a significant adult. Conversely, children develop negative self-esteem when adults who are important to them are nonaccepting and nonsupportive.

Rogers (1951) believed that the support given a child should be given freely and without "strings" or conditions. He called this special adult support *unconditional positive regard.* When you give unconditional positive regard to a child, you do not require the child to earn your interest, time, and concern. You give your support freely to the child simply because she exists.

Unconditional positive regard is not permissiveness; it does not mean that you have to accept everything a child does. Some behaviors — hurting others, putting oneself in danger, destroying property—must be stopped, and responsible, supportive adults restate and firmly enforce necessary rules and limits.

Specific Adult Practices Affect Self-Esteem

Adults influence a child's self-esteem by using specific practices as they interact with the child. Supportive adults use strategies that *enhance* or help children develop positive self-esteem. Nonsupportive adults use strategies that *demean* children and help them develop negative self-esteem.

Strategies That Enhance Self-Esteem

1. *Use positive discipline.* State expectations for behavior and give reasons. When limits are tested, focus on explaining the consequences of the behavior and on

the child's responsibility for the consequences. In this way, you will communicate your belief that the child is competent enough to regulate her own behavior.

Example   Miss Piehl has asked the children to listen to her before they embark on a walk but notices that two of the children are not listening. She says, "I want you to be quiet and listen to me so that you know what to do on the walk."

2. *Develop reasonable fair limits. State them well and enforce them firmly.* Good limits are an essential part of positive discipline and express an adult's support. Limits are a form of adult control on the child, and the child gradually internalizes them and develops self-control. In the process she will view herself as competent, because she remembers a limit, and as worthy of the adult's time — both dimensions of positive self-esteem (Coopersmith, 1967).

3. *Require children to be autonomous and to take responsibility for their own behavior.* Hales (1979a, 1979b) investigated variables related to self-esteem and found that girls' self-esteem was higher if parents required them to assume responsibility at home. Perhaps children who are responsible for certain tasks feel that they are an important part of their family system.

Making a child feel that her activity is worthwhile and interesting enhances positive self-esteem.

4. *Encourage children to take credit for doing something well. Avoid constantly pointing out what a child has done incorrectly.* Feedback from adults about how well or how poorly a child has performed a task is an important source of information about the child's competence (Bandura, 1977, 1981). When adults focus on what a child has done well they help a child recognize her competence, and competence is one dimension of positive self-esteem.

Example   Mrs. Herbach knows that Sarah recognizes and can name a square and a circle but that she does not know what a triangle is. She places a large square, circle, and triangle on a bulletin board and has the same shapes in a box. She says, "You know the names of some shapes, Sarah. I want you to reach into this box, take out one shape and put it on top of the same shape on the board." When Sarah correctly matches squares, Mrs. Herbach says, "You're right!" When Sarah pulls out the triangle and matches it, Mrs. Herbach says, "You've matched the *triangles!*"

5. *Acknowledge and help a child work through feelings of fear, anger, and jealousy.*

Example   Seven-year-old Lisa is jealous of her new baby brother and mutters to her father, "I wish that stupid baby would go back to the hospital!" Her father responds, "You don't like having Todd here, do you, Lisa?"

He communicates a message of support and willingness to treat her concern seriously. The real test of support of a child comes when the child is sick, hurt, unhappy, angry, jealous, fearful, or anxious.

6. *Engage in joint activities willingly. Show a genuine interest in the child and her activities.* Adults who show an interest in children believe that children's activities—playing with measuring cups, fingerpainting, playing computer games, building a campsite, or playing in sand—are valid and interesting for the child. By showing concern about a child's welfare, activities, and friends, an adult communicates her belief that the child is a person worthy of the adult's attention.

Coopersmith (1967) found that parents of high- and low-self-esteem children spent the same amount of time with their children. He explained this puzzling finding by noting that the mothers of high-self-esteem children spent time willingly with their children and seemed to enjoy the interaction. Mothers of low-self-esteem children, on the other hand, appeared to spend time with their children grudgingly. Consider Jane's experience with her mother.

Example   Jane's encounters with her mom are permeated with acceptance. While making cookies, her mother points out the steps in the recipe, explains new cooking terms, and shows her how to measure an equal amount for each cookie. She asks Jane if she would like to learn to make another kind of cookie sometime.

7. *Avoid making value judgments about a child's physical attributes. Treat boys and girls as equally competent.*

Example   Mr. Johnson needs help in carrying a bale of hay. He asks for two strong *children* and then chooses a girl and a boy.

8. *Treat the child's family group and culture with respect.*

Example   Mr. Johnson knows his class well. Several children live in single-parent families. When discussing the topic of families, he shows pictures of each child's family and says, "There are lots of people in some of your families, and some of your families are small."

Example   Anna announces that she is making tortillas when she works with play-dough. Mr. Johnson replies, "It was nice of your mom to show us how to make tortillas. Tortillas are a special kind of bread."

Strategies That Demean or Degrade Self-Esteem

1. *Nonsupportive adults use negative discipline.* They are sarcastic with or threaten children. They use hurtful punishment when rules are broken. Hurtful discipline demeans children by humiliating them. It leads the child to conclude that the adult views her as incapable of regulating her own behavior.

2. *Nonsupportive adults do not set limits well.* Some adults set almost no limits, some set too many limits. Many adults do not know how to state clearly even reasonable limits. Poorly defined or stated limits are not helpful because children have no way of knowing whether a behavior is appropriate or inappropriate. They are left to guess on their own, and frequently make the wrong decision.

Example   During naptime, Leslie decided to get up and walk over to the puzzle table, and another child followed her. The problem was that the teacher had forgotten to tell the children to stay on their cots during naptime. She had never actually stated the limit.

3. *Nonsupportive adults do not require children to be self-responsible.* They do not take the time necessary to help children assume responsibility. Chores are not specified or, even if they are, there is no penalty for not doing the chore. Nonsupportive adults often fail to require children to take responsibility when they have hurt someone or damaged property.

4. *Nonsupportive adults tend to concentrate on what children cannot do.*

Example   Mark and his grandfather are looking at Mark's math homework. Grandpa says, "You should concentrate more. Then you could get them right. That one is wrong. This one is wrong and this one is wrong." Mark says, "But look, Grandpa, I got these right." Grandpa replies, "But you got all the others wrong, and that's what you should worry about."

Constant feedback about what is wrong is demeaning because it communicates the adult's belief that the child is incompetent. Because younger children rely so heavily on what adults think about their abilities, Mark is very likely to feel incompetent, a component of negative self-esteem.

5. *Nonsupportive adults imply that fearful, angry, jealous, or sad feelings are bad or wrong. They do not support the child in dealing with the feelings.* Suppose that Lisa's dad had said, "Don't ever let me hear you say that again. He's here to

stay, so you can just get used to the idea!" This response would deny Lisa the right to jealous feelings. Denying her feeling is akin to denying Lisa herself, because even negative feelings are real and are a part of the child. Lisa's father would imply that jealousy is wrong, and Lisa would likely feel that something about herself was wrong as well.

6. *Nonsupportive adults give their time grudgingly and make a child believe that his or her activities are not interesting.*

Example   Marty asks her mother to show her how to make chocolate chip cookies. Feeling obligated, her mom does teach her but at the same time clearly communicates resentment, annoyance, and irritability by talking quickly and answering Marty's questions abruptly. Marty is likely to conclude that she cannot be very likeable because her own mother does not like to do things with her. Merely being together is not as important to the development of self-esteem as what actually goes on between adult and child when they are together.

7. *Nonsupportive adults make value judgments about physical attributes and do not treat boys and girls as equally competent.*

Example   Mrs. Olsen, a substitute teacher, tells Tom, "Sit outside the circle while we play 'Duck, Duck, Goose,' because you'll have trouble running with that brace on your leg."

Example   Mrs. Olsen allows only the boys to work with woodworking tools: "You girls don't know how to use tools."

SPECIAL FOCUS: Helping Children Develop Positive Self-Esteem

In summary, responsible, supportive adults help children develop positive self-esteem when they:

☐ use positive discipline.

☐ develop reasonable limits, state them well, and firmly but kindly enforce them.

☐ require children to be autonomous and to assume responsibility for their own behavior and choice of activities.

☐ encourage children to take credit for doing something well. Avoid constantly pointing out what a child has done incorrectly.

☐ acknowledge children's right to feel sad, angry, afraid, or jealous and support them in working through the feelings.

☐ engage in joint activities willingly and treat a child's activities as worthwhile and interesting.

☐ avoid making value judgments about a child's physical attributes and treat both boys and girls as equally competent.

☐ regard a child's family group and culture as valid.

8. *Nonsupportive adults imply that a child's family group and culture are undesirable or deviant.*

Example   Several of the children in Mrs. Olsen's class live only with their mothers and do not see their fathers. One child lives with his grandmother, and another lives in a foster home. Mrs. Olsen defines a family as a father, a mother, and children and ignores other types or forms of family groups when the topic of "families" is discussed.

SPECIAL FOCUS: Positive Discipline: A Powerful Tool for Developing Positive Self-Esteem

Example   Sam leaves sand toys in front of the slide even though he knows the rule about keeping the space in front of the slide clear. Another child lands on a shovel after zooming down the slide. Consider the following possible response from Mr. Saunders:

1. "Sam, get over here and pick up these toys. How many times have I told you not to put toys in front of the slide? You can just forget about playing in the sandpit until you learn the rules."

2. "I want you to move the toys back to the sandpit, Sam, and keep them there. James hurt his leg because he landed on the shovel that you left in front of the slide."

From the chapter on discipline you have read that some adults use negative, coercive, hurtful discipline, while others use positive, non-hurtful discipline. You also have seen that children who experience negative hurtful discipline often lack self-control, frequently disobey adults, tend to be aggressive, and are generally not helpful or cooperative. Positive discipline is related to higher levels of compliance (obedience), helpfulness, and cooperation and to lower levels of aggression. As you might suspect, the type of discipline used by adults also affects a child's self-esteem.

Researchers have found that positive discipline has a significant and positive influence on a child's self-esteem (Coopersmith, 1967; Hales, 1979a, 1979b; Openshaw, 1978). Negative, harsh discipline has a negative effect on a child's self-esteem. Children who experience *coercive* discipline often lack self-confidence, feel inadequate, derogate (belittle) themselves, and feel incompetent (Freedman, Carlsmith, & Sears, 1970; Openshaw, 1978).

Why does positive discipline contribute to positive self-esteem?

1. *Positive discipline is the hallmark of supportive, responsible caregiving.* Adult attitudes toward a child tend to be internalized by the child. A positive adult attitude about a child is reflected to the child in positive discipline.

2. *Responsible adults show support by firmly but gently enforcing reasonable limits* with children as Mr. Saunders does in example 2. Reasonable limits are a part of positive discipline and convey an adult's support to a child. In ex-

ample 1, however, Mr. Saunders conveys a lack of support by ridiculing Sam in public. Sam is likely to interpret his teacher's actions by feeling demeaned.

3. *To feel good about himself, Sam must feel competent.* Mr. Saunders, in example 1, implies that Sam is incapable of understanding how his behavior affected James—that Sam is not competent enough to change his own behavior and must be forced to change. In example 2 Mr. Saunders conveys his confidence in Sam's ability and competence to hear an explanation, to evaluate his own behavior, and eventually to regulate it. Adult attitudes of acceptance, support, and belief in children's competence are reflected to young children and result in their positive self-evaluation.

SUMMARY: KEY CONCEPTS IN THIS CHAPTER

1. The *self* is a cognitive construction. *Self-esteem* is one part of a person's self. Self-esteem is the evaluation a child makes of her own abilities. Competence, control, and worth (significance to others) are dimensions of self-esteem.

2. Self-esteem develops as a consequence of *social interaction* with significant others over a period of time. Children tune into the opinions that adults hold toward them and eventually internalize the adults' attitudes. Children develop opinions about themselves that closely resemble adult attitudes.

3. Children develop positive self-esteem when important adults are *accepting* and *supportive.* Adults also influence a child's self-esteem by using specific practices as they interact with the child. Supportive adults use strategies that *enhance* self-esteem; nonsupportive adults use strategies that demean or degrade children and result in negative self-esteem.

4. Positive discipline has a significant and positive influence on a child's self-esteem.

OBSERVE: CHILD GUIDANCE IN ACTION

Observe an adult as she interacts with children. Using the information in the Special Focus box, "Helping Children Develop Positive Self-Esteem," determine how well this adult supports the development of self-esteem. For example, does the adult use positive or negative discipline? Are children required to be self-responsible? Does the adult encourage the children to take credit for things done well, or does she concentrate on what they cannot do? Does the adult seem to enjoy or be annoyed at spending time with the children? Use the following format to record your observations.

EPISODE 1
Briefly describe the adult strategy. Be specific.

Describe the child's reaction.

EPISODES 2, 3, 4 Use the same format.

Summarize your findings. From the data you have collected, describe the degree to which this adult supports the development of positive self-esteem.

REFERENCES

BANDURA, A. (1977). Self-efficacy: Toward a unifying theory of behavioral change. *Psychological Review, 84,* 191–215.

BANDURA, A. (1981). Self-referent thought: The development of self-efficacy. In J.H. Flavell & L.D. Ross (Eds.), *Development of social cognition.* New York: Cambridge University Press.

CONNELL, J.P. (1980). *A multidimensional measure of children's perceptions of control.* Unpublished master's thesis, University of Denver.

COOLEY, C.H. (1902). *Human nature and the social order.* New York: Scribners.

COOPERSMITH, S. (1967). *The antecedents of self-esteem.* San Francisco: W.H. Freeman.

EPSTEIN, S. (1973). The self-concept revisited or a theory of a theory. *American Psychologist, 28,* 405–416.

FELKER, D. (1974). *Helping children to like themselves.* Minneapolis: Burgess.

FREEDMAN, J.L., CARLSMITH, J.M., & SEARS, D.O. (1970). *Social psychology.* Englewood Cliffs, NJ: Prentice-Hall.

GECAS, V. (1971). Parental behavior and dimensions of adolescent self-evaluation. *Sociometry, 34,* 466–482.

GECAS, V. (1972). Parental behavior and contextual variations in adolescent self-esteem. *Sociometry, 35*(2), 332–345.

GECAS, V., CALONICO, J.M., & THOMAS, D.L. (1974). The development of self-concept in the child: Mirror theory versus model theory. *The Journal of Social Psychology, 92,* 67–76.

HALES, S. (1979a, March). *A developmental theory of self-esteem based on competence and moral behavior.* Paper presented at the meeting of the Society for Research in Child Development, San Francisco.

HALES, S. (1979b, March). *Developmental processes of self-esteem.* Paper presented at the meeting of the Society for Research in Child Development, San Francisco.

HARTER, S. (1981). A model of intrinsic mastery motivation in children: Individual differences and developmental change. In W.A. Collins (Ed.), *Minnesota symposium on child psychology,* (Vol. 14). Hillsdale, NJ: Lawrence Erlbaum.

HARTER, S. (1982). The perceived competence scale for children. *Child Development, 53,* 87–97.

HARTER, S. (1983). Developmental perspectives on the self system. In P. Mussen (Ed.), *Handbook of child psychology,* Vol. 4. New York: Wiley.

JAMES, W. (1963). *Psychology.* New York: Fawcett. (Originally published 1890).

LEWIS, M., & BROOKS-GUNN, J. (1979). *Social cognition and the acquisition of self.* New York: Plenum Press.

MEAD, G.H. (1934). *Mind, self and society.* Chicago: University of Chicago Press.

OPENSHAW, D.K. (1978). *The development of self-esteem in the child: Model theory versus parent-child interaction.* Unpublished doctoral dissertation, Brigham Young University, Provo, UT.

ROGERS, C.R. (1951). *Client-centered therapy.* Boston: Houghton-Mifflin.

ROSENBERG, M. (1965). *Society and the adolescent self-image.* Princeton: Princeton University Press.

ROSENBERG, M. (1979). *Conceiving the self.* New York: Basic Books.

SARBIN, T.R. (1962). A preface to a psychological analysis of the self. *Psychological Review, 59,* 11–22.

WHITE, B.L. (1975). *The first three years of life.* Englewood Cliffs, NJ: Prentice-Hall.

WHITE, R.W. (1959). Motivation reconsidered: The concept of competence. *Psychological Review, 66,* 297–333.

WYLIE, R. (1974). *The self-concept: A review of methodological considerations and measuring instruments,* Vol. 1 (rev. ed.). Lincoln: University of Nebraska Press.

WYLIE, R. (1979). *The self-concept: Vol. 2. Theory and research on selected topics.* Lincoln: University of Nebraska Press.

UNIT THREE

Theoretical Approaches To Child Guidance

T his unit contains chapters on different theoretical approaches to child guidance—the Rogerian approach, the behavioral approach, and the Adlerian approach. Each of the three chapters in this unit presents the major tenets or concepts of one of these theories. In each chapter you will see how the principles of the theory have been put into action in a specific program. Programs like PET and STEP have been designed to teach adults to use principles of a particular theoretical framework in their work with children.

The three theories were chosen because they illustrate divergent views on how children grow and develop. At the same time, however, a thread of similarity ties the behavioral, the Rogerian, and the Adlerian approaches together. This thread is the emphasis within each theory on the use of positive discipline.

In chapter 9, "The Rogerian Approach to Child Guidance," you will read about the basic tenets of Rogerian theory, developed by Carl Rogers. Gordon (1970) has put these basic principles into action in Parent Effectiveness Training (PET), a program designed to help adults interact more effectively with children. You will learn about some of the basic PET skills—active listening, I-messages, and the "no-lose" method of conflict resolution.

In chapter 10, "The Behavioral Approach to Child Guidance," principles common to all branches of behaviorism are presented. You will note that behavioral theory has evolved during this century from Watson's (1928, 1958) classical conditioning model to Skinner's (1953) reliance on principles of operant conditioning to social learning theory (Bandura, 1977). Most recently, social learning theorists have emphasized cognitive processes and have questioned the role of reinforcement in learning.

Behavioral theory is perhaps best known for the technology of behavior modification. You will read about several different approaches to behavior modification. You will also read about Patterson's program (1975, 1977), an example of a program of behavior modification that uses positive discipline and emphasizes a child's embeddedness in a family system.

In chapter 11, "The Adlerian Approach to Child Guidance," the principles of Adlerian theory are presented. A very useful Adlerian concept to many adults who work with children has been the idea that some children have faulty perceptions of how to become members of a group and use inappropriate methods to gain membership. You will note that the STEP program (Dinkmeyer & McKay, 1976), designed to teach Adlerian child guidance skills, shows adults how to help children change these faulty perceptions. The STEP program, like the PET and Patterson's program, emphasizes the use of positive discipline strategies.

9

The Rogerian Approach To Child Guidance

Chapter Overview

After reading and studying this chapter, you will be able to:

- ☐ *Identify and discuss* five concepts basic to Rogerian theory.
- ☐ *Describe* chacteristics of a fully functioning person.
- ☐ *Explain* how an adult can help a child become a fully functioning person.
- ☐ *Describe* the PET program as a specific program based on Rogerian theory.
- ☐ *Identify, discuss, and practice* three of the skills taught in the PET program.

ROGERIAN THEORY

Background

Rogerian theory was formulated by Carl Rogers, who was born in 1902 in Chicago. Rogers studied to be a minister but in the end became an educational psychologist. He worked in both clinical and academic settings. He counseled children and their parents at the Child Study Department of the Society for the Prevention of Cruelty to Children in Rochester, New York.

Rogers also functioned as a teacher. It was during this period, from 1940 to 1963, that he developed and disseminated his views on counseling and therapy (Rogers, 1961).

Rogerian theory, like behavioral, Adlerian, or interactional theory, can be used as a guide to adult interactions with children. An adult who successfully uses Rogerian principles usually agrees with basic Rogerian concepts of personality development and understands counseling and communication techniques that have grown out of Rogerian theory. This chapter presents major Rogerian concepts, discusses principles of child guidance based on Rogerian theory, and examines a specific and very popular child guidance program based on Rogerian theory.

Rogerian Concepts

Self

The concept of self is the central idea in Rogerian theory. Rogers believes that people live in a world of constant change and that in the center of this world is a set of ideas a person develops about himself, the self-concept. This concept of self is based on how the person typically responds to the countless events in the world and on how he feels about himself in relation to these events.

Consciousness

Unlike Freud, who believed that people are dominated by unconscious drives, Rogers believes that humans are ruled by a conscious perception of themselves and the ever-changing world in which they live. Rogerian theorists firmly believe that individuals possess the ability to control their own actions. They believe that the awareness, or conscious perception, of self and the abillity to represent experiences form the basis of the capacity of self-direction.

Individual Perceptions are Private and Subjective

Every individual exists in a certain context and the events that occur in this context have meaning to that person as they are perceived by that person and not by anyone else. Thus, Rogerians believe that one's perception of experience is private, personal, and highly subjective. A person's view of the world is known only to him.

This Rogerian concept has implications for adult-child relationships. If a person's view is so private, then it would be presumptuous for an adult to impose his own view of a situation on a child. For example, Joel storms into the classroom and shouts, "I hate that Cristy!" If his teacher replies, "Joel, you know that you really like Cristy. She's your friend," then she is imposing her view of the situation and is telling Joel that his perception is wrong. Joel is enraged at the time and his personal perception, according to Rogerians, should not be denied.

Actualization

Rogerians believe that people have a tendency to develop all of thier abilities, to move forward, and to realize their full potential. The ultimate goal for a human, in the Rogerian framework, is to become a fully functioning person, and Rogerians posit the existence of a force that helps an individual to adapt and to grow.

Positive Regard

The need for *positive regard*—support, acceptance, and approval from others—is present in all people. Positive regard from others is internalized by a child, who soon comes to regard himself as positive. Rogerians believe that a child who is not accepted by or who does not receive the approval of adults freely and fully is hampered in development of the self. The child's energy is expended trying to attain the elusive adult approval rather than in actualizing his potential and in becoming a fully functioning person.

Characteristics of a Fully Functioning Person

When a child receives positive regard from adults and when adults refrain from forcing the child to deny experiences or personal perceptions, then that child moves in the direction of becoming a fully functioning person. A fully functioning person is open to experience, lives fully in each moment, and trusts his own judgment (Rogers, 1961).

Openness to Experience

A fully functioning person is "tuned in to" or aware of all feelings. This person is open to all feelings, including love, fear, anger, jealousy, and pride. Feelings are accepted as a part of the self. This person has no need to defend herself from "threatening" experiences because experiences are not viewed as threatening.

In terms of the adult-child relationship, this means that adults should not deny to the child the right to feel a certain way. If Joel is really angry, for example, the adult should not tell him not to feel angry. The adult certainly should not let Joel hurt someone because he is angry, but the adult does not have the right to tell Joel to deny that he is angry.

Living Fully in Each Moment

A person who lives fully in the moment does not twist experiences to fit inaccurate perceptions. Because he perceives the world more accurately, a fully functioning person is more realistic and much less defensive in dealing with new people, problems, and situations.

Trusting One's Own Judgment

Because a fully functioning person is aware of and open to all feelings and can, therefore, perceive reality more accurately, he behaves in ways that "feel right" to him. Such people think for themselves and trust their ability to make decisions. They do not need other people to tell them how to act, since they have the ability to appraise situations accurately and they trust themselves to develop good solutions to problems.

Adults can help a child become a person who trusts his own judgment by allowing the child to think for himself and by avoiding the tendency to tell him how to feel and think about problems. Adults can also accept a child as a person who is capable of changing behavior and resist imposing adult solutions on the child's problems. When adults impose their solutions and deny the child the opportunity to work through his own solutions, Rogerians believe that the development of decision-making ability is severely hampered and that the child will be less likely to become a fully functioning person who trusts in his own judgments.

Helping a Child Become a Fully Functioning Person

Rogerian theorists maintain that it is possible for parents, teachers, and therapists to help another person become a more fully functioning person. Rogers (1957) lists several conditions that are necessary and sufficient for positive personality development and change.

Two People Must Be in Psychological Contact

Put succinctly, the adult and the child have to have a relationship. Rogers labels this

condition an assumption because a relationship is necessary before an adult can have any influence at all on the child's personality development.

Recognize a Child's State of Incongruence

There must be a discrepancy between the child's actual experience and the picture that the child has of himself. For example, Charles views himself as someone others like to play with. One day, however, two of his friends do not allow him to play with them at the playground. They chase Charles away from the sliding board. Being rejected by two friends is incongruent with Charles's view of himself.

Be a Sensitive Supportive Person to the Child

The adult does not pretend to feel a certain way, but is aware of and open to all feelings about a child. The adult does not deny feelings. In spite of basic respect for each child, Mrs. Morgan discovers that she has mixed feelings about their behavior. She realizes that she gets angry when Laurie hits other children, that she likes certain children more than others, and that she occasionally does not feel like listening to a child when she is extremely busy. She does not deny these feelings but accepts them as real. She is genuine, congruent, and integrated.

View the Child as a Separate Person and Allow His Feelings

Rogerians stress the need to accept the existence of all kinds of feelings in children, not just the friendly, cooperative feelings. This acceptance is signaled mainly through verbal and nonverbal expressions of support, warmth, and empathy (Coletta, 1977).

Mrs. Morgan, for example, realizes that Susan is jealous of all the attention being showered on her new baby brother. When Sue says, "I hate that baby! I wish he would go back to the hospital," Mrs. Morgan simply says, "You'd like to see Sam go back."

Try to Experience and Demonstrate an Accurate, Empathic Understanding of the Child's Experience

Two things are essential here. One, the adult has to understand the child's fear or rage or jealousy. The child's world and experience must be clearly understood by the adult without the adult getting caught up in the child's feeling. Second, the adult has to be able to communicate this understanding to the child and make the child feel understood. Unless an adult can communicate empathy through words or behavior, the helping process, according to Rogerians, cannot take place.

Rogerian Theory and Child Guidance

Sensitive, supportive adults who want to help children develop positive personality traits can look to Rogerian theory for guidance. Supportive adults accept themselves, accept children, and have the skills to communicate this acceptance to children.

Self-Acceptance

The first essential step in effective Rogerian guidance is *self-acceptance*. Rogerians believe that only after accepting himself as a real person with legitimate feelings can an adult accept a child's feelings as legitimate.

A lot of adults assume a role when they live or work with children. These adults tend to forget that they, too, are humans with feelings. They think that the ideal adult always likes children and never feels angry, or certainly never admits to such feelings. They expect themselves to be perfect and then they are puzzled, annoyed, and frustrated when confronted with feelings that do not fit their picture of the perfect parent, teacher, camp counselor, nurse, or other professional.

Acceptance of Children

Another step toward changing the patterns of the relationship with a child is to accept the child as a separate person with his own feelings (Mead, 1976). When the adult has and communicates an understanding of the child's feeling, the child can accept the feeling and use his experience as an accurate guide to behavior. The child is freed of the need to defend feelings and is, instead, helped by the adult to work through those feelings.

Adults in the guidance system should realize that their feelings toward children can and do vary. They will not feel the same way about all the children in a group, and their feelings about individuals in the group will vary from time to time.

Certain variables affect an adult's feelings toward a child (Mead, 1976). One of these is the child. Some children, like some adults, are more attractive, friendly, co-operative, and helpful than others. Another variable is current adult concerns. For example, when Mrs. Morgan realized that she was sick one afternoon, she found herself becoming more annoyed than she usually did with Donny's insistence on being the first to go outside. Events in the adult's world impinge on the adult's situation. Many parents who accept a young child's question-asking at home do not tolerate it in other situations, in church, for example.

Communicate Acceptance of Children

Central to the principle of adults changing how they interact with children is the ability to communicate feelings of acceptance or nonacceptance in a caring way. Adults in the guidance system, according to Rogerians, need to be taught how to listen effectively to children and how to express their own adult feelings in a nonhurtful manner. Gordon (1970, 1974) has put these Rogerian principles into action by creating specific programs designed to help adults interact more effectively with children.

PARENT EFFECTIVENESS TRAINING: A SPECIFIC ROGERIAN GUIDANCE PROGRAM

Parent Effectiveness Training, known widely as PET, is a program of child guidance based on Rogerian theory. It was begun in 1962 by Thomas Gordon, who had been trained as a Rogerian therapist. Gordon, in his clinical work with children and their families, found that many adults experiencing interpersonal problems with children were simply uninformed about more effective interpersonal skills. Gordon's objective in starting the PET program was to teach adults some of the skills used by professional Rogerian counselors. In PET, adults learn some of the skills deemed necessary and sufficient by Carl Rogers to effect a positive personality change.

The PET course is taught in a group setting. There are eight weekly sessions, each 3 hours long. The course is taught in a variety of community settings by instructors who have been trained by members of Gordon's Effectiveness Training Institute. PET is not therapy. It is a class through which adults learn a variety of ways to deal with adult-child problems. Gordon has also instituted a program of Teacher Effectiveness Training (TET) that incorporates most of the PET skills.

The fundamental Rogerian principle that people can change their methods of interacting with others is the backbone of PET. Gordon (1970) helps adults change ways of interacting by teaching the basics of what goes on in all relationships between two people and by teaching specific new interactional skills. Two of these skills, *active listening* and *I-messages,* are communication techniques. Another PET skill for demonstrating acceptance is the *no-lose* method of conflict resolution.

Skills Taught in PET

PET Skill: Active Listening

"Gee, Mom. I want to stay home from school like Joanne." (10-year-old Sue)
 "That stupid coach! I hate him!" (14-year-old Luke)
 "I don't want to play cards with Grandpa. He makes fun of me." (6-year-old Mark).

In each of these cases the child "owns" a problem. *Active listening* is a skill used by professional counselors and taught to adults who take the PET course. It is a way of encouraging children to solve their problems by themselves. In each incident the child needed to know that the adult recognized his feelings. Active listening is appropriate when the child owns the problem, when he has some need that is not being met.

An adult accomplishes a number of things by listening actively to children. Listening closely, carefully, and accurately allows an adult to discover what the child's message is. Active listening puts a Rogerian principle into action; by listening actively and nonjudgmentally, adults communicate recognition and acceptance of children and their feelings. Adults who listen actively and do not offer a quick solution also communicate trust in a child's ability to work through his own problem and to find a solution by himself.

When to Use Active Listening

Gordon (1970) believes that there are many times when children send us messages saying that all is not right in their world, that something is troubling them, that they "own a problem." At such times they need adults who can actively listen to these messages.

A child who is hurt wants the adult to understand that he is hurt. For example, Andy fell off his tricycle, scratched his knee, cried, and ran to his Dad.

Active listening response: "You've scraped your knee and I'll bet that hurts." (A nonactive listening response would be: "Stop the crying, Andy. You're not hurt that badly.")

A child who feels anxious, insecure or frightened also needs to have these feelings acknowledged. Jack began to cry when his mother left him at school for the first time.

Active listening response: "You don't like your mom to leave and you feel sad without her." (A nonactive listening response would be: "You know that your mother will be back," or "There really isn't anything to cry about.")

The nonactive listener has denied the child the right to feel a certain way. The adult who is an active listener has identified and acknowledged Jack's feelings, not denied them.

Sometimes, a child sends a "coded" message in the form of a seemingly straightforward question. Such a question usually hides certain feelings that need attention. Mike, for example, watched a news show about the spaceshuttle *Challenger* (Febru-

ary, 1986). He watched the ship explode, killing seven astronauts. He asked his mother, "Have you heard from Dave this week, Mom?" (Mike's older brother is a navy pilot.)

Active listening response: "Yes, Mike, I have. It was a terrible thing that happened with *Challenger*." (A nonactive listening response: "No, I haven't heard from him. Leave me alone now.")

The active listener has realized that Mike might be afraid of something. She has responded by actively listening for feelings and reflecting those feelings to Mike.

PET Skill: Sending I-Messages

Gordon (1970, 1974) believes that every member of the guidance system, adult as well as child, has a right to have needs met. There are times in the adult-child relationship when a child does something that annoys the adult because it interferes in some way with satisfaction of the adult's needs. For example, Tina, who was in charge of cleaning the paintbrushes, has left the brushes on the table instead of washing them. Mrs. Mrogan has a problem of being annoyed because of the messy

---

SPECIAL FOCUS: How to Listen Actively

Think about the last time you had a problem and confided in someone who really listened. They did not deny your problem or feelings. They did not judge you. They did not offer you a quick solution. They did listen and seemed to understand what you were feeling. Think about how you can show the same courtesy to children. When a child owns a problem, we adults often fail to listen at all. Instead, we immediately try to solve the problem for the child. Gordon (1970) suggests that active listening be used by adults who believe that children are capable of solving their own problems. Active listening requires that an adult listens to a child's feelings in a nonjudgmental way and be able to feed back the feelings accurately to the child.

How to Use Active Listening

Listen carefuly. Do not interrupt. Try to understand what the message means and what the child is feeling.

Example Charles has been rejected by some other children at the watertable this time. "Teacher, Jim and Sam won't let me play in the water. Make them let me play with the boats." Mrs. Morgan realizes that the content of this message is that Charles wants to play in the water. She also understands that Charles is feeling very angry with the other two boys.

Use your own words to let the child know that you understand how he is feeling. Feed back your understanding to the child for verification.

Mrs. Morgan: "You want to play with the boats and Jim and Sam told you to go away. That made you angry." Charles: (verifies the adult's understanding of his feelings) "Yeah, they said that I always splash the water on them when I play."

Suspend judgment. Avoid preaching, giving advice, or trying to persuade the child to feel differently. Merely feed back your perception of the child's feeling.

Mrs. Morgan: "You didn't know that the other boys get angry when you splash them with water."

Active listening, then, is effective when the listener really wants to hear the child's message, wants to help at that point in time, can accept the child's feelings (whatever these feelings are), trusts the child to work through the problem, and views the child as a separate person. Believing that a child is a separate person with a right to his own feelings is necessary before an adult can help a child (Gordon, 1970).

---

table and of having to clean the brushes by herself. How can Mrs. Morgan get Tina to consider the adult's needs? What communication technique is appropriate when the adult, and not the child, "owns a problem"?

Active listening is not appropriate in this case because it is not the child's problem. Nor is it appropriate to send demeaning messages. Mrs. Morgan is annoyed but resists her impulse to say, "You're so sloppy and thoughtless, Tina. You never help at cleanup time." This message would be accusatory, demeaning, and anger arousing.

I-messages, another specific communication skill taught to adults who take the

PET course, are used when the adult and not the child owns the problem. In general, I-messages should be simple statements of facts, should be adult-oriented, and should not accuse the child of creating the adult's feeling (Gordon, 1970).

SPECIAL FOCUS: How to Deliver an I-Message

1. Tell the child how you are feeling because of what he has done. Are you angry, frustrated, disappointed, frightened?

Mrs. Morgan: "Tina, I was angry this morning . . ."

2. Name the behavior that is a problem for you. Be specific. It is not fair to expect a child to guess what he did that seems to be a problem for you. Avoid accusing the child.

". . . when you left the paintbrushes on the table instead of washing them . . ."

3. Tell the child how his behavior tangibly affected you. Did it cost you money, waste your time, cost you effort? Specify the effect. This is different from naming the feeling.

". . . because I had to spend extra time of my own to clean them."

     Gordon believes that Mrs. Morgan's I-message to Tina is likely to effect a change in Tina's behavior for two reasons. First, Mrs. Morgan has been *self-responsible*, i.e., she has taken responsibility for her own feelings of frustration and for expressing her feelings to Tina. Second, Mrs. Morgan's I-message is nonjudgmental and has not demeaned and accused Tina.

    Practice this skill by writing your own I-message. Think about a time when a child did something that created a problem for you.

1. Name the specific behavior:

2. Say how you felt at the time:

3. Say how the child's behavior tangibly affected you:

Now put all this information together into an I-message.

PET Skill: No-Lose Method of Conflict Resolution

Mrs. Morgan has noticed that despite reasonable, clearly stated limits for cleanup time, children inevitably leave block accessories (small figures of people, animals, and transportation toys) on the floor in a heap. Conflict between adults and children is inevitable and should not be denied because conflict is not necessarily bad. There are times in any relationship when conflict arises simply because the needs of people in a relationship do not match. Gordon advises that adults accept conflict and learn how to deal with it productively. He advises that we avoid the following two ineffective methods for resolving conflict (Gordon, 1970; Mead, 1976).

I Win, You Lose Method   This is an ineffective way to try to resolve conflict. In it the adult wins and the child loses. If Mrs. Morgan had used this method, she would have used power assertion (chapter 5 gives a detailed description of power-assertive, negative discipline). She might have yelled at the children to place the toys on their assigned shelves and might have resolved this conflict by punishing the children harshly when they failed to pick up the small toys. In any case, she would have used power to resolve the conflict, something to which Gordon is adamantly opposed.

You Win, I Lose Method   This is also an ineffective way to try to resolve conflict. The child wins and the adult loses. Mrs. Morgan would be angry because of the untidy block corner but would avoid trying to reach a solution. The result would be a messy block corner, an adult who remained unhappy and angry, and children who learned that they do not have a responsibility to participate in routines.

The problem with these two methods is that many people view conflicts as battles that someone has to win and someone has to lose. To counter this idea, Gordon (1970) proposes a third method of resolving the inevitable conflict in a relationship. He calls it the "no-lose" method of conflict resolution and sees it as a good alternative to the ineffective methods just described.

No-Lose Method   Gordon considers the no-lose method of conflict resolution central to the PET program. This method of resolving conflicts avoids the use of power, so nobody wins or loses. The adult and child together work on a mutually agreeable solution to the problem. Because the child has had a part in choosing a solution, Gordon (1970) believes that he is likely to carry out the solution.

An adult who uses the no-lose method acknowledges that the child's needs are important and communicates trust in the child's ability to carry out decisions. Using this method, therefore, requires that adults truly accept the child's feelings and needs as valid and important. Using this method also requires that the adult be adept at active listening and sending I-messages.

SPECIAL FOCUS: How to Solve Conflicts by Using the "No-Lose" Method

Mrs. Morgan decided to try the no-lose method of resolving the conflict of the messy block corner. She had heard about the method at a workshop. She learned that it involves simple problem-solving and negotiation in which both parties participate. The steps that she learned were:

1. *Identify and define the conflict.* Mrs. Morgan brings up the problem at group time. She avoids using accusatory statements.

Mrs. Morgan: "We have a problem. Every day at cleanup time I get angry because the little block toys are not put on the right shelves. They get all mixed up and I have to spend a lot of time putting them away [this is an I-message]. What do you think we can do to fix this problem together?"

2. *Generate possible solutions.* Accept a variety of solutions. Do not evaluate solutions just now.

Tina: "We could cover the toys with a blanket."
    Mike: "You could pick a 'helper' to put the toys away."
    Charles: "At home, my Dad put some buckets in my room. My boats go in one, my cars and trucks go in one, and the animals go in one."

3. *The group then examines each idea.* Mrs. Morgan's group decides that covering the toys with a blanket probably is not the best thing to do and that picking a "helper" to do all the work is not fair to one person. The group agrees that having some plastic buckets for each accessory might work.

4. *Work out ways of implementing the solution.*

Mrs. Morgan: "I think that having the buckets will probably work, but how will you know which bucket to put the animals and people and cars in so that they don't get all mixed up in one bucket?"
    Tina: "I know! Let's do it like we do it in the art corner. Let's put pictures of things on the buckets."
    Mrs. Morgan: "That's a good idea, Tina. When you come to school tomorrow, one of your jobs will be to paste pictures on the buckets. We'll do that before you even begin to play in the block corner. Then we'll place the buckets in the corner of the block corner. Then we'll check to see how the buckets are working. Thank you for helping to figure out how to fix this problem."

5. *Follow up to evaluate how the solution has worked.* Mrs. Morgan observes the block corner cleanup for a few days and notices that most of the children put the toys in the appropriate buckets. She discusses this with the group and thanks them again for their help in making the solution work.

The important thing in this whole process is that Mrs. Morgan does not view this conflict as a power struggle but as a way for the group to work out a solution satisfactory to everyone. The result is a fairly tidy block corner, an adult whose need for help in cleaning up is met, and a group of children who know that their teacher accepts their feelings and trusts them to develop and carry out solutions to problems.

SUMMARY: KEY CONCEPTS IN THIS CHAPTER

1. *Rogerian theory* was developed by Carl Rogers, a counselor, teacher, and writer. Rogerian theory is the basis for child guidance techniques used by adults who agree with its ideas about personality change.

2. The concept of *self* is central in Rogerian theory. Rogerians also believe that peo-

ple are capable of conscious perception of experience, that perception of experience is private and subjective, that people have the capacity to develop to their fullest potential, and that humans have a need for positive regard from others.

3. Rogerian theorists maintain that it is possible for adults to help children become more *fully functioning persons,* persons open to all feelings, who perceive reality accurately, and who trust in their own judgment. Rogers (1957) discusses six conditions in a helping relationship that are both *necessary* and *sufficient* for positive personality change and development.

4. Thomas Gordon (1970) has put these Rogerian principles into action by creating a program, PET, designed to help adults to interact more effectively with children.

5. PET teaches about the importance of accepting oneself and the child in the adult-child relationship. PET also teaches about the need to demonstrate this acceptance to the child through the communication techniques of *active listening* and *I-messages.* Acceptance can also be demonstrated through the use of the *no-lose* method of conflict resolution.

OBSERVE: CHILD GUIDANCE IN ACTION

Observe an adult who "owns a problem," i.e., is clearly annoyed with something a child is doing or has done. Pay special attention to what the adults says to the child. Use the information from this chapter to determine whether this adult has used an I-message with the child. Use the following format to record your observation. Observe at a child development center, in a grocery store, at a restaurant, in a laundromat, or in some other appropriate setting.

Date: _____

Time: _____

Child's first name: _____

Child's age: _____

Setting: _____

Your name: _____

EPISODE 1
Briefly describe the problem that the adult seemed to be having with the child.

Write as precisely as possible what the adult said to the child.

Answer the following questions and use them to decide whether the adult statement was an I-message.

☐ Did the adult state the child's *behavior?* _____

☐ Did the adult state his own *feelings?* _____

☐ Did the adult describe the *tangible effects* of the child's behavior on the adult? _____

Be prepared to discuss your observation with your classmates.

REFERENCES

COLLETTA, A.J. (1977). *Working together: A guide to parent involvement.* Atlanta: Humanics.

GORDON, T. (1970). *Parent effectiveness training.* New York: Peter H. Wyden.

GORDON, T. (1974). *Teacher effectiveness training.* New York: David McKay.

MEAD, D.E. (1976). *Six approaches to child rearing.* Provo, UT: Brigham Young University Press.

ROGERS, C. (1957). The necessary and sufficient condition of therapeutic personality change. *Journal of Consulting Psychology, 21,* 95–103.

ROGERS, C. (1961). *On becoming a person.* Boston: Houghton-Mifflin.

SHULTZ, D. (1976). *Theories of personality.* Monterey, CA: Brooks/Cole.

10

The Behavioral
Approach
To Child Guidance

Chapter Overview

After reading and studying this chapter, you will be able to:

☐ *List and explain* the major principles of behavioral theory.

☐ *Identify* major theorists in behavioral theory and *explain* the view of each on how learning takes place.

☐ *Describe* different approaches to behavior modification.

☐ *List and give examples* of positive discipline techniques used by behaviorists to change behavior.

☐ *Analyze* a situation calling for discipline and determine which positive discipline technique(s) would be most appropriate.

MAJOR PRINCIPLES OF BEHAVIORAL THEORY

Principle #1: All of development occurs through learning from the environment. This is the principle that unites all of the branches of behaviorism. The major belief common to all learning theorists is that human behavior is learned (Cairns, 1983; Gorer, 1955; Langer, 1969). Learning theorists believe that children's behavior is gradually molded or "shaped" as they interact with their environment. For example, behaviorists believe that a child who is afraid of dogs has *learned* to fear dogs through specific fear-inducing interactions with her environment. Similarly, a child who is aggressive has *learned* how to be aggressive through specific interactions with other people. Learning, then, is the principle or tenet around which behavioral theory is organized (Fogel, 1984).

Principle #2: Behaviorists or learning theorists do not believe in "stages" of development. Recall from your basic child development courses that developmental theorists like Jean Piaget (1952, 1970, 1983) view development as a series of phases or stages, each stage being qualitatively different from the one that came before or after. Developmentalists also believe that children are capable of learning only what their current developmental level or stage will allow them to learn.

Contrast this view with the view of a learning theorist. In learning theory, development is viewed not as a series of phases or stages but as a gradual accumulation of knowledge. Behaviorists believe that children slowly accumulate or acquire (i.e., learn) ways of responding. They believe that the principles of learning are universal and that factors like age or developmental level are irrelevant. Principles of learning, behaviorists believe, are applicable to a 2-year-old human, a 40-year-old human, a dog, or a rat.

Principle #3: Behavior can be changed if a child's environment is changed (Mead, 1976). Behaviorists maintain that the most effective way to change or modify a child's behavior is to alter the child's environment. Behaviorists use a variety of techniques in modifying a child's environment, but the basic idea is to change the way that people in the environment respond to the child's behavior.

Example Jane's parents have noticed that Jane has begun to use language they consider obscene. At first they scold her for using these words, and she then seems to use them even more frequently. Puzzled, they ask their friends how they have handled this "problem." "Well, what we found was that we had to change before our son cut out that way of talking. Yelling at him seemed to make the cursing actually worse. One thing that did work was to tell Pete that some words were better to use when we want to say how we feel and that we wanted him to use better words. Some words are better left unsaid in certain situations. We named the obscene words. Another thing we did was to stop giving Pete attention when he used foul language and to talk to him when he used more acceptable words. It took a couple of weeks but gradually the obscene words were used less often."

BEHAVIORAL THEORY: FROM CLASSICAL CONDITIONING TO SOCIAL LEARNING THEORY

Watson: Classical Conditioning

John Watson (1878–1957) is credited as one of the first major experimental child psychologists. Early in his career Watson was a researcher in physiological psychology and carried out research with animals. Believing that techniques used with animals could also be used with humans, Watson carried out a series of experimental studies with newborn humans.

In their studies of human infants Watson and his associates investigated emotional development. They wanted to demonstrate that a child's emotions and personality are "shaped" by the environment through conditioning. They hoped to show that emotions could be learned through *classical conditioning*. From 1917 to 1920 Watson carried out a series of studies at Johns Hopkins University. You have probably read about the most famous of these in your basic psychology textbook. It is Watson and Rayner's (1920) study of aversive conditioning with Albert, a 9-month-old human infant. The study is usually used to illustrate how children can *learn* responses like fear through classical conditioning.

Albert, Watson noticed, had an emotional reaction to a sudden loud noise created by a steel bar. Albert did not have an emotional response to a white rat or a rabbit. Watson's goal was to find out whether he could condition Albert or teach him to fear the rabbit. He did this by showing the animal to Albert and at the same time making a loud noise with the steel bar. This pairing of the animal with the feared loud noise took place seven times. Albert, afraid of the loud noise, also learned to fear the animal. Watson and Rayner claimed success in classically conditioning an emotional response in a human infant.

Watson's proposal that the conditioned response was the key to understanding behavior was based on this single study with one subject. His work generated many other research studies, but lately his "Little Albert" study has been heavily criticized (Harris, 1980).

Watson's teaching and research stopped abruptly in 1920. Cairns (1983) maintains that Watson's views became more extreme with the passage of time. All behaviorists believe that the environment has a large impact on development, but Watson's view was one of extreme environmentalism. He believed, for example, that rearing children was simply a matter of conditioning "habits."

Watson wrote a bestselling book, *Psychological Care of the Infant and Child,* and many articles for magazines in the 1920s and 1930s. His writing influenced child-rearing during that time. He probably induced a lot of stress and guilt in parents by telling them that the fate of their children was totally in their hands (Stevenson, 1983). He gave parents "rules" for childrearing. For example, he advised against too much "mother love" and suggested that parents be cool and aloof with their children, refraining from displays of affection. He believed that children who received affection would become too dependent on attention from others.

Watson's advice, in retrospect, seems ludicrous, especially when one considers research showing the need for lots of contact between babies and adult caregivers for healthy development. Watson, however, wrote his articles long before this research was done, and parents during the 1920s and 1930s had no way of knowing how inaccurate Watson was.

Skinner: Operant Conditioning

B.F. Skinner (b. 1904), who carried on the work initiated by Watson, believes in a radical form of behaviorism. Skinner's major concern is with changing or modifying behavior rather than with thoughts or feelings. Skinner is perhaps best known for his reliance on the principles of *operant conditioning* to change behavior.

Stevenson (1983) notes that Skinner carried reinforcement theory to an extreme. Much of his time has been spent in the study of those contingencies between a child's response and its reinforcement that either weaken a behavior or make it stronger. He wanted to know what schedule for giving reinforcement would most effectively weaken, strengthen, or maintain a given response. He concluded that an organism's behavior remains stable if the proper schedule of reinforcement has been used but that new behavior will result from withholding reinforcement or reinforcing different responses.

Skinner's early work on operant conditioning was with caged rats, but the principles of reinforcement derived from this work were eventually applied to children and other people. Bijou and Baer (1961), for example, analyzed child development and behavior in a Skinnerian framework. They, like Skinner, did not consider a child's motives or feelings.

Skinner's principles of reinforcement have been used by teachers, hospital personnel, and others who want to regulate someone's behavior. Some researchers now believe that Skinner's operant conditioning will have its greatest impact in applied settings like schools and hospitals in the form of *behavior modification* (see the Special Focus box, "Steps in Using the Reinforcement Approach to Behavior Modification"). Skinner's work has been heavily criticized. For example, Chomsky (1959) argues vigorously that Skinner's view that language develops through reinforcement is inaccurate.

Bandura: Social Learning Theory

Social Learning Theory (SLT) is one branch of general learning theory. A major social learning theorist is Albert Bandura. This section focuses on Bandura's view of social learning theory (1977) and highlights differences between the social learning theorists's view and Skinner's version of how learning takes place. Social learning theorists emphasize the social nature of learning and acknowledge that cognitive factors affect learning and that the concept of reinforcement must be reexamined.

Modeling

Like all learning theorists, social learning theorists acknowledge that learning is a significant part of development, but they also believe that learning takes place in a *social* setting. They remind us that children are social beings and are heavily influenced by observing the behavior of other people, a concept that Skinnerians ignored.

A central component in social learning theory is *modeling* or *observational learning*. Bandura and Walters (1963) demonstrated that children could learn or acquire new behavior by observing another person performing the behavior and that the child need not perform the behavior for learning to occur.

Children can learn many new skills by observing the behavior of others: things as simple as preference for one vegetable over another, facial expressions, or table manners. They can learn how to hurt others by watching television heroes fighting,

Reproducing a behavior learned through observational learning.

how to treat others with dignity, how to share, or how to be selfish. We often think about actually watching a model—a real person who is physically present. However, children can also learn from models on television, in video games, in books (Maccoby & Martin, 1983; Stevenson, 1983).

Cognitive Processes in Observational Learning

Certain cognitive factors affect observational learning. Observational learning takes place by symbolic processes within the child. It involves several factors:

1. *attentional factors*—whether the child can discriminate and interpret the event.
2. *retentional factors* — whether the child can remember the event.
3. *reproductive factors* — whether the child can reenact the event.
4. *motivational factors*—whether the child wants to learn the material (Bandura, 1969; Cairns, 1983; White, 1970).

A child, then, does not observe somebody doing something and automatically imitate the action. Whether she learns the material depends on a variety of other factors.

Role of Reinforcement in Observational Learning

The major difference between Skinner's learning and Bandura's social learning theories is their view on reinforcement. Skinnerians maintain that reinforcement is

SPECIAL FOCUS: Which Models Will Children Imitate?

Children become increasingly accurate in their ability to imitate models as they grow older (Yando, Seitz, & Zigler, 1978). As they get older, children observe many models of how to do things and how to behave, but they do not imitate all of them. Children seem to be fairly selective in who or what they imitate. Several factors account for their choices (Maccoby & Martin, 1983).

Children imitate models who are nurturant, powerful or prestigious, and skillful when compared with the child's level of skill. Children have contact with adults who possess these characteristics. Their parent(s) are powerful in their ability to control resources. Adults are nurturant and are skillful in doing things that a child must learn to do—eating with utensils, writing, reading, using money. Other adults may also be viewed as nurturant, powerful, and skillful and therefore be imitated. Behaviors modeled are frequently in the best interest of a child—how to swim, how to negotiate a point in a discussion, how to organize things—but some behaviors are *not* in her best interest. While a child can learn from an admired sports figure that exercise and a sensible diet are good for her, for example, she can also observe a sports figure she admires using some harmful substance like chewing tobacco or steroids. Children imitate prestigious, skillful models, but the behavior modeled is not always in the best interest of a child or adolescent.

Children imitate a prototype of behavior after observing several models. Perry and Bussey (1979) detected an important phenomenon in modeling. They found that children often do not imitate just one model but seem to observe a large number of models performing an action and then build a *prototype,* a composite of the behavior of the group. Children seemed, in this work on sex-typed behavior, to infer from a group of models, rather than just their parent, which sex-typed behavior they considered appropriate. Maccoby and Martin (1983) suggest that a child might then observe another model, say a parent or someone on television, and imitate the new model only if the model's behavior "matches" the child's prototype.

Example Joseph observes lots of male models in real life and on film and develops a prototype of "how males act with babies"—they hold them and smile. They seem to like playing with babies. He imitates male models who hold babies and like to take care of them. He then observes his friend's father, who refuses to hold a new baby. Joseph does *not* imitate this model because the model does not fit his prototype.

Children imitate the behavior of a model if value is attached to the behavior. A child's ego ideal is an important determinant of what she imitates. Children have aspirations, and their aspirations affect the models they choose to imitate. One child might aspire to be a concert violinist. She goes to concerts with her mom and dad, takes lessons, and observes the practice time spent by a friend of the family who is a concert violinist. She observes lots of violinists and builds a prototype of models who practice a lot. She imitates this behavior because the models are similar to her ego ideal, i.e., what she wants to be.

necessary for learning, while social learning theorists emphasize that children do not have to be reinforced for learning to occur. A social learning theorist would argue that a child can learn new behavior just by watching someone else. The person observed frequently has little or no contact with the child and therefore cannot deliver reinforcement (Maccoby & Martin, 1983).

Example   Cheryl watched an adult volleyball player spike the ball when near the net. Cheryl learned, or acquired, the new behavior simply by observing the model. She did not need to be reinforced to learn how to spike. She did have to watch the player, remember the action, and store it in her memory.

What, then, is the role of reinforcement in observational learning? If reinforcement is not needed to learn a behavior, is it necessary at all? Social learning theorists would reply, "Yes, reinforcement definitely plays a part in the learning process." Once you've learned *how* to do something by watching someone or reading about it, then reinforcement enters the picture. Whether you actually imitate or produce the behavior depends on how you look at the consequences of that activity for the person you observed. Whether you imitate that behavior also depends on how you view possible consequences for yourself if you perform the behavior.

Example   Cheryl observed that the crowd at the volleyball game cheered for the adult who spiked the ball. The player herself gave a cheer and jumped up with her arms raised in delight. Cheryl thought to herself, "H-m-m, that player was cheered. People like what she did. Maybe I'll get cheered too if I try spiking sometime."

Social learning theorists would predict that Cheryl was highly likely to imitate the spiking action that she learned through observation because she perceived positive consequences for the person observed and foresaw similar consequences for herself (Bandura, 1977).

BEHAVIOR MODIFICATION

Behavior modification is a technology. It involves altering environmental events so that behavior can be changed. Behaviorists believe that if they change the way the environment responds the child will behave acceptably and not unacceptably (Franklin & Biber, 1977; Redd & Sleator, 1978; Stevenson, 1983).

Programs reflecting a behaviorist perspective emphasize behavioral change, or behavior modification. A person who develops a behavior modification program believes that it is not necessary and is even irrelevant to focus on a child's developmental level when trying to change a behavior. Instead, the keys to behavioral change are the principles of learning—the laws of classical and operant conditioning (Franklin & Biber, 1977).

The aim of a behavior modification program is to achieve measurable changes in observable behavior. Behaviorists believe that the most efficient way to change behavior is through a systematic planned administration of reinforcement on a *contingency basis.*

Example   Jim is observed to hit other children. The aim of a behavior modification expert is to decrease the hitting (observable behavior) by 90 percent (the measurable change). Jim is reinforced whenever he works cooperatively with other children. This reward is contingent on Jim's showing cooperative behavior. He is not reinforced when he hits. The behavior modificationist believes that this program will gradually shape Jim's behavior.

Professionals have been using behavior modification and behavior therapy for several decades. For example, Mary Cover Jones (1924a, 1924b) used conditioning to reduce fear in children. Similarly, children with *enuresis* (bedwetting) were treated successfully with conditioning procedures (Mowrer & Mowrer, 1938). Behavior modification has been extremely popular in the past 20 years. It has been widely used in schools, hospitals, and institutions to change everyday behaviors.

Different Approaches to Behavior Modification

Behavior modification usually conjures up images of an adult reinforcing and punishing a child. This is Skinner's reinforcement approach, but it is only one of the many approaches to behavior modification. Others include *modeling, imagery, cognitive,* and *aversive* approaches (Stevenson, 1983).

Modeling Approach to Behavior Modification

Example   Suppose that Josey is afraid of mice. A behavioral therapist is called in to help her and has Josey watch other children play fearlessly with a pet mouse. They pet the mouse, change its food while it is in the cage, and let the animal run up and down their arms. Josey observes this for several days, finally begins to relax, and eventually asks if she can change the mouse's water while another child holds the mouse.

This therapist has used modeling to decrease a child's fear (Bandura, Grusec, & Menlove, 1967). Modeling can also be used when children avoid certain situations, e.g., calling someone on the phone. The child can observe another child making a telephone call without fear.

Cognitive and Imagery Approaches to Behavior Modification

Children, like adults, find themselves in situations that make them anxious—"show and tell" time at school, having to order something in a restaurant, performing at an athletic event, taking a test.

Example   Mr. Rodrigo noticed that 6-year-old Jenny seemed quieter than usual one morning, the day she was to take a battery of standardized tests. She told him she "was scared." He used a behavior modification technique, the imagery approach, when he encouraged her to imagine being in the testing room, holding her pencil, and filling in the little circles. He reminded her that her class had practiced for this test. She imagined herself looking at pictures, thinking about good answers, and then marking the paper.

Other therapists use the cognitive approach to behavior modification. The focus here is on changing a child's thinking about a situation.

Example   Susan, scheduled to give her first speech on Tuesday, asks her mom on Monday night if she can skip school on Tuesday. Susan admits to some anxiety and is encouraged by her mom to say positive things about herself and her speech: "My speech is written and it is good. I have practiced it three times."

Aversive Approach to Behavior Modification

Aversive therapy is used as a "last resort," when other therapy has failed to change a child's behavior and when the child is clearly in danger of hurting herself. Self-mutilation by children has been successfully treated by using aversive therapy (Lovaas, Freitag, Gold, and Kassorla, 1965).

Reinforcement Approach to Behavior Modification

This is probably the best known of the behavior modification approaches. Skinner and his followers formulated general principles of behavioral change and showed how to apply these relatively simple principles to a variety of behavioral problems.

SPECIAL FOCUS: Steps in Using the Reinforcement Approach to Behavior Modification

A behavior therapist follows specific steps in altering a child's environment:

1. *Assess the problem.* Determine conditions associated with a problem behavior by carefully observing the social environment. For example, a behavioral therapist is consulted by Ms. Riley about Steven's disruptive behavior at group times. The therapist observes that Steven is indeed disruptive but also observes that Ms. Riley gives Steven lots of attention after Steven has been disruptive. She is reinforcing the disruptive behavior. The therapist also notes that there are several times during the day when Steven works quietly with others but that nobody ever pays attention to him then.

2. *Choose desired (target) behaviors.* After observing the undesirable behavior of the child and the adult's behavior or classroom conditions fostering it, the therapist made recommendations on how to alter the environment. She specified target behaviors (shouting and running away) that needed to be changed and then made the recommendations.

3. *Determine the reinforcer.* Ms. Riley was asked to reinforce Steven's positive behaviors (remaining with the group) but first had to determine the type of reinforcer that might be valuable to Steven. She realized that the reinforcer had to have value to Steven.

4. *Specify short-term behavioral goals.* "Decreasing disruptive behavior" is a big goal, so the therapist recommended that it be broken into smaller steps. Instead of requiring Steven to sit for the entire group time before receiving a reward, Ms. Riley or the aide reinforced Steven after brief periods during the story.

5. *Monitor constantly and allow adequate rehearsal and practice.* Monitoring requires continuing observation. The undesirable behavior should gradually drop out if the program is a good one. If the behavior does not drop out, then the program should be examined and changed.

BEHAVIORISTS USE POSITIVE DISCIPLINE TECHNIQUES

Responsible adults who believe in the behavioral approach to child guidance use a variety of positive techniques to change a child's behavior. Some of these have already been discussed and will only be listed here. Others will be described in somewhat more detail.

Modeling

(See previous discussion in this chapter.)

Positive Reinforcement

Example   When Marie used the sliding board correctly, Mrs. Whitney said, "You came down the slide just right!"

Marie's brother said, "Hey, thanks for helping me move the sprinkler, Marie!"

Marie's mother had a small chart on the refrigerator. Marie was to brush her teeth every morning. When she brushed her teeth, Marie was allowed to paste a sticker on the chart. She got to exchange a filled chart at the end of the week for a trip to the planetarium.

Marie's brother, teacher, and mother all used positive reinforcement. A *positive reinforcer* is something that increases the strength of a response, the probability that a response will be given or given more frequently. Stevenson (1983) notes that almost anything can serve as reinforcement for the human child. A "thank you," a smile, a pat on the back, a raisin, a sticker on a chart, a trip to the zoo are but a few examples.

Marie's mother used a *token reinforcement* when she gave Marie a sticker for toothbrushing. Many classrooms are token economies, i.e., the adults make a deliberate attempt to modify the children's behavior by using tokens as positive reinforcement. The tokens (stickers, smiley faces, plastic chips) are supposed to "stand for" or symbolically represent the reinforcer. Therefore, tokens are the means to an end. Tokens are not meant to be an end in themselves. Adults who realize that tokens are merely gimmicks use tokens responsibly. They arrange the environment so that a child receives positive reinforcement for appropriate behavior.

Extinction

Example   Linda has been speaking in a whining voice, and this annoys her uncle. He says that he is not going to pay attention to Linda when she whines, so he completely ignores her when she whines. In the past her uncle has reinforced Linda's whining by scolding, looking at her, or giving her what she wanted so that she would be quiet.

An adult who uses *extinction* refuses to reinforce (ignores) a response (whining, in this case) so that the child gives that response less frequently (Birnbauer,

SPECIAL FOCUS: Positive Reinforcement: Can a Child Get Too Much of a Good Thing?

Example   Mary is a student who enthusiastically applies her knowledge of child development when she takes a summer job as a camp counselor. As she works with her group of 10-year-olds, phrases like "Good job!" "You're really good at that!" "Super work!" "You're so helpful!" frequently punctuate her interaction with the children. She has been noticing lately, however, that this praise does not seem to be working as well as it did early in the summer. Why has this happened?

Adaptation Level

Mary uses encouragement or praise, which is a good technique, but does not realize that children seem to adapt to a particular level of praise (Maccoby & Martin, 1983). Her campers become so accustomed to her lavish praise that she finds herself having to use even more. Praise should not be used indiscriminately. Instead, it should be used when appropriate and possibly even sparingly so that a word of praise carries real meaning.

The same advice applies to rewards (Maccoby & Martin, 1983). Rewards, like M & Ms, that are given too frequently lose their reward value. Children expect to receive the reward and if it is not offered might think they are being punished. Many adults have been trapped into a cycle of having to escalate the value of treats so that children still view the treat as a reward. What started out as a legitimate reward, e.g., a trip to McDonald's for practicing a musical instrument, can become, in an adult's eyes, a bribe.

Potential Negative Motivational Effect of Rewards

Example   Joanna is in fourth grade and is excited about participating in gymnastics. Her mother rewards Joanna for going to practice. Joanna then stubbornly refuses to participate. What went wrong?

Positive reinforcement, praise or rewards, is not inherently bad. On the contrary, positive reinforcement is an appropriate technique. In cases like Joanna's, however, positive reinforcement can actually "backfire" and lose its effectiveness as a motivator. Joanna is at first spontaneously interested in gymnastics, and explicitly rewarding her for this activity decreases her interest (Lepper & Greene, 1979). Joanna is motivated internally and she perceives her mother's "reward" as an attempt to control her. Her waning interest is really resistance to external control (Maccoby & Martin, 1983).

Praise and rewards are appropriate and positive techniques. If overused or used inappropriately they can be counterproductive and have negative side effects.

1978). It is unwise, however, to ignore a child when she is hurting herself, others, or animals or when she is disturbing someone.

Time Out

Example   "That's a hit, Tom. Time out." Tom's coach sends Tom out of the game when he punches a friend. Tom sits in a special time out spot in the stands for 5 minutes.

Time out occurs when a child is taken out of a situation because he acts inappropriately (hitting a teammate) and is placed where he will not be reinforced for the behavior. This technique is described more fully in chapter 5.

Response Cost

Example Roger's mother uses a token reinforcement system to help him remember to put his dirty clothes in the clothes hamper. Each night, if he deposits his clothes in the hamper, he gets to put a star on his "hamper chart." He receives a star for Monday, Tuesday, and Wednesday. On Thursday he leaves his clothes on the floor. He loses a star from the chart.

Roger's mother combines the token reinforcement system with a technique known as *response cost*. She imposes a "fine" (losing a star) when Roger behaves in an inappropriate way (leaves clothes on the floor).

DRO: Differential Reinforcement of Other Behavior

Linda's uncle uses extinction and Tom's coach uses response cost responsibly and appropriately and, as a result, Linda whines and Tom hits his teammates less frequently. The adults should combine these techniques with prompting and reinforcement of other more acceptable behavior that is incompatible with the unacceptable behavior. It is not enough to ignore Linda when she whines. She must be prompted to use a better way of talking and then should be reinforced for using this "other" behavior as well as ignored for whining. Likewise, Tom should be told that he is expected to play cooperatively and then should be reinforced for this behavior that is incompatible with hitting. DRO is viewed as a way to describe and reinforce an acceptable behavior to a child even as you try to weaken a less acceptable behavior through extinction or response cost.

PATTERSON'S PROGRAM: A BEHAVIORAL
CHILD GUIDANCE PROGRAM

Like Adlerians and Rogerians, many behaviorists have developed child guidance programs based on the main ideas of their theory. Gerald Patterson is a behaviorist — a social learning theorist — who has developed a program to teach adults about basic concepts of the technology of behavioral change. He describes his program in two books. *Living with Children* (1977) is a primer that outlines the theory. It is easy to read and use. *Families* (1975) is a slightly longer, more detailed presentation that includes more explanatory material.

Patterson's program clearly illustrates principles of the behavioral approach to child guidance. It demonstrates how behavior therapy can change a child's behavior

---

SPECIAL FOCUS: Do Behaviorists Believe in Using Punishment?

Yes. Behaviorists believe that punishment is an effective technique for weakening behavior but that it is only one of several behavior management procedures (Richards & Siegel, 1978). Responsible behavior therapists realize, however, that hurtful punishment is unethical and ineffective. They point to a negative side effect of harsh punishment as an argument against its use: a child will avoid an adult who punishes harshly.

Richards and Siegel suggest some cautions to adults who believe in using punishment. These cautions alert adults that they can use positive discipline techniques even when they think that punishment seems warranted.

Do not use punishment to teach a new behavior. Punishment is not very useful for teaching something new. A better approach is to teach a new behavior by modeling or role playing.

Avoid hurtful punishment. Some forms of punishment hurt children—hitting, sarcasm, ridicule, isolation in frightening places, threats. Punishment, however, is not automatically negative and harsh. Other nonhurtful, positive forms of punishment are used every day by loving, humane, sensible adults. For example, time out, response cost, and extinction are positive forms of punishment if they are not overused and if they are applied well.

Use punishment sparingly. Do not overuse punishment and always prompt an alternative, more acceptable behavior. Mild, nonhurtful punishment is more effective if the child is also provided with an alternative behavior that will earn positive reinforcement.

---

without hurtful punishment. Patterson also acknowledges that a child is embedded in a family group and that a behavioral program will be more effective if adults modify their own behavior as well as the child's behavior. Patterson's program uses extinction, time out, and response cost as the major techniques for changing children's behavior.

SUMMARY: KEY CONCEPTS IN THIS CHAPTER

1. Behaviorist theory is undergirded by principles common to all branches of behaviorism.

2. Behavioral theory has evolved from Watson's classical conditioning model to Skinner's reliance on principles of operant conditioning to Bandura's social learning theory. Recent developments in social learning theory place emphasis on cognitive processes and have questioned the role of reinforcement in learning.

3. Behavior modification involves altering environmental events so that behavior

may be changed. There are several different approaches to behavior modification.

4. Responsible adults who believe in the behavioral approach to child guidance use a variety of positive techniques to change a child's behavior.

5. Patterson's program is an example of responsible behavior modification. It shows how behavior can be changed without the use of hurtful punishment and also acknowledges the child's embeddedness in a family system.

OBSERVE: CHILD GUIDANCE IN ACTION

In this observation you will be looking for examples of behavior a child has learned through *observational learning*. One of the best places to find such examples is the housekeeping corner or block corner in an early childhood center. There you will watch children taking on roles and performing activities that they learned by observing other people, e.g., making a birthday cake, loading asphalt into a dump truck, shaving face or legs with "pretend" shaving cream, washing a baby (doll), ordering food in a restaurant, cooking a meal. Use the following format to record your observation.

Date: _____

Time: _____

Child's name: _____

Setting: _____

Your name: _____

EPISODE 1

Describe a child's actions which indicate that observational learning has taken place.

Example Kathy, Todd, and Lisa were in the housekeeping corner where shaving equipment has been set out (no razor blades!). Todd had slathered real shave cream onto his face, spread it around, and then used the shaver to scrape away "whiskers." Kathy picked up the shaving cream can, sat on a chair and puffed cream onto her *leg*. The teacher had started to walk away but did a "double take" when she saw what Kathy was doing. "Kathy, why are you doing that?" "I'm shaving my legs. My mom shaves her legs, too."

YOUR EXAMPLE:

EPISODES 2, 3, 4 **Use the same format.**

Share your observation with your class.

REFERENCES

BANDURA, A. (1969). *Principles of behavior modification.* New York: Holt, Rinehart & Winston.

BANDURA, A. (1977). *Social learning theory.* Englewood Cliffs, NJ: Prentice-Hall.

BANDURA, A., GRUSEC, J.E., & MENLOVE, F.L. (1967). Vicarious extinction of avoidance behavior. *Journal of Personality and Social Psychology, 5,* 16–23.

BANDURA, A., & WALTERS, R.H. (1963). *Social learning and personality development.* New York: Holt, Rinehart & Winston.

BIJOU, S.W., & BAER, D.M. (1961). *Child development: A systematic and empirical theory,* Vol. 1. New York: Appleton-Century-Crofts.

BIRNBAUER, J.S. (1978). Some guides to designing behavioral programs. In D. Marholin (Ed.), *Child behavior therapy.* New York: Gardner Press.

CAIRNS, R.B. (1983). The emergence of developmental psychology. In P. Mussen (Ed.), *Handbook of child psychology,* Vol. 1. New York: Wiley.

CHOMSKY, N. (1959). Review of Skinner's *Verbal behavior. Language, 35,* 26–58.

FOGEL, A. (1984). *Infancy.* St. Paul: West.

FRANKLIN, M.B., & BIBER, B. (1977). Psychological perspectives and early childhood education: Some relations between theory and practice. In L.G. Katz (Ed.), *Current topics in early childhood education,* Vol. 1. Norwood, NJ: Ablex.

GORER, G. (1955). Theoretical approaches—1941. In M. Mead & M. Wolfenstein (Eds.), *Children in contemporary cultures.* Chicago: University of Chicago Press.

HARRIS, B. (1980). *John Watson as film producer and developmental psychologist.* Paper presented at the meeting of the American Psychological Association, Montreal.

JONES, M.C. (1924a). The elimination of children's fears. *Journal of Experimental Psychology, 7,* 382–390.

JONES, M.C. (1924b). A laboratory study of fear: The case of Peter. *Pedagogical Seminary, 31,* 308–315.

LANGER, J. (1969). *Theories of development.* New York: Holt, Rinehart & Winston.

LEPPER, M.R., & GREENE, D. (Eds.). (1979). *The hidden costs of reward: New perspectives on the psychology of human motivation.* Hillsdale, NJ: Erlbaum.

LOVAAS, O.I., FREITAG, G., GOLD, V.J., & KASSORLA, I.C. (1965). Experimental studies in childhood schizophrenia: Analysis of self-destructive behavior. *Journal of Experimental Child Psychology, 2,* 67–84.

MACCOBY, E.E., & MARTIN, J.A. (1983). Socialization in the context of the family: Parent-child interaction. In P. Mussen (Ed.), *Handbook of child psychology,* Vol. 4. New York: Wiley.

MEAD, D.E. (1976). *Six approaches to child rearing.* Provo, UT: Brigham Young University Press.

MOWRER, O.H., & MOWRER, W.N. (1938) Enuresis: A method for its study and treatment. *American Journal of Orthopsychiatry, 8,* 436–459.

PATTERSON, G.R. (1975). *Families.* Champaign, IL: Research Press.

PATTERSON, G.R. (1977). *Living with children* (rev. ed.). Champaign, IL: Research Press.

PERRY, D.G., & BUSSEY, K. (1979). The social learning theory of sex differences: Imitation is alive and well. *Journal of Personality and Social Psychology, 37,* 1699–1712.

PIAGET, J. (1952). *The origins of intelligence in children.* New York: International Universities Press.

PIAGET, J. (1970). Piaget's theory. In P. Mussen (Ed.), *Carmichael's manual of child psychology,* Vol. 1. New York: Wiley.

PIAGET, J. (1983). Piaget's theory. In P. Mussen (Ed.), *Handbook of child psychology*, Vol. 1. New York: Wiley.

REDD, W.H., & SLEATOR, W.S. (1978).The theoretical foundations of behavior modification. In D. Marholin (Ed.), *Child behavior therapy*. New York: Gardner.

RICHARDS, C.S., & SIEGEL, L.J. (1978). Behavioral treatment of anxiety states. In D. Marholin (Ed.), *Child behavior therapy*. New York: Gardner.

SKINNER, B.F. (1953). *Science and human behavior.* New York: Macmillan.

STEVENSON, H. (1983). How children learn: The quest for a theory. In P. Mussen (Ed.), *Handbook of child psychology*, Vol. 1. New York: Wiley.

WATSON, J.B. (1928). *Psychological care of the infant and child.* New York: Norton.

WATSON, J.B. (1958). *Behaviorism* (rev.). Chicago: University of Chicago Press.

WATSON, J.B., & RAYNER, R. (1920). Conditioned emotional reactions. *Journal of Experimental Psychology, 3*, 1–4.

WHITE, S.H. (1970). Learning theory tradition and child psychology. In P. Mussen (Ed.), *Carmichael's manual of child psychology*, Vol. 1. New York: Wiley.

YANDO, R., SEITZ, V., & ZIGLER, E. (1978). *Imitation: A developmental perspective.* Hillsdale, NJ: Erlbaum.

11

The Adlerian Approach
to Child Guidance

Chapter Overview

After reading and studying this chapter, you will be able to:

☐ *Identify and discuss* three concepts basic to Adlerian theory.

☐ *List* the four mistaken goals that some children have about how to fit into a group.

☐ *Describe,* for each mistaken goal, the child's faulty perception, what the child does, the adult's typical feeling and reaction, and a better approach for adults to take.

☐ *Explain* the Adlerian view on both hurtful and positive forms of discipline.

☐ *Describe* the STEP program as a specific Adlerian guidance program.

Mr. Seberg is concerned about several incidents that have occurred in the past few weeks. Among them was one during storytime.

Kelly: "Look, Mr. Seberg! I can stand on one foot!" (Everyone is distracted from the story and looks at Kelly.)
Mr. Seberg: "Sit down, Kelly. We're listening to a story." (She sits but after a few minutes she runs to the front of the group, grabs the flannel piece, and slaps it onto the flannelboard.)
Mr. Seberg: "Look here, Kelly. I'm getting tired of having to talk to you during storytime. Go and sit at the table until we're finished."

Another incident happened during clean up time. Jake had played with a large basket of pegs. Mr. Seberg stopped in each area to remind children that lunch was next and that they would have to put things away. He noticed that Jake had left the pegs strewn about the table.

Mr. Seberg: "Jake, you will have to put away the pegs before you eat."
Jake: "I have to wash my hands first."
Mr. Seberg: "Oh, no, you don't! First you put away the pegs." (Jake ignores his comment and goes to the sink.)
Mr. Seberg: "I told you to put away the pegs. Now turn off the water and get back to the table!"
Jake: "Okay, okay. Leave me alone."

Adlerian theorists have a unique perspective on how the personality develops. Their view of these adult-child episodes is different from that of a behaviorist or a Rogerian. An Adlerian has specific ideas on why these children acted as they did as well as on the role of the adult in child guidance.

The Adlerian theory of personality development was developed by Alfred Adler (1870–1937). Adler's life in many ways paralleled that of Sigmund Freud. Both men were from Vienna. Adler was only a few years younger than Freud. Both attended medical school, and both developed an interest in psychiatry. They held divergent views on how the personality develops. Freud maintained that each person is primarily a biological being, while Adler believed that each person is a social being. Freud believed that personalities are shaped by biological needs, but Adler maintained that personalities are shaped by individual social environments and interactions. Freud believed that people are driven by unconscious forces that cannot be seen or controlled, but Adler maintained that people actively and consciously direct and create their own growth.

Adlerian theory, like other theories described in this unit, can be used to guide an adult's interactions with children. This chapter presents some of the major concepts of Adler's theory, looks at how the theory explains children's behavior, and examines a specific child guidance program based on Adlerian theory.

ADLERIAN CONCEPTS

Humans Strive for Psychological Strength

Humans realize that they lack the physical strength of many other species. Because of perceived inferior physical abilities, people tend to develop feelings of psychological inferiority (Mead, 1976). Humans, then, exist in a state in which feelings of inferiority and helplessness are always present.

People try to buttress their sense of inferiority with feelings of psychological strength. Adler believed that people strive to become better or more perfect than the inferior creatures they perceive themselves to be (Schultz, 1976). In Adlerian theory the overall goal people seek is to rid themselves of feelings of inferiority and to become stronger and more perfect.

Each Person Has an Individual Style of Striving for Psychological Strength

Humans share the goal of becoming more perfect, but they differ in how they try to reach the goal. Each person develops a *lifestyle,* an individual style of striving for the goal. A person's characteristic style of striving affects the way in which he reacts to problems encountered in daily life.

One's style of striving develops partly as a result of the type of adult-child interaction experienced during early childhood. Adlerian theorists believe that a person's way of dealing with problems, or style of striving for perfection, is established by age 4 or 5 and therefore consider the early childhood period an important one in personality development (Dinkmeyer & McKay, 1976; Dreikurs & Soltz, 1964; Shultz, 1976).

A style of striving to overcome feelings of inferiority also develops because of how the child interprets his experiences. Thus, a basic Adlerian idea is that people are active in their own development. Adlerians believe that experiences with others certainly have an effect on one's outlook but that people are creative and tend to interpret these experiences and try to make sense of them. People are more than passive recipients of stimulation. They actively create their own style of striving.

Humans Develop Different Levels of Social Interest

Adlerians believe that humans are primarily social beings and that feelings of psychological strength are best achieved by working and cooperating with others (Adler, 1964). Individual actions affect the society as well as the individual. When an individual cooperates with others, the society benefits; and when people refuse to work together, the society suffers.

Social interest means that a person has a sense of belonging to the group and feels like a vital part of the group, realizing his role in the group's functioning. Consequently, a person with a high degree of social interest is willing to cooperate with

other group members and contributes to the functioning of the group. A person with little social interest tends to do things that benefit himself but not necessarily other group members.

Humans are born with the potential and the capacity to develop many social behaviors like cooperation and contribution to the group. A number of factors determine a child's level of social interest.

Social Interest is Influenced by a Child's Self-Esteem

Adlerians believe that a child's physical characteristics affect the reactions of others to him, which in turn affect how the child feels about himself. The opinions of significant adults have an impact on a child's level of self-esteem. Adults who view a child as competent or attractive communicate their opinions to the child, who eventually internalizes those opinions and begins to view himself similarly. On the other hand, adults who view a child as unattractive or incompetent also communicate these opinions to the child, who internalizes them and forms an unfavorable opinion of himself.

Adlerians believe that a child who develops positive self-esteem or feelings of competence and self-worth during childhood will become an adult with a strong sense of social interest. A child who develops feelings of incompetence during childhood will become an adult who lacks social interest (Mead, 1976). In short, a child who likes and respects himself and is confident about his abilities is likely to become an adult who will respect others and will work well with and help others. A child who is given little respect or who is treated as incompetent is likely to become an adult who shows little respect for others and who refuses to cooperate with and help other group members.

Social Interest is Nurtured by Interaction with Significant Adults

The capacity for developing social interest is present in all children, but social interest does not develop automatically. Adlerians believe that it must be nurtured by the environment in which a child operates (DiCaprio, 1974). Adult socializing agents influence how cooperative or helpful a child becomes because they create the atmosphere in which the child exists.

Adults model specific behaviors or patterns of interaction, which are imitated by children. Observing cooperation and group contribution is likely to result in high levels of cooperation, while observing competitiveness is likely to result in a low level of social interest.

Adults can also create an atmosphere in which respect for and cooperation with others is valued and encouraged. An atmosphere conducive to developing respect for others has reasonable, firmly enforced limits on behavior that hurts others. If adults communicate the idea that the world is a place in which competition and not cooperation is desirable, then they will not encourage children to act cooperatively. They will encourage children to pit themselves against others.

Social Interest is Affected by a Child's Accurate or Inaccurate Perceptions

Children realize how important it is for them to fit into their social group. Each child goes about "fitting in" by following his own interpretation of the group's rules for group membership. Each child makes decisions about what he has to do to be accepted as a group member (DiCaprio, 1974; Dreikurs & Soltz, 1964; Mead, 1976).

Some children are able to achieve a sense of belonging to their group by cooperating and making useful contributions. They interpret the rules of group membership accurately. Other children often interpret their world imperfectly because they lack experience or have a limited ability to evaluate their experiences. These children have a faulty perception of how to fit into the group. They tend to use ineffective approaches to gain a place, whether the group is a family, class, or other group. These children often display seemingly irrational behavior in their efforts to become group members. Such children's behavior does not help them become group members.

MISTAKEN GOALS

The episodes described in the opening to this chapter are typical of the adult-child interactions that occur when a child has a faulty perception of how to fit into a group. Kelly thought that she had to be the center of attention, and Jake thought that he had to be in charge or in power. Jake spent a lot of time in a power struggle with Mr. Seberg.

Dreikurs believed that a child who has faulty perceptions or mistaken goals on how to be a group member will seek group membership in one of four ways (Dreikurs & Soltz, 1964):

1. by getting the *undue attention* of others.

2. by getting *power* over others.

3. by hurting others through *revenge.*

4. by displaying *inadequacy.*

This section describes each of these ways of trying to fit into the group. Each mistaken goal is described in terms of the child's faulty perception, how the child acts based on the perception, and how an adult usually feels and reacts when a child behaves irrationally. Alternative adult reactions to help a child find a better way to fit into the group are suggested (Dreikurs & Soltz, 1964).

Undue Attention

Everyone, including a child, has a need for and a right to attention. Some children, however, make demands for *undue attention* from adults. These children seem to be unable to look at a situation and see the needs of other people. For example, Mr. Seberg was mixing a batch of playdough before school started and Kelly arrived early. Kelly asked him to help her climb "right now," ignoring the fact that he was busy and that this was a situation in which his attention was not necessarily due.

The Child's Faulty Perception
Striving for undue attention indicates that a child like Kelly has the faulty idea that she is important only when she is the center of attention. Getting the attention of others, then, is used by some children as a means of feeling that they belong.

What the Child Does
The child becomes skillful at gaining attention by using different attention-getting

techniques. Kelly is becoming accomplished at getting attention whenever she wants it. She is beginning to display annoying attention-getting behaviors. For instance:

Mr. Seberg: "I'm sorry, Kelly. You're a little early today and I have to finish my work. I'll help you later and you can play quietly with puzzles until then." (Kelly goes over to the puzzle rack and, without a single word, dumps four puzzles onto the table. She then glances quickly at the teacher. Mr. Seberg goes to the table.)

Mr. Seberg: "Kelly, why did you turn over all the puzzles? You clean them up right now!"

How the Adult Feels and Usually Reacts

Adults feel annoyed or irritated when children demand undue attention. They usually react by following their first impulse—by giving the child the undue attention demanded—as Mr. Seberg did. Giving in to the child's demands reinforces the attention-getting behavior. Kelly is likely to display similar behavior again because it has gotten her just what she seems to need. Giving in to demands for undue attention also reinforces Kelly's faulty perception of how to gain a sense of belonging to the group (Mead, 1976).

Other adults yell at or scold a child for seeking attention. The attention-seeking behavior stops only briefly and is then resumed. When Kelly failed to get the teacher's attention by asking she became angry and dumped the puzzles, and that finally worked. Mr. Seberg yelled: just the attention Kelly was after. Kelly, relentless in her pursuit for attention, does not stop until she gets it.

A Better Approach

Mr. Seberg observed Kelly in other situations and discovered that she usually did something to draw attention to herself. She acted silly at snacktime, moved around constantly on her cot at naptime, and interrupted any group in which she was participating. He concluded that her goal was to get *undue* attention and that his method of dealing with the problem did not seem to be working. Adlerians believe they can help a child discover that she can be a valuable group member without having to be the center of attention. In the following recommendations, Mead (1976) emphasizes the need for adults to change their way of reacting to demands for undue attention.

1. *Ignore the impulse to give in to the attention-seeking behavior.* For example, Mr. Seberg received an emergency phone call from a child's parent. While he talked, Kelly demanded his attention.

Kelly: "I found the book." (She repeats this several times, each time increasing the volume of her voice).

Mr. Seberg: "I'm talking to Jon's mom about something important right now. I can't read to you right now. I'll read to you later."

2. *Acknowledge the child's request but let her know that she can complete the task.* Leave the area if necessary so that she can finish the job.

Kelly (who happens to be a whiz at putting small plastic blocks together): "Will you help me, Mr. Seberg? I can't put the rest of the wheels on my car."

Mr. Seberg: "You've done a good job with two of the wheels. Try putting the others on in the same way. I'll check back with you right after you get it done."

3. *Give the child due attention.* Encourage a child to become a group member by helping him learn to cooperate and by acknowledging the needs of other group members. Mr. Seberg noticed when Kelly finished with her car, and as promised, he stopped at her table.

Mr. Seberg: "Kelly, the car is finished and you did it by yourself. Would you show me how it works?"

Power

The Child's Faulty Perception

Some children think that they are important only when they demonstrate power over others. Their faulty perception is that their personal value comes from being in charge and showing others that they are the "boss." To such a child a loss of power in relation to an adult is the same as a loss of personal value.

What the Child Does

The child develops several techniques for involving adults in a power struggle and for gaining control over them. Like Jake in the introduction, the child usually makes

an adult so angry and so frustrated that the adult turns on and attacks the child. It might look like the adult "won" when he yelled at Jake, but it is Jake, according to Dreikurs (Dreikurs & Soltz, 1964) who is in charge. He has succeeded in engaging Mr. Seberg in a struggle for power. The adult had a similar confrontation with Amy on the playground.

Mr. Seberg: "Amy, you can have two more turns and then I want you to park your trike." (Amy takes several more turns, gets off the trike, and runs over to the slide).
Mr. Seberg: "Amy, it's time to come in. Please park your trike." (Amy then gets on the tricycle and rides it to the shed. She gets off but does not put the trike inside. Instead, she walks toward the classroom. Mr. Seberg glares at her.)
Mr. Seberg: "Amy, for the last time, get over to the shed and put your trike inside."
Amy: "No!"
Mr. Seberg: "We'll see about that." (He grabs Amy's arm and steers her toward the shed.)

Amy is clearly the victor here. She has controlled and manipulated the adult, engaging him in a power struggle.

How the Adult Feels and Usually Reacts

Adults usually feel upset and angry when confronted with a power-seeking child. Some adults feel that their authority has been challenged. Like many adults, Mr. Seberg's first impulse was to fight back and to remind Amy that he was in power. Adlerians believe some children are so skillful at the power game that adults do not even realize that they are in a power struggle. To reestablish authority and to overpower the child, adults often resort to power assertive, hurtful tactics like hitting, slapping, grabbing, yelling, or threatening.

Adults who allow themselves to be drawn into power struggles with a child reinforce the child's power-seeking behavior. They serve as sparring partners, persons with whom the child practices and sharpens power-seeking skills. They also reinforce the child's faulty perception of how to become a group member. Adlerians would say that Amy's feeling of importance comes from gaining power over other people. Mr. Seberg has not done anything to help Amy clarify that faulty perception. If anything, he has reinforced her faulty perception.

A Better Approach

Whether a child continues to play the power game depends largely on how important adults react. Children like Amy need adults to guide them toward more positive ways of becoming group members. They do not need adults as sparring partners. Adlerians maintain that adults who change their ways of reacting to a defiant child have the best chance of actually helping that child. Their suggestions follow (Dinkmeyer & McKay, 1976; Mead, 1976):

1. *Resist the first impulse to fight back.*
2. *Decide to respond differently.* Adults do have a choice about how they react to children. They are not locked into one way of acting.
3. *Withdraw from the conflict.* An adult who chooses not to participate in a power struggle often surprises a child, particularly if the child has previously succeeded in fighting with the adult. Withdrawing from a power struggle is

not easy. An adult who realizes that a power play is about to begin can simply refuse to participate. A useful technique is to label the interaction as a power struggle.

Mr. Seberg: "It looks to me like you feel like fighting with me about the trike." (He refuses to fight back and communicates his intention to Amy.)

Mr. Seberg: "I don't feel like fighting, so I'm going inside to watch the movie. You may watch it too when you put your trike away."

The adult should then withdraw and avoid the urge to nag, coax or threaten the child.

Many adults believe that withdrawing from a fight means that they are failures. They think that adults have to "put the child in her place." Adlerian theorists, however, disagree (Dinkmeyer & McKay, 1976). Their opinion is that a well-timed withdrawal creates an atmosphere in which adults can help the child develop a more positive approach to group membership.

Revenge

Tom made a lot of noise and awakened several children during naptime.

Mr. Seberg: "Tom, when you talk during naptime, you wake the others. I want you to be quiet."

Tom: "You're always yelling at me. I hate you!"

The Child's Faulty Perception

Adlerians argue that children like Tom are discouraged. These children believe that they have little value or power in the group, and they do not feel liked by other group members. Their faulty perception is that they have value only when they hurt others.

What the Child Does

Just as some children work at attention-getting or power struggles, other children consume a lot of their energy convincing people that they are not likeable. Such a child does things to show people that he *is* a bad person. When a child seeks revenge, he shows extremely hurtful behavior toward others.

How the Adult Feels and Usually Reacts

An adult who has been attacked by a child feels hurt. Many adults either back away from the child or retaliate against the child's hurtful behavior. The child is not helped by the adult's actions. Retaliating and backing away reinforce both the child's hurtful behavior and his faulty perception—that he is a bad, unlikeable person of little value who has to hurt others to be a part of the group.

A Better Approach

Again, the adult should do the unexpected and resist the first impulse to retaliate or to give sermons and back away. A child who seeks revenge is a child who needs help. Self-esteem in this child is low, and adults who care about the child can help by fostering a positive sense of self-esteem in the child. Only when this child values himself and feels valued will he value others enough to refrain from hurting them. To help Tom feel accepted, Mr. Seberg decided to concentrate on Tom's acceptable behavior instead of focusing on his errors.

Mr. Seberg: "You've stayed on your cot, Tom. Thanks. But I see that you're ready to be awake. You may read a book quietly or help me mix playdough."

Demonstration of Inadequacy or Incompetence

Some of the children were making a large collage. Each child had cut various shapes and then glued them to the mural paper. Mr. Seberg noticed that Anita stood at the table for some time and then walked away.

Mr. Seberg: "Anita, would you like to put some shapes on the mural?"
Anita: "OK."
Mr. Seberg: "Which one will you cut out first?"
Anita: "You cut one out for me."
Mr. Seberg: "OK, which shape should I cut for you?"

The Child's Faulty Perception
A child like Anita feels completely discouraged and thinks that she cannot do anything well. She and others like her believe that they have nothing to contribute to the group, so they do not even try.

What the Child Does
Anita lets the adult know how inadequate she perceives herself to be. A child like this hopes that by pleading inadequacy, she will discourage others from expecting much from her.

How the Adult Feels and Usually Reacts
It is puzzling and frustrating to interact with an intelligent child who has given up and acts like he cannot do anything. Adults are often at a loss in helping such a child. The first impulse is to highlight the child's errors, the result of which is to further discourage the child. Many adults, like Mr. Seberg, give in and perform the task for the child, whether the task is drawing, cutting and pasting, tying shoelaces, or doing a science fair project. Both focusing on mistakes and performing tasks for the child reinforce the child's faulty perception that he can be a group member only by demonstrating incompetence.

A Better Approach
A knowledge of child development is useful here. If it is legitimate to expect a healthy 5-year-old to be able to cut paper with scissors, then Mr. Seberg needs to concentrate on helping Anita discover her ability and should refrain from performing the task for her. Most important, Mr. Seberg needs to learn how to encourage Anita. The adult's role becomes one of arousing self-confidence in the child so that

she can solve problems and carry out tasks on her own. He can break down tasks into smaller, easily managed parts so that Anita can achieve success.

Mr. Seberg: "You know, Anita, that I saw you cutting strips of paper just yesterday. Start here by finding a shape with straight sides . . . Good, you found the large rectangle. You cut it out, paste it on the paper, and then I'll take a look at what you've done."

Summary: Mistaken Goals

A principle of Adlerian theory is that all behavior or misbehavior has a purpose or goal and that because people are primarily social beings their main goal is to belong to the social group. Children make decisions about what behavior will allow them to attain group membership. Many times their perceptions are inaccurate and thus they display seemingly irrational behavior in their search for importance and group membership. Some children think that they are important only if they are the center of attention; others think that wielding power over others is the key to group membership. Some children view themselves as unliked and seek group membership by hurting others. Other children hide behind a shield of inadequacy or incompetence, hoping that other group members will not expect them to do much. Adults need to be aware of the mistaken goals and the behavior that results from them. Adults also need to know that they are not locked into typical reactionary responses but can choose more helpful alternatives.

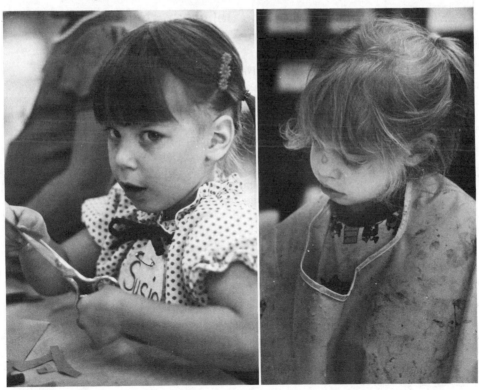

STEP: A SPECIFIC ADLERIAN GUIDANCE PROGRAM

STEP—Systematic Training for Effective Parenting—is a program developed by Don Dinkmeyer and Gary McKay (1976) based on Adlerian theory. The STEP program is a small-group discussion method of parent education for child guidance. It is organized around nine STEPs, or weekly sessions, with each session focusing on a specific aspect of adult-child interaction. Each STEP is designed to teach a specific Adlerian concept or guidance technique:

STEP 1. Understanding your child's behavior and misbehavior.

STEP 2: Understanding more about your child's emotions and about yourself as a parent. Recognizing the differences between "good" parents and "responsible" parents.

STEP 3: Learning to use encouragement instead of praise, to build your child's confidence and feelings of self-worth.

STEP 4: Improving communication by becoming an effective listener.

STEP 5: Communicating your ideas and feelings to your child. Helping your child to explore alternative ways of behaving.

SPECIAL FOCUS: Adlerians Believe in Using Positive Discipline

Adlerians Do Not Believe in Using Negative Discipline

Adlerians maintain that children who exert power over adults need to be helped to find a better way to gain a place in the group. Adlerian theorists and practitioners do not believe in using hurtful, negative discipline for several reasons:

1. *Hurtful discipline has no place in a relationship between equals.* It is obvious that children are not equal to adults in size, experience, or the ability to evaluate experience. However, Adlerians believe that all system members are equal in their right to be treated with respect. If either an adult or a child wields power over the other and uses negative discipline, then that person has demonstrated a lack of respect for the other.

2. *Negative discipline is ineffective.* Negative discipline does not stop inappropriate behavior permanently and can even make it worse.

3. *Negative discipline does not help a child clarify faulty perceptions.* If an adult punishes a child who seeks attention, power, or revenge, then the child usually persists in the inappropriate behavior because he still has the faulty perception.

4. *Negative discipline elicits similar behavior from the child.* Degrading discipline by an adult is mirrored in the behavior of the child. Adlerians say that a child who is disciplined harshly usually retaliates and increases his attempts to "get back at" the adult.

STEP 6: Replacing reward and punishment with learning from consequences.

STEP 7: Applying natural and logical consequences to the challenges of childrearing. Acting positively instead of reacting negatively.

STEP 8: Establishing family meetings that encourage democratic family relationships.

STEP 9: Developing confidence and growing as a person as well as becoming a more effective parent.

A variety of materials for the STEP program are available in a self-contained kit. Materials include an instructor's manual, a parent's handbook, charts, and posters. The core of the STEP program consists of nine cassette tape recordings, one of which is used each week as a springboard for discussion.

SUMMARY: KEY CONCEPTS IN THIS CHAPTER

1. Adlerian theory was developed by Alfred Adler, a contemporary of Sigmund Freud. Basic differences exist between Freud's and Adler's ideas on how the personality develops.

Adlerians Use Natural and Logical Consequences: Positive Discipline

Children do need and will accept guidance when adults treat them with respect and avoid using power. Adlerians recommend the use of natural and logical consequences instead of punishment. An adult who uses natural and logical consequences helps a child learn two things—that he alone is responsible for his behavior and that he also has the power to change his own behavior. Consider the following episodes. Heather refused to eat her snack.

Mr. Seberg: "Everyone needs to eat a snack. Hurry and finish the fruit." (Heather continues to dawdle.)
Mr. Seberg: "Heather, I really wish you'd eat. You're going to be hungry later if you don't."

Later, Heather was hungry and Mr. Seberg took her to the kitchen and gave her a piece of fruit. But he decided that this approach simply was not working. He was angry, and Heather was starting to test all sorts of limits. She was also becoming increasingly defiant. Mr. Seberg decided to try using logical consequences. When Heather refused, as usual, to eat the snack, Mr. Seberg did not coax or nag. He passed the basket around the table and said nothing when Heather took nothing. Later that morning, Heather approached Mr. Seberg and asked for something to eat.

Mr. Seberg: "I can see that you are hungry. We'll be having lunch in 2 hours."

He did not give in and did not give her food. In the first episode, Mr. Seberg took the responsibility for Heather's behavior. In the second episode, however, Mr. Seberg let Heather take responsibility and experience the consequences of choosing not to eat—being hungry. Heather did not starve by missing one snack, and she learned that she has the power to change the way things turn out.

2. One Adlerian concept is that humans are *goal-seeking creatures*. Adler viewed people as having feelings of inferiority, which they strive as their major goal to overcome.

3. *Style of striving* is another Adlerian concept. Each individual has a personal style of striving for the goal of overcoming feelings of inferiority.

4. *Social interest,* a feeling of group membership, is a third Adlerian concept. Adlerians believe that humans are primarily social beings and want to be part of their social group.

5. Adlerians believe that a person who develops positive self-esteem will show a high degree of social interest. Social interest is influenced by the child's environment, especially by adults who model and encourage cooperation and contribution to the group. Social interest is also influenced by a child's interpretation of how to fit into a group.

6. Adlerian theorists believe that some children have faulty perceptions of how to become a group member and seek group membership in one of four inappropriate ways: by seeking undue attention, struggling for power, taking revenge, or displaying inadequacy.

7. Whether a child continues to act on faulty perceptions depends largely on how adults react to his mistakes. One type of adult rection tends to maintain a child's irrational behavior. Another type of adult reaction helps a child find more positive ways of gaining group membership.

8. STEP—Systematic Training for Effective Parenting (Dinkmeyer & McKay, 1976) —is a packaged program complete with a variety of media to use in small discussion groups. The STEP program gives specific ways that Adlerian theory can be applied in practice.

OBSERVE: CHILD GUIDANCE IN ACTION

Observe a child's "misbehavior" and determine the child's goal: *undue attention, power, revenge,* or a *display of inadequacy.* One of the best ways to discover a child's goal or purpose in misbehaving is to observe the *consequences* of the misbehavior. Concentrate on the results of the behavior and not just the misbehavior itself.

Use the following format to record your observations. Observe at a child development center, in a grocery store, at a fast-food restaurant, or in some other setting. Observe at least two episodes of "misbehavior" in which an adult and a child interact.

Date: _____

Time: _____

Child's approximate age: _____

Setting: _____

Your name: _____

EPISODE 1

Briefly describe the child's "misbehavior."

Describe the adult's reaction to the misbehavior.

Write how the child responded to the adult's attempt at correction. Be specific.

From what you have observed, what do you think is this child's goal in misbehaving? Undue attention, power, revenge, or a display of inadequacy? Why?

Compare your observations with those of another class member. If you disagree, say why.

EPISODE 2 Use the same format.

REFERENCES

ADLER, A. (1964). *Social interest*. New York. Capricorn Books.

DiCAPRIO, N.S. (1974). *Personality theories: Guides to living*. Philadelphia: W.B. Saunders.

DINKMEYER, D., & McKAY, G.D. (1976). *Systematic training for effective parenting*. Circle Pines, MN: American Guidance Service.

DREIKURS, R., & SOLTZ, V. (1964). *Children: The challenge*. New York: Hawthorn Books.

MEAD, D.E. (1976). *Six approaches to child rearing*. Provo, UT: Brigham Young University Press.

SHULTZ, D. (1976). *Theories of personality*. Monterey, CA: Brooks/Cole.

Index